¡PRESENTE!

¡PRESENTE!

Nonviolent Politics and the Resurrection of the Dead

KYLE B. T. LAMBELET

Georgetown University Press / Washington, DC

The publisher is not responsible for third-party websites or their content. URL links were active at time of publication.

Library of Congress Cataloging-in-Publication Data

Names: Lambelet, Kyle Brent Thompson, author.
Title: ¡Presente!: Nonviolent Politics and the Resurrection of the Dead /
    Kyle B.T. Lambelet.
Description: Washington, DC : Georgetown University Press, 2019. | Includes
    bibliographical references and index.
Identifiers: LCCN 2019005026 (print) | LCCN 2019022054 (ebook) | ISBN
    9781626167278 (ebook) | ISBN 9781626167254 (hardcover : qalk. paper) |
    ISBN 9781626167261 (pbk. : qalk. paper)
Subjects: LCSH: Nonviolence--Religious aspects—Christianity. | Political
    theology. | Peace—Religious aspects. | U.S. Army School of the Americas.
Classification: LCC BT736.6 (ebook) | LCC BT736.6 .L35 2019 (print) | DDC
    241/.697—dc23
LC record available at https://lccn.loc.gov/2019005026

♾ This book is printed on acid-free paper meeting the requirements of the American National Standard for Permanence in Paper for Printed Library Materials.

20 19   9 8 7 6 5 4 3 2   First printing

Printed in the United States of America.

Cover design by Martha Madrid.
Cover photograph by Linda Panetta | Optical Realities Photography | www.OpticalRealities.org

This book is dedicated to all those whose persistent, resurrected presence disturbs and inspires the work against the violence of empire and for peace with justice, especially Mike, Eli, and Jerry. *¡Presente!* As Jon Sobrino wrote, "May their peace give us hope, and may their memory never let us rest in peace."

For if the dead are not raised, then Christ has not been raised. If Christ has not been raised, your faith is futile and you are still in your sins. Then those also who have died in Christ have perished. If for this life only we have hoped in Christ, we are of all people most to be pitied.

1 Corinthians 15:16–19, NRSV

I have often been threatened with death. I must tell you, as a Christian, I do not believe in death without resurrection. If I am killed, I shall arise in the Salvadoran people.

Óscar Romero in an interview with José Calderón Salazar
two weeks before his assassination

The security of the resurrection does not take away the desire to struggle but strengthens it. As a follower of Jesus, one tries to do this out of hope.

Ignacio Ellacuría,
"The Christian Challenge of Liberation Theology"

We have seen that the infamous SOA is not just a building; it is not just a policy. The School is a mindset with roots as old as the colonization of the Americas. It is the belief that land, resources and human rights are commodities that can be bought, stolen and destroyed. In that mindset there are no ancestors, no memory, and no imagination. Inside that set of beliefs Celina, Elba and the six Jesuits were dangerous enough to assassinate but not human enough to have a right to live.

Liz Deligio, SOA Watch activist

CONTENTS

PREFACE

I first attended the annual vigil of the School of the Americas Watch in 2005. I had graduated earlier the same year with an undergraduate degree in theology and had set about looking for concrete embodiments of the radical ideas I had encountered in the classroom. This search brought me to a Catholic Worker community in Atlanta, and with these workers I traveled to Columbus, Georgia, where the annual event was held. For most of my companions, this was a site of annual pilgrimage. For me it was a first. What I experienced on that chilly November morning at the gates of Fort Benning impacted me profoundly.

At the time the United States was fighting two wars—one in Afghanistan and another in Iraq—and in the year prior the Abu Ghraib prisoner abuse scandal had come to light. The consensus among those of us who traveled to Fort Benning was that the torture of detainees was not an aberration, the work of some "bad apples." Rather, seemingly indiscriminate torture for counterinsurgency purposes came straight from the playbook of the training manuals that instructors used in the US Army's School of the Americas (SOA) until the mid-1990s. The torture and assassinations that had plagued Latin America through the second half of the twentieth century were spreading to Iraq and beyond.

Arriving at the gates of Fort Benning early that Sunday morning, the scene was electric. Though I had participated in massive anti-war protests in Los Angeles during the buildup to the US invasion of Iraq, this felt different. Tens of thousands of people from across the country and the globe gathered in this relatively remote location. There were women religious, Food Not Bombs anarchists, Jesuit high school students, southern civil rights activists, Central American sanctuary recipients, Veterans for Peace, and many, many others. What brought this wildly plural group together was the ¡presente! litany, an hours-long protest liturgy in which the names of those who had been tortured and killed by the graduates of the SOA/Western Hemisphere Institute for Security Cooperation (WHINSEC) were sung and claimed responsively as *presente*, "present." Though the congregated mass was remarkably diverse, the people figured out a way to coordinate their bodily movements together in affirming the presence of the dead.

My first exposure to SOA Watch activism was overwhelming. Afterward, my fellow Catholic Workers and I made our way to a Chinese buffet in Columbus, and we reflected on what we had just experienced. Looking around at my companions, many of whom were wearing shirts that boldly proclaimed "NO WAR!" I suggested that the protest was a way of saying no and saying yes: we said no to war, to torture, and to empire while also saying yes to solidarity, to nonviolence, and to a communion that transcends death.

I lacked at the time the conceptual vocabulary or the analytical tools to probe my experience, but I left my first SOA Watch vigil with a constellation of questions: What political work does this theologically and viscerally powerful action do? How does it perform that work within a context of such religious, ideological, and identity-based diversity? What is the relationship between this action, the civil disobedience committed annually at the gates, and the ongoing work of lobbying for legal reform? What role does the images and stories of the martyrs play in shaping movement participation? And, most of all, what does it mean for us to claim the presence of *these* dead in *this* place?

This book, completed nearly a decade and a half after my first trip to the gates of Fort Benning, responds to these questions.

After returning to the SOA Watch's annual mobilization several times as a participant and then several more times as a researcher (participant-observer), after dozens of official and unofficial interviews with SOA Watch activists and organizers, after participating in an SOA Watch delegation to the US-Mexico border, and after combing through personal archives of several SOA Watch "prisoners of conscience," I have a better sense of the impact of the claim of presente not only on my own life but also on the lives of the transnational grassroots network of SOA Watch activists. The messianic claim that the dead are presente shapes a distinctive, transnational, and nonviolent politics.

ACKNOWLEDGMENTS

This book develops a messianic political theology that, if nothing else, proclaims it is not all up to us! Thus, it is quite appropriate to acknowledge that this project would have been impossible without the support of many people and institutions.

First and foremost, I wish to thank the countless SOA Watch activists who willingly spoke with me about their experiences, shared their analysis, and welcomed me to join them in their organizing. I especially wish to thank those, both named and anonymous, who went on the record and responded to my request for an interview. More than merely providing data, which they supplied in loads, these conversations gave energy and urgency to my research and inspired me in my own political action. In addition to interviews, I wish to thank Cynthia Brinkman, Rebecca Kanner, and Jerry Zawada for making their personal archives available to me. I am also grateful to María Luisa Rosal and Arturo Viscarra, who each helped me connect to others within the movement. I especially wish to thank Anton Flores-Maisonet, who not only eagerly connected me to collaborators in the struggle but willingly opened his home to my family and me as well. Anton, Charlotte, Jairo, and Eli were gracious hosts. Their gift of hospitality has reminded me often to offer the same charity and kindness to the activists who appear in the pages that follow.

In addition to my research subjects, this work would not have been possible without significant institutional support. As a germ of an idea, this research project began at Vanderbilt University Divinity School, where Melissa Snarr, Ted Smith, and Holly McCammon all helped nurture my nascent intuitions and sharpen my methods. While it began with term papers at Vanderbilt, the project came to full flourish at the University of Notre Dame. I cannot think of a better place to have completed the lion's share of this research, especially through the joint PhD in theology and peace studies in the Department of Theology and the Kroc Institute for International Peace Studies. Not only formationally but also financially, Notre Dame's support afforded me both the opportunity to pursue the fieldwork and the focused writing time necessary for its completion. The Louisville Institute's Dissertation Completion Fellowship also aided both financially and substantively.

Finally, my colleagues at Emory University's Candler School of Theology have proven a source of support and encouragement in the process of publishing this book.

I have benefited immensely from the comments and questions of fellow scholars who have read and responded to my work. I presented parts of my research at the annual meetings of the American Academy of Religion, the Peace and Justice Studies Association, the International Studies Association, the Fellowship for Protestant Ethics, and the Society of Christian Ethics. I received valuable feedback at each. My interdisciplinary cohort of Francis Bonenfant-Juwong, Karie Cross Riddle, and Heather DuBois patiently read and commented on every chapter of the dissertation that was the seed for this book. Their feedback has been indispensable in every way, and I am deeply grateful to each of them for their insight and companionship.

Ann Mische, Atalia Omer, Ted Smith, and Todd Whitmore—my dissertation committee—were outstanding guides as this project first developed. Their insight, individually and collectively, helped me clarify the big questions, and their encouragement kept me writing even when it remained unclear where exactly I was going. I owe special thanks to my adviser, Jerry McKenny. A project of this type, drawing on multiple academic disciplines, runs many risks. If I have avoided some of them, it is due in no small part to Jerry's careful engagement with every page of this work. Since a readings course early in my time at Notre Dame, Jerry has been a steady source of guidance, wisdom, and insight, especially on the promise and danger of messianic political theologies. As others have said, it is true here: my work is better for the advice of these fine scholars and would have undoubtedly been even stronger had I taken more of it. The errors that remain in fact and judgment are my own. I'm also grateful to the team at Georgetown University Press—Al Bertrand, Hope LeGro, Glenn Saltzman, and many others—for seeing promise in my dissertation and helping to make it a book.

Finally, I wish to thank my family who supported me in countless ways during each step of the research and writing process. Garren and Naomi accompanied me to the gates of Fort Benning (Garren more than once) and tolerated my absence during weeks of fieldwork. My parents, Patty and Brent Thompson, supported me in the midst of a long and sometimes wandering educational process. My partner, Nicole, was a constant source of questions and insight. Our dinnertime conversations have made the pages of this book countless times. It was the patience and support of each, even beyond and behind the research and writing, that has reminded me always that whatever creative agency I might express here would be impossible without the prior love and support of others. They have been for me a means of God's grace, for which I am grateful.

ABBREVIATIONS

AFL-CIO	American Federation of Labor and Congress of Industrial Organizations
CASM	Central American Solidarity Movement
GJM	Global Justice Movement
ISN	Ignatian Solidarity Network
LCWR	Leadership Conference of Women Religious
NAACP	National Association for the Advancement of Colored People
SOA	School of the Americas
SOA Watch	School of the Americas Watch
SOA/WHINSEC	School of the Americas / Western Hemisphere Institute for Security Cooperation
UCA	Universidad Centroamericana José Simeón Cañas
WHINSEC	Western Hemisphere Institute for Security Cooperation

INTRODUCTION
Join Us in This Vigil

Join us in this vigil
and you will know what it is to dream!
Then you will know how marvelous it is
to live threatened with Resurrection!
To dream awake,
to keep watch asleep,
to live while dying,
and to know ourselves already
resurrected!

Julia Esquivel
"They Have Threatened Us"

What role should the dead play in our politics? Some argue that politics is the space where the living struggle over the power to decide about the distribution of common goods. Under such a description, politics is an immanent affair that involves power relationships, give and take, and sometimes compromise. Such politics is the work of living agents, not the dead.

Yet it is impossible to deny that the dead do play a role even in this immanent affair. We honor those killed in war through public rites and national holy days. Similarly, we commemorate the great dead among us by laying their bodies in state. We memorialize the victims of tragedies through statuary and museums. These modes of commemoration and memory often serve to reinforce the power relationships that constitute the political status quo.

The appearance of the dead in politics, however, is not always stabilizing. The images of the untimely dead can shock consciences and spur social movements. The recently aggrieved are given special deference to confront policies that neglect or harm. And, at times, the distant memories of past wrongs can justify a politics of resentment that fuels genocidal violence. In each of these practices of memory, the living draw on the authority of the dead to justify a politics of radical change.

We can tolerate the dead as a memory in statuary and funerary rites, although even this memorialized presence can be dangerous. And we can allow survivors to speak with the mantle of the dead and call for specific policy changes. What we cannot accept is the dead as agents. The dead broker no compromises. The dead demand response. Thus, those who are daily crucified on the cross of economic and technological progress cannot be allowed to appear. When the "crucified people" appear as agents, they disrupt the normal, immanent routine of politics.[1] The appearance of the dead in the streets of the city—as reported by the writer of the Gospel of Matthew—is a sign that something radically new is happening in our midst.[2] And while a hope for and belief in the resurrection is an affirmation that creedal Christians repeat often in their prayers, such a resurrected presence is anything but comforting. In fact, Julia Esquivel rightly names such presence as a threat in her poem excerpted in the epigraph. Writing in exile during Efraín Ríos Montt's genocidal campaign against indigenous Guatemalans, the poet-theologian recognized that the presence of the dead is dangerous, especially to those who create the structures of death. Under what moral philosopher Charles Taylor has called our immanent frame, the agential presence of the dead raises the specter of extremism.[3]

This extremist disruption explains both the presence and repression of the dead in politics. Social movements call up images of the dead to justify their civil disobedience, just as organizations calling for global jihad point to their martyrs as exemplars. Whether anti-abortionists' crusades, Daesh's jihad, or Kach's catastrophic messianism, we imagine that a politics rooted in the agential presence of the dead falls prey inevitably to the twin temptations of either violence or quietism. In each of these cases, the presence of the dead, a messianic affirmation, seems to indicate the end of politics. Voicing the wisdom of the age, political philosopher Mark Lilla states, "We find it incomprehensible that theological ideas still inflame the minds of men, stirring up messianic passions that leave societies in ruin."[4] Lilla's worry is that religious passions, particularly religious passions heated by the fire of messianic hope in the perfection of our politics, lead to bloody outcomes. Not only secular theorists such as Lilla but also theologians and ethicists have debated the relative merits of messianism for our politics. *Messianism*, the Christian theological affirmation that the crucified and resurrected Jesus is sovereign over history, is "a stumbling block" and "foolishness," to borrow the words of Saint Paul.[5] The worry of theorists and theologians alike is that messianism quickly devolves into extremisms of violent enactment or quietist withdrawal.

On the one hand, messianism can correlate with extremist violence that attempts to enact the messianic age through human activity. For example, R. Scott Appleby and his collaborators in the Fundamentalism Project identified in messianic movements what they called an ideology of millennialism in which God will bring history "to a just (and often bloody) culmination."[6] While some version of this eschatological hope animates many peace-pursuing religious traditions, in the context of late modernity millennialism can justify an "emergency clause" that suspends normal ethical constraints on violence. This latent antinomianism justifies violent enactment. Appleby concludes that "in such a context, violence is not only permissible; it is obligatory."[7] Such violence rejects the pluralistic giving and taking of reasons. Such messianic actors aim to remake human society by their own designs, enacting the will of God through human agency. The violent enactment of the messianic age seems to flatly reject the possibility of politics.

On the other hand, messianism can correlate with a quietist withdrawal that waits for God's action. If violent extremism claims that the enactment of the messianic age is up to humans, quietist extremism claims that the initiation of the messianic age is up to God. This type of messianism seems world denying and escapist. As adherents pay more attention to the supernatural, they give less to the natural here and now. This is, perhaps, why eschatology has become an embarrassment in late modernity.[8] This embarrassment is not only evident in the critiques of Friedrich Nietzsche and Ludwig Feuerbach but also in those of theologians such as James Gustafson.[9] Messianism is a problem, on this account, because it invests too much in the future and not enough in the present. Such a quietist extremism seems to fall into the trap of promising a pie in the sky when you die and, in doing so, distracts adherents from the hard, piecemeal work of making a common life with neighbors and enemies.

In both cases, scholars critique messianism as apolitical because its extremisms spell the end of practical reasoning. Ethics and eschatology seem to be at odds.[10] Messianism brings religious ideologies to bear in pluralistic politics, it tempts an antinomian rejection of law and ethics, and it provides cover to charismatic authoritarians who operate with messiah complexes. Whether resulting in violent enactment or quietist withdrawal, messianism inevitably seems to undermine the reasoning that is the very foundation of politics. In this book, however, I argue otherwise. Rather than devolving into extremisms of violence or withdrawal, I show that the messianic affirmation of the presence of the dead not only can evade each of these problems but also can generate a nonviolent politics rooted in distinctive forms of practical reasoning.

I make this argument through an extended case study of the transnational social movement surrounding the School of the Americas Watch. Since 1990 this social movement organization has called for a fundamental change in US foreign policy and the closure of the School of the Americas and its institutional successor, the Western Hemisphere Institute for Security Cooperation, which is a training facility for Latin American military and police officers at Fort Benning in Columbus, Georgia.[11] Graduates of this training facility—including people such as Roberto D'Aubuisson, who ordered the assassination of Archbishop Óscar Romero, and Hugo Banzer, the Bolivian dictator—have gone on to commit heinous acts of violence against Latin American peoples.

The movement to close the SOA/WHINSEC was initiated after one such act of violence—the 1989 assassination of six Jesuit professors, their housekeeper, and her daughter at the Universidad Centroamericana José Simeón Cañas (UCA) in San Salvador, El Salvador. Soon after the attack, activists learned that the perpetrators were trained at the School of the Americas. For twenty-five years the movement centered its activity on an annual protest liturgy near the November 16 anniversary of the UCA massacre. In that liturgy, activists read aloud the names of those killed by graduates of the SOA/WHINSEC and proclaimed them as presente. The claim that the dead, those whom Ignacio Ellacuría named the "crucified people," are presente draws on a syncretistic mix of precedents: Christian creedal affirmations of a belief in and hope for the resurrection, Latin American leftist protest repertoires, and pre-Colombian traditions of ancestralization. I argue that this claim is messianic. Naming it as such calls up a bundle of complex associations, some of which I engage in the pages to come. But I use this ascription as a Christian political theologian to identify the interruptive reign of Jesus the Christ in history. Locating my own particularity should not be understood as a denial of either the complex plurality of messianic thought or the movement to close the SOA/WHINSEC. Rather, I name my own convictions here to allow the reader as well as the activists and authors I engage to maintain their difference. This book explores the political, moral, and theological significance of the messianic claim presente as it shapes the deliberation of this nonviolent movement. As I show, the messianic extremism of the movement does not devolve into violence or quietism; rather, it opens into practical reasoning.

Through an extended case study of the SOA Watch, I construct a messianic political theology of the crucified and resurrected people. I juxtapose ethnographic and historical materials with normative and theological analysis to argue that the dead are political agents. My thesis is that the crucified people are present as a messianic sign that the current age is being broken open, that the strictures of death are being overturned, and that resurrection is breaking in among us. This does not mean the end of practical reason, however, as some would worry or hope. Such a messianic inclusion of the dead requires neither violent enactment nor quietist withdrawal. Rather, it can generate a fruitful though unresolved tension between political effectiveness and moral faithfulness as activists respond to God's resurrecting action in "taking the crucified down from their crosses."[12]

The analysis that follows begins and ends with the *¡presente!* litany and in particular the messianic claim that the dead are present at the gates of Fort Benning. This claim, which is performed liturgically, fundamentally conditions the political task of practical reasoning that follows. To say that messianism fundamentally conditions SOA Watch politics is not to suggest that it does so in a clear or definitive way. Rather, in an apophatic register, the claim of presente stands even in judgment of the SOA Watch's political efforts. The claim that the dead are presente calls SOA Watch participants to a faithful and effective solidarity with the dead. The tension between faithfulness and effectiveness is one that is native to the political imaginations of many SOA Watch activists. In spite of the tendency of academics to pit faithfulness and effectiveness against one another, a tendency I explore in the following section, I argue that the messianic obligations generated by the *¡presente!* litany require the exercise of practical reason as people in collectives discern what to do in light of competing goods.

THE MESSIANIC DISRUPTION OF PRACTICAL REASON IN POLITICAL THEOLOGY AND STRATEGIC NONVIOLENCE

This book develops a messianic political theology that seeks to demonstrate how the liturgically invoked presence of the dead informs a collective exercise of practical reason about what to do in the face of an intractable system of violence and death. The claim that messianism and practical reason can be constructively related requires defense, however, for conventional wisdom would suggest that messianism is anything but reasonable.

The opposition of messianism and practical reason has a long history that structures the two fields of study that this book contributes to: political theology and civil resistance. In each of these literatures, the extremist risks to practical reason—quietism and violence—find expression in the maxims that animate the opposing impulses of faithfulness and effectiveness. *Messianic quietism* is a withdrawal from politics in an attempt to remain faithful because it is all up to God. *Messianic violence* is an enactment of responsibility that assumes it is all up to us. Both extremes belie errors in practical reasoning, but these errors are present not only in messianic extremes but also in academic discourses. To name my debt to these discourses, as well as to demonstrate where I hope to contribute, let me situate my argument briefly within them.

Practical reason has been classically understood as the capacity to discern the goods at stake in a particular action and the means appropriate to achieve those goods. A person with *phronesis*, or prudence, to use the scholastic terminology, is able to discern the goods or principles at play in a concrete situation, to imagine prospectively or retrospectively the results of certain courses of action, and to judge how they ought to act in such a situation to preserve and pursue those goods. Aristotle argued that such reasoning was a fuzzy science.[13] Some social theorists such as Pierre Bourdieu have expanded this claim such that practice can, at times, swing free of what we would commonly understand as reason.[14] But even taking Bourdieu's insight that practical reason is not a speculative enterprise but one that is formed through habit and power, I think the classical definition of practical reason as a form of *thinking* is worth retaining. People who act often, but by no means always, think about and justify their actions with principles in mind.[15]

In this book, my interest in practical reason has centered on the kinds of justifications that SOA Watch actors give when they think about their tactical decisions: whether to lobby or to commit civil disobedience, whether to use Christian God-talk or to appeal to cross-traditionally held values and symbols, whether to continue gathering at Fort Benning or to move their protest to the US-Mexico border. Time and again, as I demonstrate throughout the following chapters, when thinking reflexively about their tactical decisions, SOA Watch actors analyzed those decisions through the dialectical tension between faithfulness and effectiveness. This dialectic is a messianic one: SOA Watch actors wonder how to remain faithful to the dead who are presente while effectively intervening in the system of US–Latin American militarism. Balancing and specifying these demands of faithfulness and effectiveness—indeterminate obligations that are generated by the presence of the dead—is the work of practical reason. While my research subjects described this tension without any prompting on my part, the dialectic has a history that is also reflected in academic discourse.

Most prominently, social theorist Max Weber argued that conviction and responsibility, analogues to faithfulness and effectiveness, are the principle goods at stake in the vocation of politics. Reflecting on the demands of politics for his own context in the early days of Weimar Germany, Weber delineated two primary political ethics in his 1919 address "Politics as a Vocation":[16] the politics of ultimate ends and the politics of responsibility. For Weber, the *politics of ultimate ends* was oriented toward a commitment to faithful adherence to religious or ethical demands. A principled stand, this posture of political engagement says, "I've been faithful to this or that requirement, and the rest is up to God." The *politics of responsibility*, however, was concerned about the effect of its political engagement. It asks what, if any, consequences political engagement will have, and it attempts to shape action based on anticipated outcomes. It takes responsibility by prospectively anticipating and retrospectively owning the impact of political action.[17]

Weber's purpose in articulating these two ethics of political reasoning was heuristic. He was constructing a set of ideal types that by design exaggerated concrete manifestations of the same dynamics. Descriptively, Weber aimed to disaggregate two modes of political engagement and show how they are motivated by distinct principles of action. In the end, however, Weber argued that they are not opposed but together dialectically constitute the vocation of politics.[18]

What is important for my argument is to note how Weber's heuristic description becomes our contemporary dilemma. In its ideal form, the typological method ought to be evaluated on its capacity to descriptively illuminate concrete empirical cases. Surely it is helpful to see the way in which these ideal types contrast with each other and how they generate different modes of political engagement. Yet ideal types are also illuminative when they fail. And they often fail because most concrete embodiments are intractably mixed. The problem for us is that Weber's heuristic division has come to construct our ideational world and not merely describe it. Our common political sense would tell us that a quietist ethics of faithfulness to ultimate ends is simply oppositional to a violent ethics of responsibility. As I demonstrate, whether to Christian political theologians or to analysts of strategic nonviolence, these oppositions have become basic and actively structure our account of what is good, true, and right. Though Weber cannot be faulted for this error, the reception of his opposition distorts our descriptive, evaluative, and constructive capacities.

Political Theology

The primary academic discourse to which this book aims to contribute is the field of political theology. The term itself is contested. *Political theology* is currently used to describe a wide variety of scholarly projects from liberation theologies and critiques of civil religion to historical retrievals of classic figures focused on questions of sovereignty, power, and agency.[19] In its genealogy, the term came to prominence in the Anglophone world due to the work of German post-Shoah scholars Jürgen Moltmann, Dorothee Sölle, and Johann Baptist Metz and to the theologies of liberation from Latin America, Black theologians, and feminists. After the publication of translations of German political theorist Carl Schmitt's works, a classical account of the "theology of the political" has enjoyed a renaissance.[20] Who can claim the term is thus a matter of some debate. I do not intend to resolve this contestation here or to choose a side in the squabbles. Rather, I use *political theology* in the banal sense of a normative theological analysis of the dynamics of power, or politics.[21]

While it is simply a historical fact that theology and politics are co-implicating discourses in the West, the nature of their relationship has long troubled the Christian theological tradition. Is politics a sphere of human making that God, from beyond history, redeems? Or is politics itself a location where God is active in redeeming the world in cooperation with historical human activity? Or are humans responsible for building God's reign on earth? At issue for Christian theologians is the location, time, and means of God's agency.

Christian thinkers such as Reinhold Niebuhr (as well as Robert Markus, Oliver O'Donovan, Jean Bethke Elshtain, Charles Mathewes, John Milbank, and William Cavanaugh, among others) have used Saint Augustine's distinction between the two cities to indicate the contours of God's action.[22] Accordingly, the city of God is on pilgrimage, and though inextricably mixed with the city of earth, *history* is the space of human judgment in which we can anticipate but never realize the final culmination of God's salvation. Politics "during the world" is thus limited, for example, in Niebuhr's account by human sin and in O'Donovan's by human finitude.[23] God acts from eternity to enter the space and time of human contingency. The human agency that is required, therefore, is an effective responsibility of judgment. Politics is thus a space of penultimate human activity marked by fallible human judgments and conditioned ultimately by God's final action. Consequently, Augustinians tend to downplay the salvific significance of politics. While effective responsibility is the melody line (an overpowering one in Niebuhr but less so in O'Donovan), faithfulness plays harmony.[24]

Responding especially to Niebuhr, ecclesiocentrists such as theological ethicists John Howard Yoder and Stanley Hauerwas and their followers have argued that the church is the privileged location of God's action in the world.[25] Critiquing the Augustinians' fixation on politics as the province of the state, and Niebuhr's relegation of Christ to a transcendent and inapplicable norm, they argue that the living body of Christ is God's vision for the world. God acts metonymically through the church, meaning the church is the privileged site that stands in for God's agency in the world. Therefore, this is not a politics that is captured by the logic of effectiveness; rather, it is a politics that depends on God's redemptive agency to complete the enduring faithfulness of God's people. Thus, the "responsibility" of the Christian citizen is to wait faithfully and in obedience. Effectiveness is an idol that should be resisted.[26]

If Augustinians have tended to emphasize effectiveness and ecclesiocentrists faithfulness, liberationists have attempted a resolution of the antinomy. Prominently, Gustavo Gutiérrez has developed a theology of liberation rooted in the experiences of the poor and responding with fidelity to the long Christian theological tradition of what is now termed a preferential option for the marginalized.[27] In addition to Latin American liberation theology, Black liberationists, womanists, and feminists, among many others, have constructed liberation theologies responsive to particular contexts of oppression.[28] These projects hold in common an attempt to forge a relationship between political action and fidelity, variously construed, to the Gospel. For Gutiérrez, drawing on the example of Óscar Romero, "concern for effective action is a way of expressing love for the other."[29] Echoing this blending of faithfulness and effectiveness, Leonardo Boff and Clodovis Boff have argued for an "effective love," suggesting that (1) if we are followers of Jesus, we should love the poor as Jesus did; (2) if we love the poor, we must love them in their actuality, not through our own paternalistic projections of them; and (3) we therefore must love them effectively, attending to their needs and the alleviation of their suffering.[30] Helpfully, Gutiérrez and the Boffs insist that Christians should keep in play both faithfulness to the example of Jesus and effectiveness in carrying out that example.

Augustinians have tended to focus on responsibility, ecclesiocentrists have tended to focus on faithfulness, and liberationists have attempted to keep both principles in play. This book engages each of these literatures. For example, in chapter 2 I interact extensively with William Cavanaugh, who is both an Augustinian and an ecclesiocentrist, and in chapter 5 I take up womanist and Black theological engagement with redemptive suffering. This book especially develops the liberationist impulse to keep both faithfulness and effectiveness in a dialectical tension. Just as the SOA Watch movement that began in the wake of the UCA massacre, this project draws from the work of liberationists Ignacio Ellacuría—president of the UCA and target of the SOA-trained Atlacatl Battalion—and his colleague and interpreter Jon Sobrino, who escaped assassination only by virtue of being at an international conference at the time of the attack. Drawing on this liberationist stream, however, this book pushes in a messianic direction by referencing the political theologies that draw a thread from Saint Paul to Walter Benjamin, Jacob Taubes, Johann Baptist Metz, and Giorgio Agamben. Before returning to this messianic lineage more fully, let us turn to a second field this book contributes to—namely, strategic nonviolence.

Strategic Nonviolence

Not unlike the political theology just surveyed, analysts of nonviolent action have similarly been exercised by the relationship between principle and strategy, faithfulness and effectiveness. Peace studies scholar David Cortright narrates the development of the theory and practice of nonviolence as a gradual maturation away from religious roots and toward a scientifically verified political practice.[31] Starting with Mahatma Gandhi's appropriation of his Jain and Hindu commitments for political purposes, Cortright then moves to Martin Luther King Jr.'s melding of Gandhian nonviolence with Niebuhr's Christian realism. Together, they produced a "realistic pacifism." While Gandhi and King both held a fidelity to both their religious commitments and a desire for effective social change, Cortright identifies a paradigm shift following the civil rights movement. With public intellectual and War Resister's League activist Barbara Deming and political theorist Gene Sharp, effectiveness and faithfulness were split, and a focus on the techniques of strategic nonviolence emerged as the preferred subject of analysis.[32]

While Deming maintained a moral concern, late in his career Sharp largely discarded faithfulness and its religious baggage. What became important for contemporary analysts such as Erica Chenoweth and Maria Stephan is not the moral superiority of nonviolent struggle, its ability to honor the humanity of the enemy, or the purity of the nonviolent activist.[33] Rather, what became important is that *nonviolence works*. Deming argued that nonviolent action allows activists to maintain control of the political situation in a way that violence prevents.[34] Sharp argued that nonviolence removes the support of oppressors by enlisting third parties to back opposition movements.[35] Chenoweth and Stephan agree with both but identify a "participation advantage" that allows nonviolent movements a lower barrier to entry and thus a wider base of support, increasing the cost of repression.[36] In each case, regardless of the causal variable identified, effectiveness is the primary measure of value.

Whereas many political theologies leave faithfulness in play, even though some scholars have attempted to diminish its import or fixated on it to the exclusion of questions of effectiveness, strategic nonviolence has largely eclipsed issues of moral principle. This eclipse is not without exceptions, such as Sean Chabot's call for the development of social movement phronesis and Chaiwat Satha-Anand's rejection of the supposed principled, pragmatic binary.[37] But though analysts of strategic nonviolence might allow for moral arguments and even theological affirmations to be used instrumentally in supporting the effectiveness of a nonviolent campaign, they are largely unconcerned with the moral dynamics of nonviolent social change.

As I argue in chapter 3, this eclipse of ethics within strategic nonviolence is due to two trends in the theorization and practice of nonviolence, both of which I take to be positive developments. The first development is the use of social scientific methods in the study of nonviolence. Sociologists and political scientists, theorists of social movements and civil resistance, have analyzed the dynamics of nonviolent contention through large-N quantitative studies that allow a comparative view of the relative success of these movements. These methods are uniquely—some might say narrowly—oriented to questions of effectiveness. The second development is the pluralization of the reasons that actors take up nonviolent tactics. Nonviolent struggle has diffused across a wide, even global variety of cultures and political contexts. The internal reasons that people take up nonviolence are thus irreducibly plural. While I take both trends to be positive, I do not believe that analysts of nonviolence should cease offering moral analysis. As I demonstrate in the following chapters, moral and theological examination of a plural movement such as the SOA Watch makes for a richer analysis in descriptive, evaluative, and constructive registers. Thus, while I draw on the literature of strategic nonviolence, I also critique its evasion of ethics and suggest a method by which normative work might be done, especially with cases of ethical pluralism.

An Alternative: Developing a Messianic Political Theology

Both academic literatures of political theology and strategic nonviolence run the risk of collapsing the dialectic between faithfulness and effectiveness. Rather than allowing Weber's illuminative heuristic to remain ideal, scholars have tended to flatten the theoretical tension between the two principles to one or the other, either faithfulness or effectiveness. This book develops an alternative, a messianic political theology that performs faithfulness to the dead through effective political action with the living.

The messianic political theology I develop draws on the long messianic tradition articulated by Saint Paul; crystalized in the twentieth century by Walter Benjamin, Jacob Taubes, Johann Baptist Metz, and Giorgio Agamben; and recently taken up by Christian ethicists such as Ted A. Smith and P. Travis Kroeker. As Benjamin oracularly suggested in his theses "On the Concept of History," every moment of the present is "shot through with splinters of messianic time."[38] Benjamin imagined politics as a sphere of violence where bodies piled ever higher. Yet, precisely because of the mortification of politics, politics itself can become a site of divine action. Divine agency interrupts the catastrophe of history, even to resurrect the dead. Human responsibility emerges under this interruptive account of divine agency: because it is not all up to us, we engage in politics that we cannot achieve but through redemption. The messianic political theology that I develop works in this political theological tradition and brings it into dialogue with the martyrs remembered by the SOA Watch, especially Ignacio Ellacuría.

As I demonstrate in the following chapters, such messianism is not without its problems.[39] The messianic obligations that follow from the presence of the dead underdetermine the concomitant political actions (chapter 2). Furthermore, these affirmations can become problematic in pluralistic political spaces (chapter 3). Messianic appeals can engender forms of antinomianism through appeals to a higher law that abrogate other norms (chapter 4). And messianism can fund forms of authoritarian charisma that foreshorten rather than enable practical reason (chapter 5). Yet I argue that each of these problems often associated with messianic political theologies emerge when the dialectic of effectiveness and faithfulness is resolved on one side or the other. In critical dialogue with the praxis of the SOA Watch, I develop a messianic political theology of the crucified and resurrected people that leaves considerations of faithfulness and effectiveness in play. I argue that to emphasize one principle of practical reason to the exclusion of the other is a mistake that leads to problematic political judgments and unfaithful practices.

My account refuses the collapse of practical reasoning into pure effectiveness or faithfulness in two ways. First, I include liturgy as a key mediating performance. It generates obligations of solidarity that issue forth into effective political action. The historical antinomy between faithfulness and effectiveness is thus put to productive use by liturgy, which because it is at once earthly and eschatological, refuses their final separation. Second, and related, this liturgical inclusion presupposes a cooperative account of divine and human agency in which God's action is the ground and possibility of creative human agency.[40] It is especially easy to see this at work in liturgical protest, as I develop it in chapter 2, but in all human activity, God's prior action is presupposed. I reject competitive accounts of divine and human agency that would suggest either God is active or it is all up to us. Instead, I suggest that the messianic political theology developed here offers a promising alternative to such accounts. While this argument is implied throughout this book, I take up this second point most fully in the conclusion.

THE PRESENCE OF THE DEAD AND THE SCHOOL
OF THE AMERICAS WATCH

The extended case study that follows tells a story of the emergence and maintenance of a nonviolent movement for social change, the School of the Americas Watch. As with all stories, this one has a beginning, a middle, and an end, but, as I tell it, it does not conform to a simple diachronic arc. Because the chapters drop the reader into the middle of the action, as it were, it is helpful to selectively narrate the story of the School of the Americas Watch here.

Before the SOA Watch, and even before the SOA existed, the US Army founded the Latin American Ground (LAG) School in the Panama Canal Zone in 1946. Following World War II, the LAG was one site of ascendant US power among its neighbors to the south, a bulwark in the US effort to contain communist influence in the Western Hemisphere. Between 1946 and

1959, LAG—which was renamed and reorganized in 1949 as the US Caribbean School—trained nearly eight thousand students, and in the following decade, it trained over thirteen thousand.[41] The training school for Latin American military officers gained its name the School of the Americas in 1963. It remained in Panama until the terms of the Panama Canal Zone were renegotiated in the early 1980s, and the SOA moved to Fort Benning, a sprawling US Army base in Columbus, Georgia, in 1985.

Throughout its history, whether named the LAG, the SOA, or the WHINSEC, this training facility has remained a key component in the US–Latin American military system. It has functioned as a conduit for the movement of (mostly) men, munitions, and money that enable the development of relationships of patronage and cooperation between the United States and its southern neighbors. From its founding in Panama to its renaming in 2001, the School of the Americas trained over sixty thousand troops.[42] Since its name change, the SOA/WHINSEC has trained over twenty-two thousand more graduates, as of 2017.[43] From its earliest instantiations, participants in the school have taken courses in military tactics, weaponry, and procedures. While the subject of the courses and the sending countries of the students have changed over time, what has not changed is the school's place in the system of US empire. Through the relationships built at the school, the United States has pursued its economic and security interests among its southern neighbors. These interests, though often clothed in the language of human rights and economic development, have never been benign. Rather, US influence in Latin America has been accompanied by civilian repression, torture, and death.

Just as the school has a history preceding the movement, so do the protests against it. When the SOA was based in Panama, members of the Sisters of Mercy report protesting at the facility. And once the school moved to Fort Benning, members of the intentional Christian community Koinonia Farm based in Americus, Georgia, participated in a regular vigil at the site. Even Maryknoll priest and activist Roy Bourgeois, who would later become one of the cofounders of the SOA Watch movement, participated in an action at Fort Benning prior to the arrival of the SOA, protesting the training of Salvadoran troops there in 1983.[44] These activists decried the ways in which the SOA's military training insulated and facilitated the impunity of Latin American officers and trained them in the counterinsurgency doctrines of the Cold War.

These protesters, among many others, were part of the Central American Solidarity Movement (CASM), which followed on the heels of the anti-war and New Left movements of the 1960s and 1970s.[45] The CASM had a particularly religious orientation. Many of its leaders were former and current missionaries who had worked in Central America and, because of that work, were uniquely positioned to speak with some authority about the experiences of violence and repression that plagued Central and South America.[46] The religious identity of the actors not only allowed their biographical availability but also informed the kinds of tactics they used. Many drew on a long tradition of protest repertoires of the Catholic left, repertoires that included using liturgy as a form of nonviolent direct action. By calling on the theological resources of their tradition, activists prophetically indicted the governmental policies that meant death for their Latin American allies.[47]

Though Catholic leftists and CASM activists had some awareness of the SOA, it was not until the assassination of six Jesuits, their housekeeper, and her daughter at the Universidad Centroamericana in San Salvador in 1989 that the SOA emerged as a focus of activism.[48] The assassinations proved a moral shock that mobilized CASM activists even as the wider movement had begun to wane.[49] Roy Bourgeois joined with other CASM activists to target the SOA. The training facility had come to their attention through media coverage when Rep. Joseph Moakley (D-MA) led a congressional investigation of the UCA massacre.[50] What Bourgeois and his colleagues started in the wake of the UCA massacre would grow into a movement that involved tens of thousands of participants over a twenty-five-year span.

As the CASM waned, the SOA Watch grew. It blended a mix of legislative and nonviolent direct action tactics to build a sustained movement calling for the closure of the SOA and for a fundamental change in US foreign policy in Latin America. The movement was rooted in an annual mobilization near the anniversary of the UCA massacre (November 16), and it was during such protests that the SOA Watch began to use the ¡presente! litany.[51] After slowly building momentum in the mid-1990s, the movement began to enjoy some legislative successes.[52] These successes were especially forthcoming when activists unearthed "torture manuals" that commended Vietnam War–era methods of interrogation and civilian repression in Latin American contexts. Activist pressure produced its most significant result in 1999 when the US House of Representatives voted to cut funding to the school, a move that would have effectively closed the facility.[53] This victory was scuttled, however, when the Department of Defense initiated a plan to close the facility and rename it the Western Hemisphere Institute for Security Cooperation. This plan won over legislators who were wary of being tied to the SOA but were willing to continue supporting its aims under a different name.[54]

While the movement to close the school still had momentum, a dramatic shift in political opportunity occurred following the attacks on the World Trade Center and the Pentagon on September 11, 2001. This shift in political opportunity meant both an increase in the repression of popular protest and a flourishing of dissent. As the George W. Bush administration made the case for and prosecuted its wars in Afghanistan and Iraq, the latent anti-war movement had a resurgence, and the SOA Watch was well poised to capital-ize on it. The SOA Watch's annual vigil grew to attract more than twenty thousand participants annually in the mid-2000s.[55] The SOA Watch became, as one activist described it, "one of the things that . . . anchored [our] annual activist calendar, in that era of having [an] actual annual activist calendar."[56]

These years of movement growth, however, would not last. In the late 2000s the movement's numbers began to decline. With the election of US president Barack Obama, leftist movements struggled to generate the same level of oppositional energy. And the initial reasons for protest, such as the US military's support of the Salvadoran government and the moral outrage over the UCA massacre, no longer held the same urgency for participants. Movement leaders faced a decision: should they continue to focus on the SOA/WHINSEC or, acknowledging that US military training had diffused to other locations, should they consider focusing on another target? As I show in chapter 3, the influx of new people with new concerns led to a reevalua-tion of the SOA Watch's focus and to a more deliberate attending to immi-gration. Though immigration concerns had long animated the movement, shifts in movement leadership brought a greater attention to the push and pull factors of immigration. As military repression and economic exploita-tion increased in Latin America due to the foreign policy advanced through the SOA/WHINSEC, emigrants fled violence and oppression. This change in focus led in 2016 to a change in location for the SOA Watch's annual mobili-zation. Rather than going to Fort Benning, as it had done for twenty-five years, the SOA Watch led its transnational network of activists and organiz-ers to the US-Mexico border.

This all-too-brief narration of the history of the SOA Watch leaves out many details, but I hope it gives the reader some signposts as we traverse twenty-five years of movement activity. Each chapter takes up some aspect of this history, and together they tell a story about the movement's emer-gence and maintenance as well as a story about the movement's transition in light of new obstacles and opportunities.

METHODS FOR ATTENDING TO THE PRESENCE OF THE DEAD

The work that follows is what anthropologist Michael Burawoy has called an extended case study.[57] Through the dialogical juxtaposition of theory and case, I use the empirics of the case of the SOA Watch to disrupt and challenge the theory developed by both political theologians and analysts of strategic nonviolence.[58] I juxtapose the theoretical resources of academic discourse with the material culture of embodied practices. As such, my work does not resolve this juxtaposition but conceives of the relationship of theory and practice as the relationship between caption and graphic. Rather than truth content being located on one side or the other, in image or word, I argue that it is located in the charged space between.[59]

In taking up empirical, and particularly ethnographic, methods of data gathering and analysis, I follow the lead of Christian theologians and ethicists who have recently turned to ethnographic data as a source for Christian theology.[60] While the ethnographic turn has animated multiple streams of analysis, Christian Scharen and Aana Marie Vigen's edited volume consolidates these streams into a coherent development within the fields of Christian theology and ethics.[61] For them, and for this book, *ethnography* is a rigorous mode of attention that allows researchers to privilege the epistemological and ontological presuppositions of people in their own contexts while bringing to bear the theoretical resources of academic discourse.[62] While this book is not rightly named an ethnography, in the disciplinary sense of anthropology, it is *ethnographically informed*, in that it draws significantly on interviews and participant observation.

My entry into the SOA Watch movement was not first as a researcher but as a participant. To suggest that the result of my analysis is objective in any substantive sense would be self-deceiving. More accurately, this work is a project in reflexivity in which I have analyzed my own intuitions and experiences in light of the experiences of other movement participants and scholarly resources.

Thus, I draw on four data sources. First, the theory I have already outlined provides lenses with which I approach the case. Second, I have engaged in historical research that draws on the studies of US empire, the relationships between US foreign policy and Latin American domestic politics, and the Central American Solidarity Movement.[63] While these general studies provide the background, I also draw from both scholarly and advocacy literature on the SOA/WHINSEC and the SOA Watch.[64] Third, I have conducted a series of unstructured interviews with SOA Watch activists. In these interviews I elicited activists' own accounts of the dilemmas of practical reasoning that they encountered in their political engagement and probed the evaluative principles at work within those deliberative processes. As some social scientists have rightly argued, interviews are limited insofar as they take at face value interviewees' self-disclosure.[65] Thus, fourth, I have engaged in participant observation with SOA Watch activism. Whereas interviews allowed me access to SOA Watch activists' justification of their past actions, ethnographic participant observation allowed another vantage point that disclosed behavior and ideologies at work within a wider sociocultural ecology. Interviews and ethnography work together to provide richer data than one source alone might. Both the ethnographic practices of interviews and participant observation have required my own engagement in the tasks of practical reasoning. As a participant, I have drawn on my own coming to judgment as a data source, one subjected to reflexive analysis.

Utilizing these sources, I engage in three heuristically separable but overlapping analytical tasks across this book: description, evaluation, and construction. To be sure, these tasks mutually determine each other. There is no pure description; the descriptive narratives I have selected serve evaluative and constructive ends. Yet separating these tasks allows the reader a critical vantage point to contest the analytical moves I make and put the data I have assembled to different ends. The *descriptive task* is that of historically representing the development of structures and agents across time. I describe how shifts in political opportunity impact activists as well as how they tactically innovate within those changing contexts. I describe the ideologies that activists draw on to justify their decisions and place those justificatory systems in a wider historical and theological context. The *evaluative task* is that of ethically coming to judgment on the goodness and rightness of the actions that activists take.[66] I render judgments on the ways in which SOA Watch actors resolve, or fail to resolve, the dilemmas that follow. The *constructive task* is that of theologically giving an account of the movement of God within history. While this constructive account would not be possible without the empirics of the case, it is also not tied to them in a reducible way. Rather, it is my constructive intervention to narrate the relationship between the activity of the SOA Watch and the activity of God. Thus, what follows is not an ethnography in a strict sense. More accurately, it is a work of constructive political theology that draws on ethnographic materials.

SUMMARY OF THE FOLLOWING CHAPTERS

¡Presente! Nonviolent Politics and the Resurrection of the Dead proceeds in two parts. The first part sets up the problem of a messianic political theology—initially theoretically, as I have done in this introductory chapter, and then empirically. The second part takes up three dilemmas that arise with such a messianic politics—dilemmas related to pluralism, law, and leadership. Thus, the second chapter, "Crossing the Line: Liturgical Protest and the Tasks of Practical Reason," extends the preceding theoretical discourse to explore the history, theology, and politics of the *¡presente!* litany as a carrier of messianism into the movement. I identify the litany as "liturgical protest," tracking a genealogy of its emergence from Latin American leftist street chants, Roman Catholic litany of the saints, and pre-Colombian and syncretistic veneration of the ancestors. I argue against political theologians such as William Cavanaugh who have conceptualized the movement of liturgy

into politics unidirectionally, as though Christian forms of worship only influence political forms of common life rather than the other way around. So while I find a creedal, and messianic, affirmation of the presence of the crucified and resurrected people at the center of the ¡presente! litany, I argue that this affirmation underdetermines the moral and political actions that follow. Because the liturgical protest and the messianic presence it invokes are not stable in their formative powers, the movement must engage the exercise of practical reasoning to determine what faithful and effective politics requires.

The need for practical reason in the face of messianic extremism structures the three chapters that follow, comprising the second part of the book. Each chapter takes up a persistent challenge for messianic political theologies—pluralism, law, and leadership—and proceeds to both examine how the SOA Watch encounters these challenges and propose possible avenues of development. Chapter 3, "Communities of Resistance: The Power of Nonviolence in a Context of Pluralism," takes up the challenge of pluralism and the role of nonviolence in mediating it. Though emerging initially from the Central American Solidarity Movement and the Catholic left, the SOA Watch became increasingly plural as waves of newcomers from the anti-globalization and anti-war movements swelled the movement's ranks. Nonviolence has served a number of critical roles in coordinating these diverse constituencies, even as it has been questioned and critiqued. I argue against the temptation among analysts of strategic nonviolence to evade normative questions in the presence of such pluralism. Rather, I show how moral analysis can continue to illuminate the practical reasoning at work in the SOA Watch and how attention to the dynamics of pluralism enhances that analysis. Messianism of the crucified and resurrected people need not devolve into quietism; instead, it can fund a coalitional politics of memory and resistance.

The fourth chapter, "Divine Obedience: A Messianic Political Theology of the Higher Law," takes up the messianic challenge to law in its many registers. Situated in a context of legalized violence—that is, the US–Latin American military system in which the poor are daily crucified—SOA Watch actors have sought to transform that violence through lobbying within the legal system and acts of civil disobedience that transgress the same system. I argue that a messianic politics of the higher law serves to hold these diverse legal repertoires together. Appeals to the higher law have been used to justify antinomian rejections of the law of the land, a latent temptation within SOA Watch organizing. However, I show that practical reason allows discernment of obligations under a higher law, which serves to transform a legal regime of violence and death into one that promotes justice and life.

The relativizing of positive law under a higher law presents a problem for SOA Watch actors—that is, how to motivate participation in the messianic absence of clear structures of obligation. The fifth chapter, "Following the Martyrs: Moral Exemplarity, Charismatic Leadership, and the Politics of Sacrifice," analyzes the role that the exemplary dead play as paradigms of moral excellence. Through what I call technologies of iconography, SOA Watch organizers have cultivated the admiration of the exemplary dead and held them up as models to follow. These exemplary dead are deemed particularly paradigmatic in their sacrifices, even to the point of death. I identify the messianism embedded within this valorization of sacrifice and show how it enables not only acts of moral courage but also, ambivalently, the consolidation of the authority of charismatic leaders. I critique the tendency of messianic political theologies to produce a messiah complex. While I argue that sacrifice will be an inevitable part of any struggle for justice, I make a chastened case for its role in nonviolent movements, listening particularly to women and people of color in their critiques of such celebrations of sacrifice.

Together these chapters develop a messianic political theology of the crucified and resurrected people: one that is rooted in the performance of obligations in the *¡presente!* litany and issues forth into effective political action that is faithful to the crucified people. This messianic political theology devolves into neither extremisms of violence nor quietism. The liturgy grounds and expresses the messianism of the movement, but it also underdetermines the actions that follow from it and can conceal the real differences that persist among the participants. The exercise of practical reasoning allows participants to think through and deliberate about what faithfulness to these dead demands. Even as practical reason indicates concrete actions, these actions are continually brought under the judgment of a messianic horizon in which the God of resurrection is acting.

I conclude the book with a constructive theological account of political theology under the creedal affirmation of the resurrection of the dead. Drawing on the political theology of Ignacio Ellacuría, I argue that the messianic presence of the dead can generate an effective and faithful politics, a politics "threatened with Resurrection!"[67] This politics can offer guidance for those whom the dead have called forth to confront entrenched violence and hope for resurrection life.

NOTES

Epigraph: Esquivel, "They Have Threatened Us," in *Threatened with Resurrection*, 63.

1. The term *crucified people* was coined by Ignacio Ellacuría and refers to "that collective body that, being the majority of humanity, owes its situation of crucifixion to a social order organized and maintained by a minority that exercises its dominion

through a series of factors, which, taken together and given their concrete impact within history, must be regarded as sin." See Ellacuría, "Crucified People," in *Ignacio Ellacuría*, 208.

2. Matthew 27:51–53.

3. Taylor, *Secular Age*.

4. Lilla, *Stillborn God*, 3.

5. 1 Corinthians 1:23. *Messianism*, as I use it here, means the Christian theological affirmation that the crucified and resurrected Jesus is Lord. There are, of course, other forms of messianism, and I engage with some of them in this book.

6. Appleby, "Rethinking Fundamentalism," in Calhoun, Juergensmeyer, and VanAntwerpen, *Rethinking Secularism*, 232.

7. Appleby, 233.

8. Metz, *Faith in History*, 101–2.

9. Nietzsche, *Genealogy of Morals*; Feuerbach, *Essence of Christianity*; and Gustafson, *Ethics*. See also Kroeker, *Messianic Political Theology*, 97–99.

10. Schweitzer, *Out of My Life and Thought*, 56–59. See also Kathryn Tanner, "Eschatology and Ethics," in Meilaender and Werpehowski, *Oxford Handbook of Theological Ethics*.

11. The School of the Americas was renamed the Western Hemisphere Institute for Security Cooperation in January 2001. In the following, when I refer to the school before it officially closed in 2000, I refer to it as the SOA. After 2001, I refer to the facility as the SOA/WHINSEC, acknowledging the continuity with the SOA even as the name has changed.

12. This phrase was developed by Jon Sobrino, one of the survivors of the UCA massacre, and drawn from Ignacio Ellacuría. See Sobrino, *No Salvation*, 8.

13. Aristotle, *Nicomachean Ethics*, secs. 1.6, 2.2.

14. See Bourdieu, *Practical Reason*; and Bourdieu, *Logic of Practice*, 86.

15. Social scientists have recently had vigorous debates about whether cognition is mostly automatic or deliberative. See Vaisey, "Motivation and Justification"; and Cerulo, "Mining the Intersections." I follow Ann Mische to suggest that in certain social spaces, such as social movements, we can find heightened forms of deliberative cognition. See Mische, "Finding the Future."

16. Weber, "Politics as a Vocation," in Gerth and Mills, *From Max Weber*.

17. This is a type of "strong" responsibility in which the outcome of history is all up to human action. See McKenny, "Responsibility," in Meilaender and Werpehowski, *Oxford Handbook of Theological Ethics*.

18. Weber, "Politics as a Vocation," 127. The apparent contradiction between Weber's stark contrast between these two principles of action and his latter synthesis of the two has been the site of some scholarly debate. See, for example, Starr, "Structure." Weber's purpose was not merely descriptive. As many critics of Weber have noted, the ideal typological method is normatively freighted. And, certainly, this case is no different. Weber is using the contrast between the ideal types of the politics of ultimate ends and the politics of responsibility to suggest a preference for a responsible ethics of effectiveness in the political sphere. Yet I do not aim to settle an argument about Weber here. My purpose in recalling Weber's contrast is not to intervene

in Weberian scholarship but to show how this dichotomy has elective affinities not only with the tensions of practical reason described by SOA Watch activists but also in the two principal literatures to which this book contributes. For example, see Lovin, "Limits of Freedom"; and Sharp, "Ethics and Responsibility."

19. Lloyd and True, "What Political Theology Could Be."

20. Schmitt, *Political Theology*; and Schmitt, *Concept of the Political*.

21. Of course, this definition has a certain Schmittian resonance. However, I would suggest that Schmitt merely identified what the Christian theological tradition has long born witness to; that is, theology and politics have always been bound up from the earliest moments, a theme I take up specifically with regard to liturgy in chapter 2.

22. Niebuhr, "Augustine's Political Realism," in Cavanaugh, Bailey, and Hovey, *Contemporary Political Theology*; Niebuhr, *Nature and Destiny*; Markus, *Saeculum*; O'Donovan, *Desire of the Nations*; O'Donovan, *Ways of Judgment*; Elshtain, *Augustine*; Mathewes, *Theology of Public Life*; Milbank, *Theology and Social Theory*; Cavanaugh, "From One City to Two"; Cavanaugh, *Migrations of the Holy*; and Cavanaugh, "Church in the Streets."

23. The phrase *during the world* is recovered by Mathewes, *Theology of Public Life*. See also Niebuhr, "Augustine's Political Realism"; and O'Donovan, *Ways of Judgment*.

24. It is beyond my scope to here resolve the differences between Augustinians such as Niebuhr and O'Donovan. The salient point is that politics is the time of human judgment, one that is always marked by sin and finitude and is therefore penultimate. This position, in all its diversity, has clear affinities with Weber's politics of responsibility.

25. Yoder, *Politics of Jesus*; Yoder, *Body Politics*; Hauerwas and Willimon, *Resident Aliens*; and Hauerwas, *After Christendom?* The work of John Howard Yoder should not be cited without mention of his serial sexualized violence perpetrated across his career. I cite him here to indicate, simply, his historical influence. Readers wishing to consider Yoder more carefully should consult Goossen "'Defanging the Beast'"; Guth, "Doing Justice"; and Scarsella, "Not Making Sense." See also Lambelet and Hamilton, "Engage Survivors More."

26. See especially Yoder, *Politics of Jesus*, chap. 12.

27. Gutiérrez, *Theology of Liberation*; Gutiérrez, *We Drink*; and Gutiérrez, *On Job*.

28. See, for example, Cone, *God of the Oppressed*; Schüssler Fiorenza, *In Memory of Her*; Copeland, *Enfleshing Freedom*; Cone, *Cross and the Lynching Tree*; and Douglas, *Stand Your Ground*.

29. Gutiérrez, *We Drink*, 108.

30. Boff and Boff, *Salvation and Liberation*, 4.

31. Cortright, *Peace*.

32. Deming, *Revolution & Equilibrium*; and Sharp, *Politics of Nonviolent Action*. This shift is often narrated as a transition from principled to pragmatic nonviolence, a narration I critique in chapter 3. See also Lambelet, "Nonviolent Struggle."

33. Chenoweth and Stephan, *Why Civil Resistance Works*.

34. Deming, *Revolution & Equilibrium*.

35. Sharp, *Politics of Nonviolent Action*.

36. Chenoweth and Stephan, *Why Civil Resistance Works*, chap. 2.

37. Chabot, "Making Sense," in Schock, *Civil Resistance*; and Satha-Anand, "Overcoming Illusory Division," in Schock, *Civil Resistance*.

38. Benjamin, "On the Concept of History," in Jennings and Eiland, *Selected Writings*, 397.

39. Keller, *God and Power*.

40. Tanner, *God and Creation*. It should be noted here that Tanner's understanding of divine action is distinct from Benjamin's and that of other messianic thinkers. Whereas Tanner affirms the creative agency of the human grounded in the agency of God, Benjamin has a more critical view of the possibilities of human agency. Yet I would suggest there is a compatibility insofar as Benjamin affirms the redemptive possibilities embedded within sites of mortification, of the ruins, of memory. It is beyond the scope of this book to fully develop this theoretically, but I hope to demonstrate the compatibility through the case.

41. Gill, *School of the Americas*, 72–74.

42. Gill.

43. US Army, "WHINSEC Information Brief."

44. For more on this history of activism preceding the SOA Watch, see chapter 2.

45. Smith, *Resisting Reagan*.

46. Nepstad, *Convictions of the Soul*, chap. 4.

47. See, for example, Jason Bivins's treatment of brothers Dan Berrigan and Phil Berrigan and the Catonsville Nine in *Fracture of Good Order*, chap. 4.

48. I take up some of the details of these assassinations in chapter 2. But for more, see the excellent study by Lassalle-Klein, *Blood and Ink*.

49. Smith, *Resisting Reagan*, chap. 12; and Keogh, "Survival."

50. Moakley, "Interim Report"; and Colman McCarthy, "Soldiers' School for Scandal," *Washington Post*, January 28, 1990.

51. The use of what I call liturgical protest came to define the politics of this movement. I explore the protest liturgy more fully in chapter 2.

52. I treat the relationship between different legal repertoires, as well as these legislative processes, more substantively in chapter 4.

53. House of Representatives, Foreign Operations, Export Financing, and Related Programs Appropriations Act of 2000, 106 Cong. Rec. H6700-6709 (July 29, 1999), https://www.congress.gov/congressional-record/1999/07/29/house-section/article/H6676-2.

54. Gallo-Cruz, "Protest and Public Relations."

55. While these numbers are notoriously tricky to pin down, figures higher than twenty thousand have been reported in multiple sources. See Rubin, "Geography of Protest."

56. Interview with Michael Loadenthal, phone, November 11, 2015.

57. Burawoy, *Ethnography Unbound*; and Burawoy, *Extended Case Method*. For an example of a theological ethicist drawing on these methods, see Bretherton, "Coming to Judgment"; and Bretherton, *Resurrecting Democracy*.

58. West, *Disruptive Christian Ethics*; and Whitmore, "Crossing the Road."

59. Smith, "Troeltschian Questions."

60. The turn to ethnography is part of a larger turn to culture within Christian theology and ethics. For two complementary narrations of the turn to culture, see Sheila Davaney, "Theology and the Turn," in Brown, Davaney, and Tanner, *Converging on Culture*; and Ted Smith, "Redeeming Critique."

61. Scharen and Vigen, *Ethnography*.

62. Such an intuition has animated recent works across the fields of Christian and religious ethics, but exemplars for my own work include Stout, *Blessed Are the Organized*; Snarr, *All You That Labor*; Bretherton, *Resurrecting Democracy*; and especially Whitmore, *Imitating Christ in Magwi*.

63. Rosen, *Empire and Dissent*; Huggins, *Political Policing*; Schlesinger and Kinzer, *Bitter Fruit*; Smith, *Resisting Reagan*; Smith, *Disruptive Religion*; and Nepstad, *Convictions of the Soul*.

64. Nelson-Pallmeyer, *School of Assassins*; Nepstad, *Convictions of the Soul*; Gill, *School of the Americas*; and Hodge and Cooper, *Disturbing the Peace*.

65. Jerolmack and Khan, "Talk Is Cheap."

66. Bretherton, "Coming to Judgment."

67. Esquivel, "They Have Threatened Us."

CROSSING THE LINE
Liturgical Protest and the Tasks of Practical Reason

On a brisk November morning, my family and I got off I-185 at the last exit before entering the sprawling US Army base Fort Benning.[1] *Passing flags and statues celebrating the army ranger, we found a parking spot in the working-class neighborhood just north of the entrance to the base. After parking the car, my spouse and I unbuckled our daughters, aged two and five, and got them suited in their rain gear. Together we shuffled past a police checkpoint to join congregants carrying umbrellas, crosses, and placards, braving the light drizzle of a not-too-chilly Georgia rain. Other families with young children, student groups from Catholic colleges, and long-haired veterans in military regalia, along with clergy and vowed religious from a diverse set of religious traditions, had all gathered. We walked about a quarter mile to join the mass and together faced a stage assembled before three imposing fences topped with razor wire. Like ushers, Columbus police lined the street, demarcating the boundaries of the licit. In spite of the rain and, maybe, because of the panoptical vision of the authorities, the feeling was electric.*

Rousing speeches from the local representative of the National Association for the Advancement of Colored People (NAACP) and the School of the Americas Watch were interrupted by sightings of friends new and old to whom we introduced our kids and reconnected. After brief words from several speakers, an offering was taken. Musicians led the congregation, singing, "No mas! No more! We don't want your dirty war!" By the end of this SOA Watch anthem, my five-year-old daughter was singing along.

Following word, offering, and song, the litany that we'd been waiting for, and dreading, began. After silence from the stage, the crowd hushed. A cantor's lone voice rang out, "Óscar Romero, sixty-two years old." And the congregation responded in lyrical chant, "¡Pre-sen-te!" The litany continued with the singing of names: first the six Jesuits and the two women assassinated at the UCA, then the four North American church-women raped and murdered in El Salvador, and then the thousands of others killed and disappeared across Latin America. For each of these victims of the graduates of the notorious US Army training school, the congregation affirmed, "¡Presente!"

A group of dignitaries including SOA Watch cofounder Roy Bourgeois, SOA Watch staff members, and other movement luminaries led a solemn procession around the stage. They carried crosses and iconographic placards with the names of those killed by the graduates of the School of the Americas and Western Hemisphere Institute for Security Cooperation. Behind them followed mourners draped in black robes and wearing white death masks. Pallbearers, they carried mock coffins representing the Latin American dead. And behind them, hundreds of activists from across the United States and beyond slowly processed, carrying crosses marked with the names of the dead, as well as placards and banners representing groups such as the Baptist Peace Fellowship, John Carroll University, Dominican Women Religious, and Veterans for Peace.

We joined the procession, and with each name that the cantors read, we responded, "¡Presente!" while raising our crosses or fists in unison. Slowly circumambulating the stage, we eventually passed by the gate, and I helped my two-year-old daughter place the cross that I'd been carrying into the chain-link fence. Over the course of several hours, the aluminum fence was transformed into an ofrenda, *or "offering," for the dead. We continued to walk, chanting the names of the dead and claiming them as* presente *for the duration of the action.*

The only interruption of the litany came as shouts were raised near the fence. "Someone's crossing the line!" a fellow vigil participant noted excitedly, and I joined with those moving toward the fence to witness the transgression. In years prior, some number of the thousands who gathered had committed acts of civil disobedience by going over, under, or around the fence-turned-ofrenda to pray on the base grounds. Hundreds in the late 1990s, and then thousands in 2000 trespassed onto the base. But after the attacks on the World Trade Center and the Pentagon, military and law enforcement officials made civil disobedience more difficult by erecting fences and severely punishing transgressors. After September 11, 2001, for what is colloquially called crossing the line, activists faced three to six months of imprisonment and thousands of dollars in fines.

This year, it was Nashua, the peace clown, who was making his way over the fences. A repeat offender, Nashua found his way to the canvas covering the Welcome to Fort Benning sign. He unsuccessfully attempted to remove the canvas, unveiling evidence of the base, before Columbus police arrived to arrest him.

✝ ✝ ✝

When I participated in the 2014 annual vigil, the School of the Americas Watch was memorializing the twenty-fifth anniversary of the UCA. What began in 1990 as the gathering of a few friends of SOA Watch cofounder Roy Bourgeois had grown to a gathering of tens of thousands of people just a decade later. In this chapter, I introduce the vigil as a central, formative act of this nonviolent movement for social change. While the annual vigil represents one of a range of organizing tools that the SOA Watch has used to interrupt and transform the structure of US militarism, it has been a particularly potent tactic that has served a number of critical roles in the movement. I argue that the vigil is not merely a tactic but rightly understood as a form of what I call liturgical protest. This descriptor draws us, quite intentionally, into the sphere of political theology.

Observers of nonviolent movements for social and political change have long recognized the critical role of ritual in the dynamics of contention. Whether well-known cases such as Mahatma Gandhi's use of fasting or Martin Luther King Jr.'s use of prayer, or more mundane examples such as a candlelight vigil after an act of violence, ritual serves to channel the at times contradictory emotions of nonviolent actors into common political action. As peace studies scholar Lisa Schirch suggests, "It takes more than a sharp intellect, searing analysis, comprehensive planning, and quick diplomacy to build peace. These are all important components of peacebuilding, but none can transform deeply held traumas, beliefs and fears like religious ritual."[2] For Schirch, as well as other scholars, ritual is an indispensable resource for building a "justpeace."[3] But working solely in the register of ritual, a contested concept to begin with, says too little about the dynamics at work in the SOA Watch's *¡presente!* litany.[4]

More pointedly, I argue that the *¡presente!* litany, which stands at the center of the SOA Watch's annual vigil, is a form of liturgical protest. I show that as liturgical protest, the claim that the dead are present operates as a carrier of messianic content into the center of the movement. The litany performs the principle of solidarity by focusing the participants' common moral attention while embodying a messianic hope for resurrection that outstrips the human capacities for political change. As such, the litany invokes divine agency. Critics of messianic political theologies worry that such invocations can either lead to apathetic resignation (because it's all up to God in the end) or violent implementation (because we are the instrument of God's action on earth).[5] The invocation embedded in the *¡presente!* litany of a belief in and a hope for the resurrection of the dead, however, generates neither resignation nor violence. Instead, the litany performs the principle of solidarity even as it forms participants for future political action.

It is through the anamnestically remembered presence that bonds of solidarity are formed between the living and the dead. Thus, with liturgical and political theologians such as William Cavanaugh, I find that the *¡presente!* litany is formative for participants. But against Cavanaugh and his allies, I argue that this formation underdetermines the political actions that follow. Though the dead are active, in all the ways I explore in this book, they do not tell SOA Watch participants what to do next. Thus, participants must make prudential judgments about the moral demands generated by their participation. Remaining faithful to the presence of the dead requires participants to discern what effective political action is needed. In other words, as liturgical protest the litany does important communicative, formational, and invocative work, but the tasks of practical reason remain.

I pursue this argument in three steps. First, I give a fuller historical account of the development of the *¡presente!* litany over time. I track the transnational migration of the liturgical form from Latin America into its use by the SOA Watch and its development as a repertoire of contention within that movement over nearly two decades. Second, this historical background sets up an analysis of the *¡presente!* litany as liturgical protest. Drawing on recent attention to liturgy and protest among political theologians, I argue that this is an apt descriptor of the annual action at the gates of Fort Benning. Third, rather than imputing an essence to the *¡presente!* litany, my aim is to examine the formative role of the liturgical protest as well as its limits. I argue that the *¡presente!* litany communicates, forms, and invokes bonding participants together with the Latin American dead. I conclude by suggesting that in spite of these significant goods, the *¡presente!* litany is ill-equipped to determine subsequent political actions; rather, it opens into practical reason, which in turn brings even the *¡presente!* litany itself under critical scrutiny.

A HISTORY OF THE *¡PRESENTE!* LITANY

The annual vigil at the gates of Fort Benning began as a response to the outrage of Central American Solidarity Movement activists over the assassination of the six Jesuits, their housekeeper, and her daughter at the Universidad Centroamericana in San Salvador in 1989.[6] The eight murdered at the UCA were but a few of the hundreds of thousands killed in armed conflicts that rocked Latin America in the second half of the twentieth century.[7] While initially focused on the UCA massacre, over the years the SOA Watch's vigil grew to include many other victims of the graduates of the SOA/WHINSEC and, as a result, a wider focus on military training as a symptom of a structure of US–Latin American militarism. Connecting the UCA massacre to a wider structure of one-sided counterinsurgent violence, US Cold War and later drug war policies, and US military training, activists had to develop effective modes of communicating their grievances and of growing their movement. The communicative modes that activists turned to were not new. They were forms of protest that were familiar to them through years of participation in the CASM and the Catholic left and, not coincidentally, their formation in an ecumenical network of churches, mission-oriented religious orders, and activist ecclesial communities. While the CASM was the immediate movement predecessor of the SOA Watch, participants had also spent time in Catholic Worker communities and organized labor, had committed actions with the Plowshares Movement (in which nuclear weapons facilities were literally beaten with hammers to shape these weapons into plowshares), and learned from the innovations of the civil rights and farm worker movements' use of song, liturgy, prayer, and fasting as tactics.[8] Thus, in this context of an ongoing social movement, shifting political opportunities, and moral outrage, the *¡presente!* litany emerged as a fitting form of protest.

Tactical Precursors to the *¡Presente!* Litany

Due to the CASM, US-based activists throughout the 1980s had developed critical consciousness about the impact of US military and immigration policies, activist networks for the dissemination of information and strategy, and repertoires of resistance to display their moral outrage and call for change. As Christian Smith demonstrates in his work, however, by the early 1990s the movement had begun to decline.[9] The political opportunities of the 1980s had closed as peace treaties were negotiated, new issues emerged, and exhaustion after a decade of movement activity took its toll. In spite of this decline, the preexistence of the attention, networks, and repertoires of this movement led to the emergence of another—namely, the movement to close the School of the Americas.[10]

US-based social movement organizations such as Witness for Peace and Pledge of Resistance had spent the 1980s making explicit the connections between US foreign and military policy, one-sided state violence or low-intensity warfare, and immigration from Central and South America to the United States and Canada. Thus, it required no stretch of the imagination to conceive that US military training had played some role in the training of the soldiers and officers who participated in the UCA massacre.

Activists had even targeted the specific institutions that later came to the fore as symbols of US complicity in Latin American violence. Representatives from the Sisters of Mercy report protesting at the School of the Americas while it was located at Fort Gulick in the Panama Canal Zone prior to its closure in 1984 and move to Fort Benning in 1985.[11] And members of Koinonia Farm, an intentional Christian community in Americus, Georgia, had held a regular vigil at the gates of Fort Benning as early as 1982 to protest the US Army's training of Salvadoran soldiers.[12]

In 1983 Maryknoll priest Roy Bourgeois along with Oblate priest Larry Rosebaugh went to Koinonia Farm and discussed a series of actions the two were planning. Bourgeois and Rosebaugh were working with a ramshackle group of activists based at the newly formed Casa Romero in Columbus. Koinonia community member Steve Clemens remembered, "They came to Koinonia and said, 'Look, we're thinking about doing some actions at the base, and just wanted to tell you about them.' And we said, 'Well, we usually go there on Thursday nights, so we'd be happy to join you if that seemed appropriate.' You know, they never gave us the details of exactly what they were going to do."[13]

What they did do was execute a series of actions directed at disrupting the training of Salvadoran troops at Fort Benning. They passed out flyers to the Salvadorans themselves, asking them to lay down their weapons and quit receiving the training. They approached the commanding officers on the base and called on them to cease offering the training. Clemens remembered that "it just turned out that Thursday night was their fifth action. They had done four previous actions and been arrested or escorted off the base prior to that. So we talked together and decided we were going to plant a cross on the base commander's lawn. So there were like four of us, five of us from the vigil group, and then Roy, Larry, and Linda participated."[14] Clemens, along with Bourgeois, Rosebaugh, and army reservist Linda Ventimiglia, planted a cross on the base commander's lawn and then knocked on the door. A young woman, likely the commander's daughter, came to the door and informed the protesters that the commander was not home but would be back soon. Military police arrived before the commander returned, and they were all processed at the Columbus jail.

In spite of being arrested and escorted off the base, the activists kept coming back. On August 9, 1983, the activists carried out one of their most memorable actions. After locating the Salvadorans' barracks, Bourgeois, Rosebaugh, and Ventimiglia waited until lights out and blasted over loudspeakers Óscar Romero's final Sunday homily in which he famously ordered the army to "¡cese la represión!"[15] Later in his trial, Bourgeois explained his actions: "If we really believed that was my brother and sister out there in El Salvador who was going to be killed by these people being trained, could I just sit back and do it once? Could my only response be a letter to my congressperson? . . . I had two close friends, the two Maryknoll sisters, raped and killed there by the military forces of El Salvador."[16] For their actions of disturbing the peace at the military base, Bourgeois received eighteen months and Rosebaugh and Ventimiglia received fifteen months in federal prison. The sentences effectively ended the nonviolent direct action presence of CASM activists on the base through the end of the decade.

The Movement to Close the SOA Emerges

When the six Jesuits were killed at the UCA in 1989, only a handful of activists across the Central American Solidarity Movement were aware of the School of the Americas and the training that it provided to Latin American soldiers. While the group from Koinonia kept an ongoing presence at Fort Benning throughout the 1980s, other sites were identified for larger actions. The UCA massacre, however, was uniquely resonant for Catholics in the United States. As with the assassination of Archbishop Romero and the rape and murder of the four North American churchwomen in El Salvador, these UCA murders "led many American Catholics to feel a personal connection to El Salvador and a personal responsibility for U.S. policy in Central America."[17] The UCA massacre was personally relatable in a way that anonymous statistics of civilian deaths were not.

Writing in the *Washington Post*, columnist Colman McCarthy was one of the first to connect the Jesuits' assassination to the training at the School of the Americas. While many focused immediately on cutting military aid to El Salvador, McCarthy pointed out that another part of the "U.S. complicity in drenching that country with the blood of its citizens" was the US Army's School of the Americas.[18] McCarthy noted that around 650 Salvadoran officers were trained in 1989, and more than 500 more were expected in 1990. But McCarthy could not offer any specific evidence connecting the UCA massacre to US military training. McCarthy's speculation, however, proved well founded when a congressional investigation headed by Rep. Joseph Moakley discovered that several of the officers implicated in the killings, as well as members of the Atlacatl Battalion who carried out the attack, were trained at the School of the Americas, and some had been there as recently as the year prior.[19]

After reading McCarthy's article, Bourgeois decided to return to Fort Benning.[20] Ignoring the ban imposed on him after his action in 1983, Bourgeois returned to Columbus and began to recruit friends and colleagues across the CASM and the Catholic left to join him in protesting at the SOA. According to social movement theorist Sharon Erickson Nepstad, Bourgeois recognized that while people were still moved by the example of Romero and the four churchwomen, the "story of the slain Jesuits . . . had the potential to strengthen activists' waning commitment. By reviving the politicized notion of resurrection, the Jesuits' deaths could be used to remind activists that such sacrifices are not in vain as long as resistance continues."[21] The first action of the cohort gathered by Bourgeois was a hunger strike beginning on Labor Day. Bourgeois along with nine others—teachers, activists, priests, and veterans—fasted as protest, with four of the group abstaining from food for thirty-five days.[22]

Activists recognized that fasting drew some attention, but it was not enough to stop the US Army's training of Salvadoran soldiers. With "no vision of starting a movement," Bourgeois asked who could stay and continue to work to bring justice for the Jesuits. He remembered,

> Most had to get back to their jobs and families, but I asked, who can stay? Let us stay and on the anniversary of the massacre, the first anniversary of the massacre of the Jesuits and the two women, let's do an action, a nonviolent action in solidarity with them, and to try and call attention through nonviolent civil disobedience. We're going to break the law. Hopefully go to prison to cast a light on this issue that's kind of hidden.[23]

On the first anniversary of the Jesuits' assassination, Bourgeois and brothers Charles Liteky and Patrick Liteky carried out a direct action at the SOA that drew on the repertoires of the Catholic left.[24] They began with a prayer service followed by the installation of a white cross with the names and photographs of the slain Jesuits, their cook, and her daughter attached. After concluding, they took their prayers into the school and poured blood, collected from the murder scene of the UCA Jesuits and mixed with their own, on the SOA "Hall of Fame."

The ¡Presente! Litany as a Repertoire of Contention

When activists decided to target the School of the Americas as a symbol of US complicity in Latin American violence, they used the political repertoires that were familiar to them: ecclesial practices of prayer and fasting along with more conventional protest repertoires of street theater and mass mobilization. Social scientist Charles Tilly has described "repertoires of contention" as the "whole set of means [a group] has for making claims of different types on different individuals."[25] I use *repertoire* in a similar way, indicating the culturally embedded means of communicating grievances, making claims, and seeking political change.[26] As I argue later, the shape of these repertoires matters both politically and theologically. But for the moment, it is sufficient to note that the white crosses, the use of prayer as a form of transgressive protest, and the iconography of the assassinated religious leaders were a set of liturgical elements that shaped the protest repertoires that developed year after year. In 1996 more than four hundred protesters gathered to construct a symbolic graveyard for the dead, which then included many other names of those killed by the graduates of the SOA. That year SOA Watch organizers also began to use the *¡presente!* litany, which involved calling out the names of the dead and claiming them as present. In years since, the *¡presente!* litany has anchored the annual vigil and has grown longer along with the list of names of the assassinated, murdered, and disappeared.

The *¡presente!* litany is a transnational *mezcla*, or mixture, of cultural and religious artifacts, drawing on the imagery of Dia de los Muertos (Day of the Dead), the protest litanies of the Latin American left, and the canonical Litany of the Saints.[27] While identifying a singular point of origin is impossible, some version of the *¡presente!* litany has been used across Latin America to memorialize the dead by "crossing the line" between south and north, church and politics. Indigenous Latin American cultures have long traditions of ancestor veneration, traditions that were syncretistically blended with Catholicism during the colonial period. As anthropologist Patricia McAnany has shown in her work on Mayan practices of "ancestralizing," the dead were not merely lost to the past but also "ancestors were created through the performance of death-related rituals."[28] Especially, she argues, through communal practices of memorialization on the anniversary of the loved one's death, the presence of the dead was made real through ritual practice. Closer to our own era, such veneration has at times taken a political valence. Prominently, it was used at the funeral of Chilean poet Pablo Neruda after Augusto Pinochet's coup d'état in 1973. In the climate of fear that followed the coup, Chileans had few avenues to articulate their grievances. So it was a construction worker watching the funeral procession of Neruda who first shouted, "¡Pablo Neruda! *¡Presente!*" And then another, "¡Salvador Allende! *¡Presente!*"[29] The cry presente—at once a theological affirmation and a political protest—has been used across leftist movements in Latin America.

One of the CASM activists responsible for bringing the *¡presente!* litany into widespread use in the United States was John Wright-Rios. A Catholic liturgical musician, Wright-Rios heard a group of Salvadorans shouting the names of slain martyrs and heroes at a protest on the steps of the US Capitol building during the height of the CASM. It brought to his mind the canonical remembrance of the saints and the invocation "pray for us" used typically in the rite of Christian initiation.[30] The contrast between the staid musical setting in the missal and the lively shouts on the Capitol's steps generated a thought: "Yeah, I can come up with a litany of the martyrs of the struggle in Latin America and in other places. I could come up with that and accompany it with drums in a Latin style."[31] Setting the affirmation to an Afro-Colombian cumbia rhythm and melody, Wright-Rios developed the call and response of the ¡presente! litany. Quickly, the litany was picked up across the CASM and used in a movement in which, according to Wright-Rios, "everything felt liturgical."

First used at the SOA Watch's annual vigil in 1996, the ¡presente! litany was a fitting way to memorialize and celebrate those killed by SOA graduates. When musician Chris Inserra first led the litany as a cantor in 1997, she was recruited so that others could cross the line onto the base. After meeting another musician and singing with her on Saturday, the woman asked Inserra, "You know I'm going to cross the line. Would you sing these names for me?" Inserra agreed. "She taught me the simple melody of the names. And the next morning I didn't realize the role that I was stepping into, but she gave me a list of names and it took like about two hours. . . . I stood up at that microphone and sang these names of people, saying presente, and hundreds of people crossed the line. . . . And from that day forward I've been involved in the SOA Watch."[32] Inserra was hooked. She came to lead the musicians' collective and organized others to sing the names of the dead. She also improvised with the litany itself. Whereas Wright-Rios had envisioned an upbeat and celebratory musical setting, Inserra slowed the litany down, adding a few more biographical details to the reading of names and emphasizing its somber quality. She also began adding names as time went on. "People send me names, you know, the Colombia massacres and the El Mozote Massacre, I've got all that. The Ayotzinapa 43, I've got those names. . . . I've got people killed on the border, particularly as we've focused on border militarization. I've got those names. People who walk onto the stage who are survivors of torture will hand me little slips of paper, and I keep adding those names. So it grows every year."[33] What began as the witness of a few activists and priests in 1990 grew to an annual gathering of tens of thousands by the end of the decade. The vigil as a protest form drew on a number of sources but was centered on the ¡presente! litany, a transnational liturgical mezcla that blurred social and political borders, "crossing the line" in more ways than one.

THE ¡PRESENTE! LITANY AS LITURGICAL PROTEST

Given this mezcla of precedents, how might we describe the ¡presente! litany? Is it a political ritual? Is it an ecclesial liturgy? Liturgical theologian and ritual theorist Ronald Grimes distinguishes between six modes of ritual sensibility: ritualization, decorum, ceremony, liturgy, magic, and celebration.[34] Grimes's categorization does not offer types of ritual per se; rather, he identifies sensibilities that populate multiple modes of ritual action. Grimes's aim is not to make a strong distinction between, for example, ritual and liturgy but to show how modes of ritual are part of various human interactions. What sets liturgy apart for Grimes is that it has an ultimate frame of reference and is motivated by a cosmic necessity. This resonates with the participants' experience of the SOA Watch's annual vigil as they described it variously as liturgy, pilgrimage, sacrament, and worship.

I wish to argue that we should understand the *¡presente!* litany as a form of liturgical protest. While it is a political ritual as well as an ecclesial liturgy, to say it is merely one or the other is to say too little about its formative, invocational power. Liturgical protest, I argue, better captures the political and theological dynamics at work in the *¡presente!* litany. *Liturgical protest*, as I use it here, describes contentious political actions that make use of ritual systems to carry out simultaneously political and theological work.[35] An appositive phrase, each term in the descriptor conditions the other.

Activist Ascriptions of the Annual Vigil

When asked, participants have described the *¡presente!* litany to me using words such as "powerful" and "sacred," "liturgical" and "sacramental." In a 1997 editorial, the *National Catholic Reporter* described the vigil: "This was great liturgy. A congregation of over 2,000 people gathered from the four winds, wonderful music to pace and focus the long ceremony toward its central act of worship, the gospel proclaimed simply, powerful preaching to apply it, over 600 concelebrants giving physical witness to the divine presence in meal and sacrifice, a community set in motion to enact what it had just celebrated."[36] Echoing this sentiment, Wesley, an ordained minister who lives in an intentional Christian community in Georgia, reported, "It's the best worship I participate in all year."[37] Claire, a Catholic laywoman who participated in the SOA Watch's vigil years prior as a Jesuit volunteer, remembered that "the fear of facing death and the die-in [were] sacramental."[38] She continued, "I actually wrote that word in [my] journal, 'This was a sacramental experience, a way of remembering and being in solidarity with what people experienced.'" For her, the embodied performance of the litany was transformative in ways that words and talk were insufficient. She said, "That made the experience click for me in a way that talking about it hadn't."

It may be unsurprising to find that participants formed in Christian traditions find the action resonant with their experiences of worship, yet participants who do not identify as Christians made similar affirmations. Nicole Tilson, a self-described agnostic, stated an intention to return to Fort Benning to "reorient myself to that agony . . . because it's like your sorrow is what motivates you."[39] Gigi Burkhalter, another non-religiously non-identified participant, characterized the *¡presente!* litany as collective mindfulness, saying, "I really appreciated that moment of solemn-ness and doing it collectively with such a large group of people. It just is very powerful. . . . It's like how meditation can be really powerful."[40]

Though noting its power, other SOA Watch activists had a more ambivalent relationship to some elements of the annual vigil. For example, at her first vigil in 1997, Rebecca Kanner, a Jewish member of the SOA Watch Labor Caucus, resisted the idea of carrying a cross to represent the dead. "What should I do if I don't want to carry a cross?" she asked Bourgeois. "You can be a peacemaker," he responded, effectively assigning Kanner to crowd control. While I take up the dynamics of pluralism more fully in chapter 3, it is important to note here that just as the sources of the litany were diverse, so were the participants' experiences of it. In spite of this diversity, however, year after year, a plural constituency of participants have joined together in body and voice to claim the presence of the dead. The common messianic affirmation, an anamnestic remembrance, is accomplished performatively through the *¡presente!* litany even if the experience of that performance remains irreducibly diverse.

Liturgy and Protest in Political Theology

Activists, even those without explicit religious identities and commitments, have been attracted to and formed by the complex mixture of religion and politics that occurs annually at the gates of Fort Benning. For the empirically attuned analyst of social movement dynamics, this will come as no surprise. Students of Emile Durkheim have long noted the ways in which political ritual generates cohesion and commitment.[41] Yet those political theorists normatively committed to a "secular" public sphere free from the entanglements of particularist comprehensive visions will find this mezcla troubling.[42] They may worry that the particular vision of a few tends to dominate discourse in a plural context. This worry is real, and I treat it more fully in chapter 3. At this point, however, it is important to note that the allure of a neutral public discourse devoid of comprehensive visions is more evasive than the normatively committed secularist tends to admit. Talal Asad and Elizabeth Shakman Hurd have rightly argued that secularisms in all of their variety are themselves particularist political projects with a history.[43] Politics, even liberal, secular politics, is not theologically neutral. Political theologians have noted the failure of a facile distinction between religion and politics, of religious and political spheres. More pointedly, they have argued that the construction of religion *and* politics as opposing spheres obscures the ways in which politics is itself implicated in narratives of sin and salvation.[44] The *¡presente!* litany bears out the complex mixing of spheres. It is unclear which side it belongs to: Is it a religious revival? A political protest? Or both?

William Cavanaugh has taken this deconstruction of the separation of the religious and the political as fundamental for his own constructive theological work and, prescient for my purposes, for his account of the politics of Christian liturgy.[45] From his earliest writings on the Chilean church's response to the Pinochet regime, Cavanaugh's political theology can be understood as an extended analysis of the theo-politics of ecclesial practices, with a particular attention to the Eucharist.[46] Drawing on Saint Augustine's conception of the two cities, Cavanaugh argues that the church is the truly public space and that its liturgies are always already political.[47] As such, the choice is not between whether to be liturgical or not, or whether to inhabit the political or ecclesial sphere. Rather, the choice is *which* liturgy. For Cavanaugh, because the church is the privileged location of God's action, ecclesial liturgies function morally to bring participants into cooperation with God's will. The nation, by contrast, operates as a pseudo religion with its own liturgies of disciplinary formation. Thus, ecclesial liturgies and national, purportedly secular, liturgies exist in competition, with each offering different cosmological spectacles that form different types of subjects.[48]

Cavanaugh's analysis takes us some way in conceptualizing the cry of presente as liturgical protest. It unmasks the facile divide between religion and politics, refocuses our attention on the embodied and political nature of liturgical action, and demonstrates that such corporate action has an important role in disciplining moral attention. Yet Cavanaugh's position also introduces a number of problems.[49] First, he conceptualizes liturgical performances as basically competitive. Christian liturgies outperform their rivals by providing, in fellow radical orthodoxy theologian John Milbank's words, a counter-liturgy.[50] But there is some slippage here. Even while deconstructing the binaries of religion and politics, sacred and secular, Cavanaugh retains the secular nation-state as a foil with which Christian liturgies compete.[51] This conceptualization disallows any productive borrowing, dynamic movement, or mezcla as what we see in the *¡presente!* litany and, I would argue, as we see in any historical account of liturgical development.[52] Second, the regulative direction of liturgical migration amplifies this competitive conceptualization. For Cavanaugh, ecclesial liturgies begin in the church and move outward into the street. The migration is unidirectional.[53] The origin of the liturgy matters for its authority to form lives well. And the right origin is the church, variously conceived, as the privileged locus of divine action. Third, because the origin is what makes a liturgy good, Cavanaugh ends up evading the necessity of ethical discernment regarding what to do in the warp and woof of politics. Rather than having to decide what action is appropriate to a given political problem, we can merely ask after the origin of the liturgy of formation. If the origin is legitimate, then the response is good.

Whereas Cavanaugh operates with a competitive notion of church and world, the *¡presente!* litany belies a mezcla of appropriations that—rather than a migration from church to world—evidences a transmigration between world and church, and church and world. Such a transmigration should not come as a surprise. As UCA martyr Ignacio Ellacuría remarked in an essay on liturgy and liberation, "We should not be alarmed that our Christian activity is political insofar as it is concerned with the present state of society and with the urgent task of societal transformation."[54] Yet, he argued, we should also be careful not to reduce liturgy to mere politics. The challenge is to keep the liturgy and liberation in a dialectical relation. That is why we need the appositive phrase *liturgical protest* to understand what is going on here. The phrase as a dialectic pushes in two directions: liturgy as protest and protest as liturgy. Let me take each side of the dialectic in turn.

Liturgy as Protest: Litany as Repertoire

First, the *¡presente!* litany operates as a repertoire of contentious politics, liturgy as protest. Repertoires of contention, as I introduced the concept earlier, are those means by which any group has at its disposal to display grievances, make demands, and call for change.[55] These are culturally embedded routines; they take a particular historical shape that is influenced by the time and place of their users. Given the Catholic leadership early on in the movement to close the SOA/WHINSEC, it makes sense that the annual protest might take a liturgical form.

As protest, the liturgy is communicative. It makes a demand by making public the victims of the SOA/WHINSEC graduates. The liturgy says that the lives of the dead cannot be easily forgotten as the collateral damage of progress. It tells the lie on impunity and calls implicitly for a fundamental change in US foreign policy. The very act of making public those who have been killed, assassinated, and disappeared by the graduates of the SOA/WHINSEC is contentious. As political theorist Seyla Benhabib has argued, "The struggle over what gets included in the public agenda is itself a struggle for justice and freedom. . . . The struggle to make something public is a struggle for justice."[56] As a communicative act, the *¡presente!* litany makes public the victims of US foreign policy to movement participants, to the US citizenry, and to the decision-makers both at the school and in Washington, DC.

But liturgies are more than communicative acts. They are also formative. They are effective in their capacities to form a particular type of body, both the personal and corporate body. As "embodied routines," liturgies recruit the will by means of the body.[57] They focus participants' attention on objects of common concern through bodily habituation. As social ethicist Christian Scharen's research on the civic engagement of Christian congregations has demonstrated, participation in worship serves to form participants' identities toward a common "sense of the public" that, in turn, guides public work.[58] In the case of the *¡presente!* litany, participants are formed in a movement-oriented collective identity, one that includes the dead in a politicized cloud of witnesses. This focuses participants' attention on the Latin American dead, those murdered, tortured, and disappeared by the graduates of the School of the Americas. Attention, in turn, demands solidarity, which demands action. For example, Sarah, a death penalty defense attorney, reflected that the litany "was so important to the centering, reminding me of . . . the work I have always wanted to do against the military complex."[59]

As a repertoire of contentious politics, the *¡presente!* litany makes public the victims of the SOA/WHINSEC graduates and forms participants in a movement-oriented collective identity that generates bonds of obligation and solidarity between the living and the dead. Yet liturgies are not merely communicative and formative. They are principally acts of worship, locations of encounter where humans respond to the saving action of God.[60] By conceiving of liturgy as protest, we run the risk of instrumentalization as liturgy is brought into service of some other agenda than worshipful response to God's saving action. Some will worry that putting liturgy to such explicitly political use cheapens what liturgy is, drawing on its moral authority and energy but betraying its theological coherence. As social ethicist Melissa Snarr notes in her study of the use of religious ritual in the US living wage movement, "The use of religious ritual is . . . vulnerable to becoming a form of theater for political expediency, losing its larger meaning and legitimacy."[61]

Protest as Liturgy: Litany as Anamnesis

This worry, though real, misses the other side of the dialectic of liturgical protest—that is, protest as liturgy. Shifting to the other side of the dialectic, the *¡presente!* litany feels as if it is liturgy because it utilizes a number of liturgical elements. It draws on the ritual system that animates Christian, particularly Catholic, liturgy, and the *¡presente!* litany maintains its litheness in part by its ongoing connection to that system. First, the vigil is situated in time liturgically: it is held annually on a Sunday morning near the anniversary of the assassination of the UCA Jesuits. Second, it is located in liminal space, at the border of the army base, a physical border that evokes the existential and spiritual border of life and death. Third, the visuals of the procession—icons of the martyrs on placards, shirts, and twenty-foot-high puppets;

clergy in collars and stoles; the crosses that participants carry marked with the names of the victims—work to connect the participants to the sacredness of the event, not only cognitively but, fourth, through the bodily synchronization of common movement and voice. Fifth, the action has an order, a rite, that proceeds from gathering and welcome, to songs of protest, to a responsive call to commitment,[62] to speeches (homilies?) and an offering to support SOA Watch organizing, and to a culmination in the *¡presente!* litany. Finally, at the center of the action is a theological affirmation that has political content: the liturgical protest acknowledges that the dead are present to us and that in their presence make a claim on us. Here is the presentation of a word (the Word?) and the invitation to participation in what sociologist Sharon Erickson Nepstad rightly calls politicized resurrection.[63]

These markers might not allay concerns over instrumentalization. Sure, a critic might argue, the action parasitically borrows from the ritual system of Christian liturgy. This does not render it free from the charge of instrumentalization; it may only double down on the problems the charge indicates. What this critique misses, however, is that the *¡presente!* litany is doing theological work. The *¡presente!* litany is properly liturgical and, as such, is an anamnetic participation in the action of God in Christ.[64] It joins with the Apostolic and Nicene Creeds to affirm a belief in the resurrection of the body and hope for the resurrection of the dead.[65] The *¡presente!* litany operates as a foretaste of a world that is coming, where the crucified people ground up by the gears of history are resurrected as martyrs, as witnesses. It is not enough to say merely that the *¡presente!* litany affirms the doctrine of the resurrection. It is more accurate to say that it *performs* it. From one perspective, the dead are not raised at the gates of Fort Benning. There is no magic to the liturgy that orchestrates ex opere operato (from the work of the worked) the power of resurrection.[66] Neither does human action, by its own lights, produce resurrection. Rather, the liturgy makes a proleptic theological claim in faith and hope that the dead are raised with Christ. It calls on God to act, creates a disciplined liturgical space for that action, and hopes to participate with God in the work of redemption. Here protest is not merely communicative (addressing legislative and military leaders) or formative (generating a collective identity that, in turn, forms moral commitments). Encompassing both those functions and expanding them as liturgy, this protest invokes divine action; it at once remembers God's work in Christ and calls on God as a political actor to intervene in the not-yet redeemed world.

Whereas instrumentalization is the worry for liturgy as protest, ecclesial authority is the worry for protest as liturgy. Some will wonder, Who owns this liturgy? The movement itself is quite pluralistic, and the vigil is designed by a consensus-based working group. While clergy and laity of many religious traditions participate in this planning, locating an ecclesial authority remains elusive. Furthermore, we cannot reliably locate the transnational origins of the litany itself. Is it a cultural appropriation of Dia de los Muertos? A leftist chant from Chile? A version of the Litany of the Saints? Clearly, it stands not as the work of any particular ecclesial institution but rather as an "emerging ritual" in a pluralistic assembly.[67] Yet I think worries about institutional ownership get the question wrong. Even from the church's perspective, God's action is not limited to the ecclesially authorized liturgies.[68] What the question raises, rather than purity of ecclesial location, is the instability of divine action in liturgy itself. How, and in what ways, is the liturgy good? Effective? How does it respond, or fail to respond, to God's work of redemption?

EVALUATING THE ROLE OF THE *¡PRESENTE!* LITANY

These questions, of course, push us from description to evaluation. To be clear, while I now shift somewhat the analytical register, there is no clean epistemological distinction at work. Description foreshadows the evaluative conclusions I draw, and evaluation constrains the description that I am able to offer. While the heuristic separation of these tasks remains methodologically important, my own location as an observant participant in SOA Watch activism blurs the distinction. Thus, I offer my own judgments not as final conclusions but to show my work and model the deliberative process of practical reasoning, thus inviting the reader to do the same.

If my critique of Cavanaugh's normative preference for a regulative direction of liturgical migration is correct, and we therefore cannot rely on the ecclesial origin of the liturgy to determine whether it can be judged good, then we must ask a series of questions about the faithfulness and effectiveness of the *¡presente!* litany as an act of liturgical protest. Its adherence alone to a liturgical form fails to tell us whether it makes for good politics. And though the *¡presente!* litany has been historically effective in focusing moral attention, it has underdetermined the political actions that follow.[69] As a theo-political act, it does not complete the work it sets out to do. Theologically, the claim of presente is issued on a messianic horizon in which the crucified people are already raised to life in hope, though they are not yet raised. Though anamnestically remembered as present, the dead do not tell activists what to do next. Thus, the bonds of solidarity formed in the liturgical protest underdetermine the acts that follow. Politically, then, the actions that are generated by this eschatological claim remain unclear. A political program does not immediately follow from the presence of the dead. Activists and observers alike must engage the work of practical reasoning.

More than this, the litany itself can be submitted to moral evaluation as we ask whether it is a faithful and effective tactic of social change. My description of the *¡presente!* litany as a repertoire of contention suggests three functions of the liturgical protest—communication, formation, and invocation—and each of these functions present themselves as sites of moral analysis. In other words, these present three lenses that give us purchase for engaging in practical reasoning about the faithfulness and effectiveness of liturgy as a means of contentious political change.

Communicating the Presence of the Dead

As an act of protest, the first and most obvious aim of the *¡presente!* litany is communicative. Etymologically, both protest (from the Latin verb *protestari*, meaning "to publicly witness, testify, or declare") and liturgy (from the Greek noun *leitourgia*, meaning a public work) indicate public, communicative acts. The communicative message of the *¡presente!* litany most directly then is that the dead are present. Activists direct this message at several targets: their fellow protesters, the general public, the media, the military, and the government. While the presence of the dead is the central liturgical affirmation, it joins with a spate of other frames and communiqués. Fundamental among them is the call to "close the SOA": shouted from the stage; emblazoned on T-shirts, stickers, and buttons; and sung in movement anthems. Activists extend this call for policy change to a demand to resist empire and radically alter US foreign relations in Latin America and beyond.

While these other messages are related to the *¡presente!* litany, the SOA Watch's primary aim is making public those anonymous victims of violence, the collateral damage of US foreign policy and military training. By naming them in a public and provocative way, activists have placed the maimed and murdered presence of victims squarely within public vision and discourse. SOA Watch organizer Hendrik Voss stated, "The word *¡presente!* is used in the ritual at the gates of Fort Benning, Georgia, when we remember those who have suffered and have been martyred by graduates of the School of the Americas. We say their names and evoke their spirits, and their testimonies are before us when we respond, '*¡presente!* You are here with us, we do not forget and your death was not in vain.'"[70] SOA Watch activists aim to keep the memory of the victims alive by evoking their spirits. As I discuss in chapter 5, the particular moral and political shape of the testimony of the martyrs presents another deliberative site. Here, however, it is enough to note that the very act of making it public is itself an important goal of the annual action.

But is it effective? Is it faithful? To respond to the first question, we must reject a tight instrumental logic that too often dominates considerations of effect. My intention throughout this work is to disabuse us of the notions of causality that form the chassis of this logic and instead suggest that we consider effectiveness in a humbler way. The effect of our actions is often quite beyond the scope of our limited human agency. As social movement theorists rightly point out, the political opportunity structures of a particular moment constrain and enable certain forms of political action.[71] Describing the *¡presente!* litany as a repertoire of contention reflects my agenda to place it in a particular historical moment, one in which activists' capacities to create the changes they seek are constrained. Charles Tilly, who developed the conceptualization of repertoires that I am using here, is interested in both repertoires and regimes and the interaction between them. For Tilly, regimes are part of what determines which repertoires are fitting and effective. Actors do not have access to the full range of actions in all times and places. Besides these mere structural constraints, however, I wish to make a theological point about God's action. We are not the only ones acting on the stage of history. God is active as well, and including God in the scene is critical for the moral account that I am constructing here.[72] It is important to note, however, that God is not a historical agent in the same way that humans are. It is more theologically accurate to say that God's agency is the very ground of the possibility of human agency. The *¡presente!* litany gestures toward effects it can participate in but not complete. As liturgy, it communicates messianic claims (such as the resurrected presence of the dead) that are issued in hope. The question of effect, then, is a question of whether the litany fittingly participates in and responds to God's action.

In this way, the effectiveness of the communicative action of making public the victims of the SOA/WHINSEC graduates depends on a number of factors, some far beyond the control of activists. First, the effective communicative reach of the action depends on media coverage. Over the years, the SOA Watch protests have garnered some significant media attention both from mainstream as well as grassroots and independent sources. Regardless of the source, coverage has been predicated on two vectors: the size of the protest and the novelty of the protest form. In the first decade of the movement, the direct action tactics of the movement were transgressive and disruptive. Moreover, the *¡presente!* litany was a novel mode of protest and therefore interesting to media sources. But media coverage is fickle and subject to the demands of infotainment. Novelty has a limited shelf life. After twenty-five years, the action is hardly disruptive, and the Columbus police have successfully cordoned off the space with fencing and personnel such that the publicness of the event itself has been curtailed.

Second, beyond the media, the effectiveness of the communicative act depends on the receptiveness of military and government elites. There is, of course, an interaction effect between the media and the government, but it is worthwhile to separate out these targets for special consideration. The *¡presente!* litany at the center of the SOA Watch's annual vigil has been effective in generating piecemeal reformist changes to the structure of the US military's training of Latin American officers.[73] By generating intense attention to and scrutiny of the SOA, activists were successful in forcing the school to close, change its name, and revamp its curriculum in 2000–2001.[74] While the actual impact of this change is contested both within and outside the movement, I would argue that it is an important success that indicates the movement's effectiveness in identifying a target (the US Army's School of the Americas), generating attention (through the annual vigil generally and the *¡presente!* litany specifically), and organizing for change (through lobbying, letter and op-ed writing, and a host of other organizing activities).[75] To be clear, it is impossible to isolate one tactical cause of this change as the *¡presente!* litany alone did not effect the transformations that organizers sought. But I think it is plausible to say that the *¡presente!* litany and its making public the victims of the US military's training policies were an indispensable element of these policy shifts.

(Per)forming the Communion of Saints

I have already suggested that the communicative act at the center of the *¡presente!* litany is faithful in at least one way: it expresses the central creedal commitment to a belief in and the hope for the bodily resurrection of the dead. While this expression raises thorny theological questions about the timing, form, and inclusive reach of resurrection, the affirmation certainly evokes this central Christian doctrine.[76] But communicative faithfulness is not the only consideration here. Moving to the second role that I have identified of the work of the vigil, by faithfully communicating an affirmation of the resurrection of the dead, the *¡presente!* litany proleptically forms, or better performs, the communion of the saints.

We can attribute the effectiveness of the *¡presente!* litany in drawing thousands of people annually to the vigil site at least in part to its faithfulness to Christian worship. For some, such as the participants I cited earlier, the vigil was simply "great liturgy."[77] For these participants, the theological coherence of this affirmation confirms preexistent religious identities while stretching them to include within those identities an affiliation with the SOA Watch movement. But even for participants who were not able immediately to access the Catholic roots of the ritual system, the embodied synchronism of the protest form initiated them into the SOA Watch movement. When Mennonite pastor and activist Joanna Shenk went to the vigil in 2008 as a seminary student new to nonviolent, social justice activism, she struggled to know how exactly to get involved. But the *¡presente!* litany was very clearly something that she could do, something that she could participate in. She recalled,

> One thing that I remember appreciating about that action, or that liturgy, is that it was really clear what we were doing, and we were all doing it together. And, so, given where I was coming from I really appreciated that. Here's a thing that I know how to do, I know how to participate. And, yeah, so that meant a lot. I remember feeling disconcerted by seeing the people lying on the ground doing the die-in stuff. I mean, disconcerting in the way they were hoping it would be. But I'm sure that was the first time I'd ever seen that type of thing acted out. In terms of chanting the names, I think it was as much about what we were, like, remembering these people and remembering the violence, as it was for me about, like, oh, I know how to participate, I can do this; like, it's clear.[78]

The liturgical form of the protest itself integrates the pluralistic assembly into a common body of action and commitment. Whether the vowed religious sister or the black bloc anarchist, they can walk together, chant together, and raise a cross or their fists together. These synchronic movements of body and voice do not do away with real differences of identity, tactical preference, and political commitment. But the *¡presente!* litany does formative work by creating a common body, a common movement identity that integrates diverse identities into a larger whole.

The most common question I have been asked in the course of my research has been, "How many times have you been to the vigil?" The question is not specific for myself as a researcher, though my answer that I have been five times between 2005 and 2015 served to prove a degree of insider status. The question reveals the vigil's role as a rite of passage, a function confirmed off the vigil site as well. Shenk shared the experience of connecting with activists across the country: "I was really glad I had that experience because I was connecting with a lot of radical communities where people had been to the SOA and I was like, yeah, I was there, and I know what you're talking about."[79] Her participation in the vigil verified her status as a movement insider.

In this way, the *¡presente!* litany generates the solidarity that activists affirm.[80] While some participants enter the annual vigil of the SOA Watch with prior commitments to solidarity activism, others do not. The litany itself performatively enacts solidarity as a principle of action. SOA Watch activist and geographer Sara Koopman remembered that "in naming we bring their suffering and loss closer to us. Named, they are no longer abstract figures, but grievable lives."[81] By speaking the names of victims of the SOA/WHINSEC graduates, bonds are formed between the living and the dead. As

Sister Helen Prejean told participants in 2005, "*Presente* also means what we will be called to, our presence. This is as much a way of remembering and memorializing and saying we will never forget you as our openness to be summoned to help to transform this world."[82] The litany takes that which is impossible—namely, an active solidarity between the living and the dead—and through synchronic speech acts and bodily attunement makes it not only possible but also real.

The performance of the reality of the communion of the saints, the solidarity of the living and the dead, generates moral obligations. As Catholic theologian Elizabeth A. Johnson reflects on the affirmation of presente: "In Latin America the custom has grown of responding to the name of the martyrs with the affirmation *Presente*, a multivalent term asking the saint to be present, implying that the saint is present, and most basically, affirming the power of the resurrection which makes it possible for the saint to be present. It is a powerful response that commits the community to honor their memory by emulating their lives."[83] The affirmation at the center of the litany that the dead are presente thus proleptically performs the communion of the saints and generates responsibilities for participants because of the reality of that communion.[84] By incorporating diverse personal bodies into a corporate body that includes even the bodies of the dead, the liturgy focuses moral attention and begins to construct bonds of moral obligation to the dead. A theological analysis allows us to see the effects of this performance, even as the total solidarity of the saints is not yet complete.

Yet there are limits to this formation. In chapter 3, I engage more substantively with the tensions and opportunities provided by a pluralistic movement such as the SOA Watch. But here it is important to note that the liturgical form of the protest, even as it focuses the moral attention of the participants by drawing them to affirm commitments to work on behalf of those named, does not erase the abiding differences of subject position and identity. One way of getting at the formational limits that this presents is to ask, Which bodies are formed by the action?

The first and most obvious body formed is the largely Catholic, largely white, former Central American Solidarity Movement activists and members of the Catholic left. Gathered by their associations with Catholic organizations such as Pace e Bene and Pax Christi, as well as Catholic orders—Maryknoll, Sisters of St. Joseph, and Dominican Sisters, among others—these activists have been the historic core of the SOA Watch constituency. For these North American solidarity activists, many of whom have spent significant time in Latin American countries as development and human rights workers, their participation in SOA Watch activism allows them to continue responding to the call to solidarity. But the annual gatherings are also a time to reconnect with old friends and colleagues, a Catholic left reunion of sorts.

Longtime SOA Watch activist Judith Kelly reflected, "As I watched the crowd, that Sunday morning, I saw people I had met through years of delegations to Guatemala, El Salvador and Haiti. At that moment I felt an affirmation of my life as a nonviolent activist, a moment of almost divine discovery—looking at so many inspiring people who I had known through my work for peace. At that moment, for me, there was no other place on earth where I could be."[85]

A second constituency for whom the *¡presente!* litany has been formative is thousands of Catholic college students. Organizing alternative fall break trips, Jesuit colleges began sending delegations of students in the late 1990s. Reflecting on the impact of this presence, scholar-activist Jack Nelson-Pallmeyer stated, "[We have] thousands and thousands and thousands of young people that participated in the nonviolent activism and were part of this movement that are now engaged in creative work all over this country."[86] One metric of the effectiveness of this formation in movement identity is the way in which the SOA Watch's annual vigil has functioned as a "movement halfway house" by forming young people in movement identities, introducing them to local struggles, and disseminating information about tactics and analysis.[87]

This college constituency, while boosting the numbers, also raises the question of how formative the experience actually was. While Nelson-Pallmeyer celebrated the exposure of students to the SOA Watch movement, longtime Catholic Worker Patrick O'Neill bemoaned their declining attendance. "Where are the Jesuit students now?" he asked me at the 2015 vigil.[88] Another activist who entered the movement along with anti-globalization activists in the early 2000s Michael Loadenthal declined to continue with SOA Watch activism after graduation, calling the protest "college-style-student-organizing." He explained that his sense of SOA Watch vigil participants was that they were "people who were political for two years of their lives as college freshman and sophomores, they get overwhelmed with school and withdraw from that, and then they graduate school, get a job, and withdraw from that for the rest of their lives. When I think about people who are like that, I think of people who attend the SOA Watch."[89]

So though the *¡presente!* litany has been formative for both of these groups—CASM activists and Catholic students—we must ask, Formative in what way? Some leaders in the movement have questioned whether the vigil is largely about the "shedding of white guilt."[90] Certainly, the repeated refrain "not in our name," a slogan borrowed from the anti–Iraq War movement, indicates at the same time a commitment to solidarity and a desire for relinquishment of responsibility. When affirming the capacity of the *¡presente!* litany to form a body and bodies, we have to ask, Which bodies? To categorically dismiss the *¡presente!* litany as an expressive performance of white guilt, however, would be a mistake. The participants are not and never have been uniformly North American whites, and growing numbers of directly impacted activists of color have come to participate. Significant for my evaluation of the liturgical protest, however, the less the *¡presente!* litany is connected to an actual intervention in the structures of militarism and violence, the more it appears to be simply a way to evade responsibility.

Joanna Shenk echoed the recurrent worry I have heard across the movement about the effect of the *¡presente!* litany:

> It didn't seem to me like we were actually expecting to change anything. We were just showing up there to continue to register dissent. And at its best, that's what it felt like: this big reunion of people because folks were, like, doing this work in their contexts all around the country, and hopefully working for achievable goals, or were doing agitating outside of just that week when they were together. But when they got together it was more just like this roar, "We're saying no!"[91]

One SOA Watch staff member sharpened this critique, questioning whether the vigil should be moved or changed before the numbers decline to only a few hundred. He said, "People are coming here, just the same people every year, because it's become a ritual for them."[92] Using ritual as a term of opprobrium, the staffer pointed toward the limits of the liturgy and its failure as a politically effective repertoire.

Those who wish to defend the vigil might say we are witnessing to the martyrs, and our faithfulness to that witness matters. Yet if that witness is disconnected from the actual work of redress and repair, it becomes at best mere ephemeral expressiveness and at worst a privileged expiation of responsibility. In this case, participation in the annual vigil might stand in for the ongoing mundane work of organizing for political change (conference calls, letter writing, lobbying, direct actions, online petitions, and more). Rather than forming participant commitment for ongoing engagement, in this scenario it leads participants to feel they have done the work in merely showing up. The more disconnected the litany becomes from actual effective political change, the more it serves the guilt of North American participants who wish to expiate themselves from responsibility for the violence that has plagued Latin America and the less it serves the liberation of Latin American victims of the graduates of the SOA/WHINSEC.

Invoking God's Action at the Gates of Fort Benning

The final role of the *¡presente!* litany that requires attention is the invocation of divine action. The liturgical protest makes a proleptic claim that the resurrection of the dead is now a present reality. This anamnestically calls on a resurrection power that outstrips any human capacity. By calling the names and claiming them as presente we do not raise the dead. However, by claiming resurrection power, we are calling on God to act. Similar to the laments of the Psalms, this call is a cry to God: "How long, O Lord?" (Psalm 13). Lament is neither a private expression of grief nor an out-of-control emotional outburst. Rather, as biblical scholars note, lament is possible in the context of the covenantal relationship in which the faithful wrestle with and even indict God, calling God to act.[93]

While the ¡presente! litany invokes the action of God, it does not produce it. Here, questions of effectiveness reach their terminus. God's action will not be manipulated or controlled, and even faithful liturgical practice cannot produce the effects activists may hope for. This being said, however, humans can participate in God's promise of resurrection. As such, the ¡presente! litany is rightly understood theologically as a response to God's prior action. As liturgical and historical theologian Katie Grimes has argued, though, we should be wary of a "liturgical optimism" that tempts us to place too much stock in the communicative, formative, and invocative power of liturgy.[94] There is no magic here. Rather, the claim of presente is made on an eschatological horizon in which God is active. What this invocation does not do, however, is to specify the political actions that follow. That requires ongoing, deliberative discernment about faithful, effective activism. In other words, that requires practical reasoning between faithfulness and effectiveness, as I have shown here.

CONCLUSION: LITURGICAL PROTEST AND ITS LIMITS

In this chapter I have introduced the SOA Watch movement through a historical, conceptual, and moral analysis of one of the central repertoires of the movement's activism—the ¡presente! litany. After tracking the transmigration of the litany across borders of nations and societal spheres, I argue that the litany is best understood as a form of liturgical protest that operates as a carrier of messianic content. This descriptive naming opens into a moral evaluation of the litany, with attention to considerations of both faithfulness and effect. By grounding my analysis and evaluation in the empirics of the case of the SOA Watch, I have critiqued the unidirectionality of William Cavanaugh's account of the politics of liturgy. The ¡presente! litany is a mezcla, a mixture of political and theological precedents. If my critique is successful, however, it opens up a problem: the origin of a liturgy cannot merely stand in for its goodness and rightness. Even while the dead are anamnestically re-presented in the ¡presente! litany, they do not tell activists what to do next. Evaluative questions endure. To conclude, I wish to summarize these evaluative judgments and gesture toward the chapters that follow.

Those with concerns merely about effectiveness might say the ¡presente! litany as a political repertoire has been partially successful. It used a resonant repertoire that was rich, maybe excessive, with symbolic meaning to target a specific policy change. It helped build a movement that consistently, in its heyday, brought together thousands of participants and mobilized them not only for the one-day action but for legislative work throughout the year as well. The ¡presente! litany itself was effective because it was a resonant repertoire. But, of course, it was one of many tactics, including broad coalition building, leadership development and training, and nonviolent direct action. While it was effective as a mobilizing tool, the ¡presente! litany failed to close the School of the Americas. It brought about reformist changes in the name and the curriculum, some of which were significant, but it did not achieve its initial aim.

Those with concerns merely about faithfulness might say this action was a faithful witness. It affirmed in a public and political way the significance of the creedal affirmation of a belief in or hope for resurrection. It was faithful to the creed and faithful to the memory of the victims of the SOA/WHINSEC graduates. Faithfulness, configured in this way, is continuing to keep the victims' memory alive and working for justice so that their deaths were not in vain. What we achieved does not ultimately matter, but we were there; our presence was registered.

Both of these evaluative judgments, while morally satisfying in some respects, come up short in others. First, regarding effectiveness, recourse to resonance as the explanatory variable cheapens what is actually happening in liturgical protest. It is not merely that this is a ritual form with similarities to what happens at church, a parasitic echo of an ecclesial practice. Rather, the litany is liturgical in a proper sense as it does the theological work of affirming the power of the resurrection of Christ and invoking divine action. Second, this being the case, faithfulness to a creedal conception of resurrection is not without its effect. Faithfulness has solidarity benefits, generates deeper commitment among participants, and feeds into a commitment to the spadework of policy change. Third, by keeping both effectiveness and faithfulness in play, I judge—and not all that differently than those who might focus solely on faithfulness or effectiveness—that the ¡presente! litany is good in a partial, piecemeal way. But focusing singularly on one or the other misses the dynamic interplay between these two principles of action and obscures the evaluative richness that I have demonstrated.

By keeping both principles in play, we can approach a theological appreciation of a liturgical protest that eschatologically outstrips itself. Not only does the ¡*presente!* litany *communicate* by claiming the enduring significance of the dead and *form* a cloud of witnesses, however loosely conceived, that engages in concrete policy change, it also invokes God's action. It operates within a political imagination in which Cyrus can be named the Messiah (Isaiah 45), in which the dead walk the streets (Matthew 27:52), and the saints Óscar Romero, Ignacio Ellacuría, Jean Donovan, and so many others join as agents in the prayers and protests at the gates of Fort Benning.

While these are no small accomplishments, organizers must continue to discern whether the action effectively communicates to targets and forms the collective identity of participants and whether it faithfully remembers and invokes God's action. After twenty-five years at the gates of Fort Benning, the SOA Watch engaged in significant discernment about moving its annual vigil from its venerable site to the US-Mexico border. This discernment was carried out in iterative deliberation around the foci of faithfulness and effectiveness, accountability to Latin American partners, and faithfulness to the memory of the dead (I return to this deliberation in chapter 6). In 2016 organizers led the international network of activists to Nogales on the US-Mexico border. For the first time the movement's annual vigil was held somewhere other than Fort Benning. Beyond the specifics of the location of the annual vigil, SOA Watch organizers have had to discern how to build a diverse coalition while remaining true to particular religious commitments, symbols, and discourses; how to use the law as a resource for reform and when to transgress it through civil disobedience; and how to motivate participants through appeals to the exemplary authority of saints and martyrs. These topics are the subjects of the chapters to come. Though conceptualizing the ¡*presente!* litany as liturgical protest takes us some distance in understanding the messianic presence of the dead and how it shapes the distinctive politics of the movement, it does not resolve these other dilemmas. The tasks of practical reason remain.

NOTES

1. The following is adapted from field notes generated while conducting participant observation. Unpublished field notes, November 23, 2014.

2. Schirch, "Ritual, Religion, and Peacebuilding," in Appleby, Omer, and Little, *Oxford Handbook of Religion,* 516.

3. The neologism *justpeace* is used by John Paul Lederach and R. Scott Appleby to describe "a dynamic state of affairs in which the reduction and management of violence and the achievement of social and economic justice are undertaken as mutual, reinforcing dimensions of constructive change." Lederach and Appleby, "Strategic Peacebuilding," in Philpott and Powers, *Strategies of Peace,* 23. See also

Lederach, "Justpeace," in European Centre for Conflict Prevention, *People Building Peace.*

4. Talal Asad has critiqued the apparently neutral and scientific conceptualization of ritual by carrying out a genealogy of the term and highlighting its disciplinary function in medieval and monastic contexts. He tracks the historical shift from ritual as a disciplinary tool for the formation of Christian virtue to an anthropological category of symbolic interpretation. While the former is particular and historical, the latter is universal. Asad rightly worries about this shift, particularly the way it obfuscates the operations of power at work within ritual processes. Asad, *Genealogies of Religion*, 55–79. See also McGrane, *Beyond Anthropology*.

5. I take up both of these worries explicitly in my treatment of the politics of the higher law in chapter 4.

6. For more extensive treatment of the context and history of the assassinations, see Commission on the Truth for El Salvador, "From Madness to Hope"; Doggett, *Death Foretold*; and Lassalle-Klein, *Blood and Ink*.

7. These numbers are notoriously difficult to track down because the counterinsurgency doctrines that were the source of the asymmetrical violence often failed to discriminate between combatants and civilians. But in El Salvador alone during the twelve-year civil war, fifty thousand to sixty thousand civilians were killed. David H. McCormick estimates a total of seventy-five thousand, including combatants, were killed. See McCormick, "From Peacekeeping to Peacebuilding," in Doyle, Johnstone, and Orr, *Keeping the Peace*, 282. For a comprehensive account of the impact of US involvement on these armed conflicts, see Grandin, *Empire's Workshop*.

8. Smith, *Resisting Reagan*; Bivins, *Fracture of Good Order*; Nepstad, *Religion and War Resistance*; and Shaw, *Beyond the Fields*.

9. Smith, *Resisting Reagan*, 348.

10. Stacy Keogh argues that the SOA Watch movement continued the Central American Solidarity Movement in spite of the decline that Smith identified. Certainly, this thesis seems to bear out given the breadth of the SOA Watch movement through the 1990s and 2000s. See Keogh, "Survival."

11. Sisters of Mercy, "Mercy's Involvement."

12. For more on Koinonia and its historic role in the social movements in the southeastern United States, see K'Meyer, *Interracialism*; and Marsh, *Beloved Community*, 51–86. The Koinonia vigil, interestingly, was conceived in part as a corrective to a march organized by Atlanta-based activists on January 24, 1982. See "Rally at Fort Benning Deplores the Training of Salvadoran Troops," *New York Times*, January 25, 1982. Through their participation in the Sanctuary movement or volunteering in Central America, many Koinonia members had had firsthand encounters with Central American refugees and were disappointed by the vitriolic tenor of the protest. Steve Clemens said, "After getting back from that march we decided at Koinonia to kind of start our own more of a quiet contemplative protest, so we started a candlelight vigil outside the entrance to the base." Interview with Clemens, phone, October 5, 2015.

13. Clemens, interview.

14. Clemens, interview.

15. Romero, "La iglesia."

16. Quoted by Hodge and Cooper, *Disturbing the Peace*, 98.

17. Epstein, *Political Protest*, 204.

18. McCarthy, "Soldiers' School for Scandal."

19. See Moakley, "Interim Report."

20. Hodge and Cooper, *Disturbing the Peace*, 132.

21. Nepstad, *Convictions of the Soul*, 147.

22. "Hunger Strike Ends at Fort Benning," *Washington Post*, October 8, 1990.

23. Interview with Roy Bourgeois, phone, October 21, 2015.

24. Bourgeois was particularly influenced by the Plowshares Movement. Deploying the metaphor used repeatedly throughout the Old Testament and Tanakh (Isaiah 2:4, Joel 3:10, Micah 4:3), activists have beaten on nuclear weapons facilities with hammers and poured their blood on the controls while calling for an end to nuclear weaponry. See Nepstad, *Religion and War Resistance*.

25. Tilly, *Contentious French*, 4.

26. See also Swidler, "Culture in Action."

27. Whelan, "Litany of Saints"; and Johnson, *Friends of God*, 253.

28. McAnany, *Living with the Ancestors*, xxv.

29. Ruiz, "Cry ¡Presente!," in Dykstra, *Bury the Dead*; Allende, "Isabel Allende"; Moran, *Pablo Neruda*, 196; and Ubalde, *Funeral de Pablo Neruda*. A similar cry was heard at Allende's funeral: "Allende, Allende, Allende está presente!" Stern, *Reckoning with Pinochet*, 39.

30. See Commission on English in the Liturgy, *Rites*, 1:149–50. Interestingly, the "Rite of Acceptance into the Order of Catechumens" asks adult candidates for baptism their names, and after the celebrant calls the name of each candidate, the candidate responds, "Present." Commission on English in the Liturgy, *Rites*, 1:54. My thanks are due to Kim Belcher for bringing this to my attention.

31. Interview with John Wright-Rios, Skype, November 10, 2015.

32. Interview with Chris Inserra, phone, October 7, 2015.

33. Inserra, interview.

34. Grimes, *Beginnings in Ritual Studies*, chap. 3.

35. My use of the term *liturgical protest* is not without precedent. Alain Epp Weaver introduces the concept to refer to the political activity of Zochrot, an Israeli nongovernmental organization promoting bilingual signage and pilgrimage tours of contested land as liturgical action. Weaver draws, as I do, on Cavanaugh and Lloyd to make this case. See Weaver, *Mapping Exile and Return*, 144.

36. "Editorial: Two Liturgies Match Swords with Plowshares," *National Catholic Reporter*, December 12, 1997, http://www.natcath.org/NCR_Online/archives2/1997d/121297/121297f.htm.

37. Interview with clergy SOA Watch participant, phone, October 5, 2014. Where participants are identified by first name only, they are pseudonyms designed to protect the anonymity of interviewees. By default, I conducted all interviews confidentially but gave interviewees the option of waiving anonymity. For the purposes of citation, I have continued to indicate the date, the medium, and the location of the interview where appropriate.

38. Interview with former Jesuit volunteer, Notre Dame, IN, November 4, 2014.

39. Interview with Nicole Tilson, phone, June 8, 2015.

40. Interview with Gigi Burkhalter, Skype, September 29, 2015.

41. See especially Durkheim, *Elementary Forms*. And for more recent appropriations of Durkheim for an analysis ritual in politics, see Kertzer, *Ritual, Politics, and Power*.

42. I have in mind preeminently Rawls, *Theory of Justice*.

43. Asad, *Formations of the Secular*; and Hurd, *Politics of Secularism*.

44. Cavanaugh, *Myth of Religious Violence*.

45. Cavanaugh is not alone in this project but is joined by other "radical orthodoxy" theologians such as Catherine Pickstock, John Milbank, and James K. A. Smith. For a few representative works, see Pickstock, "Liturgy, Art and Politics"; Milbank, *Theology and Social Theory*; Smith, *Desiring the Kingdom*; and Smith, *Imagining the Kingdom*.

46. Cavanaugh, *Torture and Eucharist*; Cavanaugh, *Theopolitical Imagination*; and Cavanaugh, *Migrations of the Holy*.

47. Cavanaugh, *Migrations of the Holy*, 46–68. In his argument about the truly public nature of the church, Cavanaugh draws on Williams, "Politics of the Soul."

48. "Christian liturgy and the liturgies of the world compete on the same playing field, as it were, and . . . a choice between them must be made." Cavanaugh, *Migrations of the Holy*, 120.

49. In the following critiques, I have learned especially from Jennifer Herdt and Vincent Lloyd. See Herdt, "Virtue of the Liturgy"; Lloyd, "Liturgy in the Broadest Sense"; and Lloyd, *Problem with Grace*.

50. See also Cavanaugh's description of the Christian political task as providing an alternative narration of conflict and reconciliation than that provided by modern liberal politics. Cavanaugh, "Discerning: Politics and Reconciliation," in Hauerwas and Wells, *Christian Ethics*; and Cavanaugh, "From One City to Two."

51. Jennifer Herdt makes this point while critiquing James K. A. Smith: "Even as the 'secularity' of the 'secular' is challenged, the 'secular' is retained as a singular category that designates Christianity's competitors." Herdt, "Virtue of the Liturgy," 538.

52. From our basic lexicon (gospel, ecclesia, liturgy) to our worship practice (for example, the Gospel procession) to our holidays (for example, Christmas), Christians have borrowed metaphors, phrases, and practices from whatever political practices were in vogue. See Bretherton, "Coming to Judgment," 169–73. See also Wybrew's account of the elevation of sacred books and the procession with lights and incense as Christian appropriations of Roman political practice. Wybrew, "Ceremonial," in Jones, Wainwright, and Yarnold, *Study of Liturgy*.

53. And in their regulative directionality, Cavanaugh's "migrations of the holy" seem to depart from the more historically attuned, and therefore messy, migrations that John Bossy identifies and from which Cavanaugh's title is adapted. See Bossy, *Christianity in the West*. In a fruitful, but slightly different way, in his volume *Christ*, Edward Schillebeeckx argues that the sacraments should be understood as a *bidirectional* encounter between humanity and God. This vertical account of God's action and human response might be connected horizontally to a transmigration in which liturgical forms move across societal spheres. See also Francis, *Local Worship, Global Church*.

54. Ellacuría, *Freedom Made Flesh*, 234.

55. Tilly, *Contentious French*; and Tilly, *Regimes and Repertoires*.

56. Benhabib, "Models of Public Space," in Calhoun, *Habermas*, 79.

57. Smith, *Desiring the Kingdom*, 1:85.

58. Scharen, *Public Worship and Public Work*.

59. Interview with former death penalty attorney, phone, September 25, 2015.

60. J. D. Crichton argues, in line with traditional Christian understandings of worship, that liturgy is best understood as response: "Because it is God who always takes the initiative, Christian worship is best discussed in the terms of response. In worship man [*sic*] is responding to God and this is true of the whole of the liturgy, whether it be praise, thanksgiving, supplication, or repentance, whether it be Eucharist or baptism, or liturgical prayer or the celebration of the Church's year. If this is so, worship must be seen in the context of saving history, which is the record of divine initiative." Crichton, "Theology of Worship," in Jones, Wainwright, and Yarnold, *Study of Liturgy*, 7.

61. Snarr, *All You That Labor*, 134.

62. Organizers usually invite participants to read together the "SOA Watch Nonviolence Guidelines." I take these commitments up more substantially in chapter 3.

63. Nepstad, *Convictions of the Soul*, 147. This gives political expression to Jean Luc Marion's account of the absence of the presence of Christ in his ascension and thereby the "resurrection of presence." See Marion, *Prolegomena to Charity*, 127.

64. For a complementary theological account of anamnesis—remembering again—see Metz, *Faith in History*, 169–81. See also Morrill, *Anamnesis as Dangerous Memory*.

65. Interestingly, Reinhold Niebuhr affirmed that "there is no part of the Apostles' Creed which, in our present opinion, expresses the whole genius of the Christian faith more nearly than just the despised phrase: 'I believe in the resurrection of the body.'" Niebuhr, *Beyond Tragedy*, 291.

66. Ellacuría is particularly critical of the spiritualization of the liturgy along these lines. See Ellacuría, *Freedom Made Flesh*, 239–41.

67. Grimes, "Emerging Ritual." See also Mitchell, *Liturgy*, 38–49.

68. "For the presence of God does not depend on relations of identity. To the contrary, to say that God is gracious is to say that God remains present to creatures and institutions that are *not* identical to God." Smith, *Weird John Brown*, 121.

69. As Jennifer Herdt rightly argues in her afterword to *The Blackwell Companion to Christian Ethics*, liturgy cannot replace the tasks of practical reason. Offering a charitable critique of the recent turns to liturgy in Christian ethics, exemplified by the volume in which her essay is situated, Herdt argues that liturgy does not "render otiose other aspects of the work of Christian moral reflection and practice; rather, it properly places these within the context of the life of Christian worship." Herdt, "Virtue of the Liturgy," 540.

70. Ruiz, "Cry ¡Presente!," 150.

71. Prominently, see McAdam, *Political Process*. But the insight that historical vagaries both enable and constrain action is a rather venerable idea, central to a materialist conception of history. See, for example, Karl Marx's critique of the French 1851 coup, "Eighteenth Brumaire," in Tucker, *Marx-Engels Reader*.

72. This account of responsibility builds on H. Richard Niebuhr's *Responsible Self*, in which an answer to the question "what is going on?" includes God's action.

73. The dynamic interplay between the moral and political claims made by SOA Watch activists and military elites has been incisively described by Selina Gallo-Cruz as a kind of boundary maintenance in which military officials accepted some of the moral claims made by protesters while moving the target of those policies that are rendered suspect by those claims. See Gallo-Cruz, "Negotiating the Lines."

74. Gallo-Cruz has also analyzed the SOA's "reinvention plan" to demonstrate the ways in which the Department of Defense was able to successfully evade the SOA Watch's central policy demand of closing the SOA. See Gallo-Cruz, "Protest and Public Relations."

75. SOA Watch activists responded in the early 2000s by decrying the change as mere whitewashing, saying, "Different name, same shame." But others, even leaders in the movement, have confessed disappointment with the movement's inability to claim a victory and pivot to other struggles. One said, "There's room, very central room, for a conversation about this school. But that's not a basis for a movement to close it any longer, it seems to me." Interview with anonymous SOA Watch volunteer, October 16, 2015. Meanwhile, officers at the WHINSEC have claimed that activist pressure has significantly changed the curriculum of the school. A former assistant dean of academics at the WHINSEC stated, "[SOA Watch members] have done a lot and they don't realize it. They have made this institute the US DOD's best human rights and International Humanitarian Law training institution. They have allowed SOA and now WHINSEC to place into the military lexicon human rights in a positive light. They took a $4 million institution and made it the agenda at the national level. *Father Roy Bourgeois is the father of WHINSEC*." Cited by Blakeley, "Still Training to Torture?," 1444, emphasis mine.

76. See Thomas Long's careful introduction to these issues in his *Accompany Them with Singing*, 46–56.

77. National Catholic Reporter, "Two Liturgies."

78. Interview with Joanna Shenk, Skype, October 2, 2015.

79. Shenk, interview.

80. In utilizing the language of performativity, I draw explicitly on Judith Butler's account of the performativity of identity and particularly her more recent work on assemblage and the performative politics of nonviolence. See Butler, *Frames of War*, 165–84; Butler, "Ethics and Politics"; and Butler, *Performative Theory of Assembly*.

81. Koopman, "Cutting through Topologies," 838.

82. Puppetista.org, Puppetista Activists @ SOAW.

83. Johnson, *Friends of God*, 254.

84. In chapter 5 I analyze the promise and challenge of exemplarity that Johnson identifies.

85. Ruiz, "Cry ¡Presente!," 150.

86. Interview with Jack Nelson-Pallmeyer, Harrisonburg, VA, October 16, 2015.

87. Social movement theorist Aldon Morris defined a *movement halfway house* as "an established group or organization that is only partially integrated into the

larger society because its participants are actively involved in efforts to bring about a desired change in society." See Morris, *Origins*, 139.

88. Unpublished field notes, November 22, 2015.

89. Loadenthal, interview.

90. Interview with an SOA Watch staff member A, phone, June 16, 2015.

91. Shenk, interview.

92. Interview with SOA Watch staff member B, phone, September 8, 2015.

93. O'Connor, *Lamentations*; and Pemberton, *Hurting with God*. For the implications of this for political theology, see Katongole, *Born from Lament*. See also Lambelet, "'How Long O Lord,'" in Cover, Thiede, and Burns, *Bridging Scripture*.

94. Grimes, "Breaking the Body."

3

COMMUNITIES OF RESISTANCE
The Power of Nonviolence in a
Context of Pluralism

During a light breakfast of eggs and corn tortillas, Anton asked, "Are you going over to prayers?"[1]

"Sure," I responded and quickly finished my breakfast taco.

We made our way to the small chapel behind the Floreses' home. Anton prepared the space by lighting candles and incense. The walls were adorned with tapestries depicting a variety of Christian symbols that were crafted by Anton's mother-in-law, as well as icons depicting Jesus in various biblical scenes. In the center of the circle of couches and chairs was a small table and on it a roughly cut wooden crucifix.

Slowly people entered the space. Those who gathered were a mixture of Alterna community members, the intentional Christian community of which the Floreses were a part, and Buddhist Peace Pilgrims, a group that for the last fifteen years had walked from Atlanta to Fort Benning to participate in the SOA Watch's annual vigil. Brother Utsumi and Sister Denise sat opposite one another in the circle. The twelve of us sat silently.

After gathering in silence, Utsumi and Denise began to chant: "Namu myōhō renge Kkyō."

Repeating the daimoku, the central mantra of Nichiren Buddhism, Utsumi and Denise used drums and a bell as they chanted their prayers. The words were unfamiliar to me, but I felt the drum in my body. I felt the prayers. I also felt my mind wandering here and there, thinking about the upcoming protest, thinking about my research, thinking about other tasks I had before me. Brother Utsumi led the prayers. The small Japanese man had come to Atlanta, the birthplace of Martin Luther King Jr., in 1989 to pray for an end to nuclear weapons. He now is the spiritual leader of the Atlanta Dojo and the Peace Pagoda in east Tennessee.

After chanting for ten minutes, Utsumi opened the floor. The protocol at this point was unclear to me, and we sat a few moments in silence.

Anton pulled up a quote on his phone from Dom Christian de Chergé, a French Trappist prior who had served a monastery in Algeria. He read,

> *If it should happen one day—and it could be today—that I become a victim of the terrorism that now seems to encompass all the foreigners living in Algeria, I would like my community, my church, my family, to remember that my life was given to God and to Algeria; and that they accept that the sole Master of all life was not a stranger to this brutal departure.*
>
> *I would like, when the time comes, to have a space of clearness that would allow me to beg forgiveness of God and of my fellow human beings, and at the same time to forgive with all my heart the one who will strike me down.*
>
> *I could not desire such a death; it seems to me important to state this: How could I rejoice if the Algerian people I love were indiscriminately accused of my murder?*
>
> *My death, obviously, will appear to confirm those who hastily judged me naïve or idealistic: "Let him tell us now what he thinks of it!" But they should know that . . . for this life lost, I give thanks to God. In this "thank you," which is said for everything in my life from now on, I certainly include you, my last-minute friend who will not have known what you are doing. . . . I commend you to the God in whose face I see yours. And may we find each other, happy "good thieves" in Paradise, if it please God, the Father of us both.*

Anton offered little interpretation of his reading but said that Christian's final testament is something he had been thinking about with regard to the attacks in Paris and elsewhere and the kind of rhetoric that had since been turned against refugees fleeing from war and violence.[2] After Anton read the statement, Denise and Utsumi chanted for several more minutes and brought the prayer service to a close.

As we slowly departed, I was struck by the unspoken pluralism of this time and space. Here we were engaged in Buddhist prayers in a clearly Christian space. But no one seemed particularly bothered by it or felt the need to talk about it. This could be due to the fact that these are long-standing relationships that have been developed over the years (Anton has participated in the pilgrimage since at least 2002), and there's an easy way to sink into the familiarness of these rhythms. Or it could be because all the participants in the prayer service share a political commitment to work against militarism and for the closure of the SOA/WHINSEC. Whatever the case, with shared commitment and long-standing relationships, there seemed to be a respect for the religious practices of the other that didn't require sameness. In their particularity, they allowed for respect, appreciation.

My feeling in the space was not discomfort but curiosity and wonderment: I wonder what was happening here. I wonder what the words are that our Buddhist prayer leaders were chanting. I wonder how the Buddhist, Christian, and other participants were making sense of this experience.

I was struck by the mezcla, the mixture, the easy syncretism of these traditions. It was not an abandonment of tradition in any sense; rather, it marked the boundary point of traditions, the place where traditions, deeply held in practice, came to meet each other, and learn from each other, intersect with each other.

† † †

How might we make sense of what was occurring in this space, in the wee hours of a Thursday morning late in November 2015? To set a little context, I was privy to this experience while conducting fieldwork in the days prior to the SOA Watch's annual vigil. My hosts, Charlotte and Anton Flores, were also hosting the Buddhist Peace Pilgrims, a group of a dozen or so folks from across the globe that walks the hundred miles each year from Atlanta to the gates of Fort Benning. The pilgrims have stopped for many years in LaGrange, Georgia, at Alterna, the intentional Christian community of which the Floreses are a part. For Alterna members—"a bilingual community of Christ followers devoted to faithful acts of hospitality, mercy, and justice"[3]—hosting the Buddhist Peace Pilgrims was an expression of their Christian life. For the Buddhist Peace Pilgrims, the international, interreligious prayer service described here was but one stop on a multisite pilgrimage for peace, one that has culminated for sixteen years in the Sunday vigil described in chapter 2.

On one level, this site of interreligious collaboration reveals an "overlapping consensus" in which participants affirm a mutual commitment to nonviolent agitation for the closure of the School of Americas/Western Hemisphere Institute for Security Cooperation.[4] Yet there is something more dynamic, more emergent happening here. In the late-night conversations, the early morning prayers, and the coordinated bodily movement of walking together, year after year, participants are habituated into forms of solidarity that transcend the normal expectations of tolerant collaboration and evince the possibility of what political theorist William Connolly has called deep pluralism.[5] Strikingly, the Buddhist Peace Pilgrims have found significant ways to participate in the *¡presente!* litany that was introduced in chapter 2. Even as the litany carries the messianic affirmation of the presence of the dead, it emerges from a mezcla of sources and animates plural religious and political practices. Utsumi and Denise provide the drumbeat that paces the chants of the *¡presente!* litany. Some years they have been joined by the radical anarchist marching band Cakalak Thunder. While this certainly represents an overlapping consensus, it also indicates something more.

It is important to note, though, that religious diversity is one among many differences that animate and challenge SOA Watch organizing. Differences of subject position, theory of change, citizenship, and relative proximity to the US military system are all part of the pluralistic terrain of the movement to close the SOA/WHINSEC. These divisions must be encountered and constructively deployed—not merely overcome—to build a sustained movement for social and political change.

Difference is not only a practical but also a theoretical challenge. The problem of pluralism has animated several scholarly discourses that are pertinent here. Social movement theorists have recognized that strategic alliances are necessary for building the broad-based coalitions that are often pivotal for movement success.[6] Political theorists, following or challenging John Rawls and Jurgen Habermas, have debated not only the appropriate role of religion in the public sphere but also the possibilities and limits of moral consensus in the midst of plural societies.[7] Critical anthropologists and phenomenologists of the secular, following Talal Asad, have argued that the concepts and practices that construct "religion" and the "public sphere" are determined by relations of power, which must be unveiled and critiqued.[8]

Each of these discourses intersect with the primary theoretical conversation that this chapter engages—namely, recent analyses of nonviolence. With Gene Sharp's intervention into the field in the 1970s and even more significantly with studies such as Erica Chenoweth and Maria Stephan's *Why Civil Resistance Works* in the last decade, the analysis of nonviolence has taken a strong strategic turn.[9] These scholars have facilitated a shift from a concern for the moral coherence of nonviolence to an attention to effective strategies of nonviolent change. One of the motivations for this shift, I suggest, is an awareness of the abiding pluralism of nonviolent movements for social and political change. By focusing on what works, analysts have been able to avoid the messy and at times contradictory reasons actors give for engaging in nonviolent political action in the first place. I maintain however, that this evasion of ethics within the analysis of nonviolence is a mistake. The internal diversity of many nonviolent movements, including the movement to close the SOA/WHINSEC, can take us some distance in explaining the evasion. It is genuinely difficult to understand the complex moral dynamics at play in plural movements. But this is especially true when those dynamics jump the bounds of our immanent frame. The messianic affirmation that the crucified people are present disrupts the normal logics of politics: tolerance, compromise, and consensus. Rather than avoiding the irreducibly plural moral terrain of nonviolent movements, we need analytical tools to describe and evaluate the practical reasoning that nonviolent actors engage in.

In this chapter, I take up an analysis of power, pluralism, and nonviolence in the movement to close the SOA/WHINSEC. As each of these terms are contested and evade simple definition and as I use them in particular ways, it will help the reader for me to specify those uses now. First, regarding *power*, I use the term to indicate, constructively, Hannah Arendt's notion of the strength and capacity that comes from acting in concert with others and, critically, the way that power resides differentially with individuals on the basis of their subject position.[10] The first use is conditioned by the second: the capacity to act in concert is diminished or enabled by the ways in which patriarchy, white supremacy, and other forms of cultural and structural violence are ignored, engaged, resisted, and remedied. Second, I use the term *pluralism* to describe the interstices of difference that are a part of the SOA Watch movement. While differences of religion are one of these interstices, so are subject position, theory of change, citizenship, and relative proximity in the US–Latin American military system. Third, variable commitments to nonviolence are themselves one of the internal differences within the SOA Watch. Nonviolence does not mean one thing; as a principle of action, it animates a number of different discourses, dispositions, and practices. Ultimately, I argue that we ought to understand *nonviolence* as a tradition of moral praxis.[11]

The prayers detailed in this chapter's opening ethnographic vignette are one of numerous sites of deep pluralism in which overlapping interstices of difference are bridged through the practice of nonviolence. My thesis is that remaining faithful to the bonds of solidarity affirmed by and formed in the *¡presente!* litany requires coalition work across these differences, and one of the primary tools of that coalition work is various levels of commitment to nonviolence. Chenoweth and Stephan rightly argue that nonviolent movements are effective by virtue of their capacity to generate the participation of a variety of actors or, in other words, by their power to act in concert. The way this gets worked out, however, is a deeply contextual, relational, and affective matter. Nonviolence is not merely a tactic that can be used instrumentally, though it is that. It is also an embodied principle that animates a pluralistic coalition, rendering differences as opportunities for strength rather than as mere liabilities to be overcome.

Thus, nonviolent coalition building requires ongoing discernment about what these differently located individuals and groups can reasonably work for together. This discernment takes place within, but is not limited to, the terrain of power in which wider societal associations and identities grant legitimacy to certain modes of speech, action, and identity, and discredit others. SOA Watch actors have had to remain attentive to the deforming impact of power and privilege within the movement itself, not just in the structures of empire that it contests. It is not enough to suggest that differences can be held at bay by focusing simply on what tactically works; rather, there are resources in the differences.

This chapter proceeds in three steps. First, I examine more fully the pluralism of the SOA Watch coalition by giving an organizational history of the movement. I show how three overlapping eras have typified SOA Watch organizing: an early stage was characterized by coalitional base building, which opened into a second season of internal critique focused on mainstreaming an anti-oppression analysis, and that led to a third period of attention and accountability to those directly impacted by US militarism. Narrating SOA Watch history in this way allows me to disrupt any simple "subtraction story" in which the movement's religious character is progressively displaced and instead to explore the complex pressures of power, pluralism, and nonviolence.[12] The second part of the chapter takes up these pressures in a theoretical register through engagement with recent literature on strategic nonviolence and civil resistance. While I show how the turn to strategy emerges, at least in part, from a recognition of pluralism, I argue that a narrow focus on what works that excludes ethics hampers our analysis. Third, I bring the first two sections into critical juxtaposition to show how nonviolent power functions within the SOA Watch movement to coordinate the tensions between faithfulness and effectiveness.

While I agree with advocates of strategic nonviolence that effective movements are successful because they gain wide participation, I show how moral commitments to nonviolence can function in different ways: as a discipline, as a tactic, and as an embodied principle. This contributes to my argument that paying attention to the *moral* dynamics of nonviolent movements is more, not less, important under the conditions of pluralism. Such attention is especially important for messianic political theologies, which have a history of producing violent movements. Nonviolence is an indispensable brake on this ambiguous historical tendency.[13]

A HISTORY OF COMMUNITIES OF RESISTANCE

We had gathered in a large industrial-looking auditorium in the Columbus Convention Center, with folding chairs arranged on concrete floors, large beams holding up the timber frame ceiling.[14] There were seats for somewhere around a thousand facing the stage; three quarters of those seats were filled by folks who were talking, reading flyers, or watching the crowd file in. An SOA Watch staff organizer María Luisa Rosal called the group to order. After a brief testimonial—she came from Guatemala with her mother as a refugee after her father was disappeared during the internal armed conflict—she began to do a roll call to see who was in the room.

"If you've been to the vigil for twenty-five years, please stand," she called out. No one visible from my seat stood, but people were looking around to see who had been here every year since the beginning. Cheers went up from the crowd to acknowledge someone who had stood up.

María Luisa continued through the roll call. "If you've been to the vigil for fifteen years, please stand." More folks stood, mostly gray-haired, white activists.

"If you've been to the vigil for five years, please stand." Many more stood but still less than half of the attendees.

"If you're a student, please stand." A significant number of the attendees stood. Those movement veterans who weren't students sat down.

"If you're an educator, please stand." The roll call continued, with participants indicating their affinities by sitting or standing when called.

"If you're a human rights advocate, please stand.

"If you're an immigrant rights activist, please stand.

"If you're an environmentalist, please stand.

"If you're women religious, please stand.

"If you're clergy or part of our communities of faith, please stand.

"If you're part of our LGBT and queer communities, please stand.

"If you're a peacemaker, please stand."

At this point, most folks were standing, and the slow rumble of cheers and hollers had built into swelling shouts and applause.

†††

How does a plural movement such as the SOA Watch emerge and sustain itself over twenty-five years? How does it attract diverse participants while feeding the associations, networks, and affiliations that have been the historic base of the movement? The movement to close the SOA/WHINSEC inherited the symbolic repertoires and strategic dilemmas of its immediate movement predecessor, the Central American Solidarity Movement. In chapter 2, I examined how the SOA Watch took one of these repertoires, the *¡presente!* litany, and made it a cornerstone of its activism. A reader unfamiliar with the SOA Watch may conclude from that analysis that the movement is Christian or, if not Christian, at least "religious." This conclusion, however, would be incorrect or, more carefully, incorrect without significant qualification. Rather than merely solidifying the Christian identity of the movement, its use of this liturgical repertoire created a dilemma, one that was crystallized by sociologist Christian Smith in his analysis of the CASM regarding the question of whether to "maintain a religious identity or diversify."[15]

There is not one answer to this question, and as Smith argued with reference to the CASM, when the tension was resolved, it was done in an ad hoc manner. For some, such as one of the staff organizers I spoke with, the SOA Watch is "*not* a religious movement."[16] Though admitting the significant religious constituency and that one of the movement's founders was a Maryknoll priest, these actors argue that the movement has grown to embrace a wider public and a less religiously laden concept of solidarity. But for others, their participation in the SOA Watch is foundational for their own religious practice, "a high point of [their] liturgical year."[17] For these actors, the gates of Fort Benning are a site of annual pilgrimage, and the *¡presente!* litany constructs their faith in fundamental ways. While this diversity of viewpoints has endured throughout the history of the SOA Watch, its affiliations and alliances have changed over the years.

We could make sense of the shifts in religious affiliation in SOA Watch by telling a story of gradual secularization. The movement started through acts of public witness in which religious (largely Christian) actors worked out their convictions in public. As the movement grew, it made alliances with other movements, its staff professionalized, and its framing took on a more secular valence. In short, what began as a religious movement became a secular one. Yet this narrative is what philosopher Charles Taylor identified as a "subtraction story" in which the religious veneer is inevitably sloughed off, and the secular core remains.[18] While this is one way the actors make sense of the movement's historic changes, it tells too simple a story.[19] It is incorrect to say that the movement operates by a kind of public reason that is free of God and God-talk or that the religious commitments and practices of the movement were simply and inevitably replaced by secular ones. There was nothing inevitable about the development of the movement over time, and a religious affiliation (or lack thereof) is but one of myriad interstices of difference that have impacted SOA Watch organizing. Rather, deeply held religious and secular commitments have required a sustained space of deliberation, convergence, and collaboration.

Not only religious affiliation but also subject position, political ideology and commitment, as well as citizenship and relative proximity to the impact of the violence of US–Latin American militarism all animate the types of collaboration enabled and constrained by SOA Watch organizing. All these relations are transacted on the terrain of power. But the differences of power that distort and deform can also be converted into the power to act in concert. These differences offer sites of conflict but also sites of collaboration, alliance building, and even creative, improvisational synthesis. Thus, the pluralization of the movement over time is not a subtraction story of lamentable loss or praiseworthy replacement but one that includes losses and gains, challenges and opportunities.

In the following section, my primary aim is to complicate the subtraction story by arguing that the history of SOA Watch organizing is less one of secularization and more one of pluralization. Pluralism presents certain challenges for the movement but also affords opportunities. Difference and the conflict that sometimes attends it can be the seedbed for transformative change.

Coalition Building (1990–2009)

Participants in the SOA Watch's actions in the year following the UCA massacre were largely friends and acquaintances of movement cofounder Roy Bourgeois. Readers will recall the two actions carried out immediately after the massacre: a thirty-five-day fast beginning on Labor Day of 1990 and a direct action on the one-year anniversary of the assassinations. The demographic composition of these actions is indicative of the early organizing model. At the fast, the core participants were five Catholic priests (Maryknoll, Dominican, and Jesuit), two of whom were also veterans of the Vietnam War; two male Salvadoran refugees; two female human rights activists (one, a Catholic Worker; the other, a staff member at the Resource Center of the Americas); and two Catholic laymen.[20] At the direct action on the first anniversary of the UCA massacre, Bourgeois and his friends Charles Liteky and Patrick Liteky led the charge. In large part, these white, middle-aged Catholics organized against US militarism because of their personal experiences working with Latin American people.

As anthropologist Lesley Gill summarizes,

> The core group of activists who initiated the anti-SOA movement were veterans of the 1980s struggles to end U.S. government support for murderous Central American regimes. They drew inspiration from the teachings of liberation theology and firsthand encounters with the victims of Central American political violence, and this inspiration lived on among them, even as Central America ceased to be a major political issue in the United States. The activists were middle-aged, church-affiliated, religious people. Many were (or had been) priests, nuns, and pastors who had worked as missionaries in Latin America, where they bore witness to the human consequences of the dirty wars, or they were involved with Central American refugees in the United States, primarily through the church-based Sanctuary movement.[21]

Unsurprisingly, SOA Watch activists used the networks that were available to them to mobilize support for their campaign.

The coalitional strategy of the SOA Watch in the 1990s was to target and gain support from obvious constituencies, what activists sometimes call low-hanging fruit. The movement was bolstered by an early endorsement by the Leadership Conference of Women Religious (LCWR), the organization that represents 90 percent of Catholic women religious in the United States. In 1994 the LCWR's national assembly passed a resolution calling for the closure of the SOA, an action it would repeat in 1996 and 1998.[22] And in August 1996, more than four hundred LCWR members gathered at the gates of Fort Benning prior to their national assembly in Atlanta, according to action organizer Sister Mary O'Brien of the Congregation of Saint Joseph, to "call national attention to the urgent need to put an end to an institution of violence by closing the School of the Americas."[23] Other Catholic organizations also lent their support. Pax Christi, for example, gave movement cofounder Bourgeois the Pope Paul VI Teacher of Peace Award in 1997.[24]

While primary support came from Catholic organizations, other groups were also present from an early stage. Historic civil and human rights groups such as the NAACP issued resolutions of support.[25] And similar to the Catholics who mobilized in part because of their justified outrage at the targeting of religious leaders, labor groups were moved by the stories of organizers who were assassinated by repressive Latin American militaries.[26] The SOA Watch Labor Caucus formed out of a 1998 action in Tacoma, Washington, and in 1999 the Executive Council of the American Federation of Labor and Congress of Industrial Organizations (AFL-CIO) issued a statement joining the call for the closure of the SOA.[27] Veterans and veterans' groups also played a significant role in SOA Watch organizing. Additional support came from religious groups beyond the Catholic Church: the Presbyterian Church USA General Assembly passed a resolution calling for the closure of the school as early as 1994, and the monks from Nipponzan Myohoji, the Atlanta Dojo highlighted at the beginning of this chapter, started participating in the vigil in the late 1990s and began their Peace Pilgrimage in 1999.

This history of organizational coalitions shows how a movement initially supported by a small network of white, Catholic leftists grew to embrace a much larger, and more plural, constituency. In 1998 journalists James Hodge and Linda Cooper reported that the vigil drew "a sea of people . . . as far as the eye could see." They continued: "Activists completely filled the green space in front of the U-shaped apartments where Bourgeois lived. Students were sitting and standing on apartment rooftops. And what a rainbow coalition it was, with participants ranging from toddlers to the Grandmothers for Peace and including Buddhist monks, residents of Nagasaki, Native Americans, Latin Americans, and members of the NAACP, which earlier that year had joined the call for the school's abolishment."[28] The increase of organizational affiliations corresponded with the greater annual attendance at the vigil. By 1998 the numbers had swelled to nearly seven thousand people. The vigil's attendance would reach its height in 2007 and 2008 with an estimated twenty-five thousand participants each year.[29]

One of the mechanisms that contributed to these soaring numbers was the outreach to and training of young people, particularly those enrolled in Jesuit educational institutions. After his 1995 arrest for a direct action at Fort Benning, SOA Watch member Robert Holstein began organizing Jesuit colleges and universities to send delegations of students to the annual vigil. A former Jesuit turned lawyer, Holstein used his own money to fund buses for many of the delegations. Over time the Ignatian Family Teach-In for Justice formed and planned a two-day education and strategy conference prior to the vigil. The teach-in was a major attraction for politically engaged students at Jesuit institutions. Because six of the UCA martyrs were themselves Jesuits, and because the weekend mixed education with action, it was an ideal location of pilgrimage.

The Ignatian Solidarity Network (ISN) grew out of the Jesuits' presence at the SOA Watch's vigil and began coordinating the annual teach-in and a number of other programs throughout the year. But in a development that reveals the limits of such coalitions, the SOA Watch alliance with the ISN began to fracture, and in 2009 the ISN ceased sponsoring the annual vigil. Similar to other breakups, the reasons for the eventual split between the SOA Watch and the ISN are themselves part of the source of conflict. Across multiple interviews, I heard two basic explanations. From the perspective of some SOA Watch supporters, the Jesuits' departure from the annual vigil was a failure of prophetic vision. The perception was that ISN member institutions were increasingly uncomfortable with the confrontational tactics of the SOA Watch and, more important, the wide range of progressive causes represented at the vigil. One former ISN intern reported that she heard feedback that the vigil "made [students] uncomfortable. There were a lot of strange people there."[30] The issue that became neuralgic for the alliance, however, was Bourgeois's support of women's ordination.

Bourgeois had long been a supporter of women's ordination in the Catholic Church. In fact, he came under fire while planning the 1990 fast that started the anti-SOA movement for concelebrating a mass with three women at a church in Minneapolis.[31] While the archbishop of Saint Paul and Minneapolis barred him from priestly duties in the diocese, no other ecclesial action was taken at that time. Though Bourgeois made women's ordination an issue of concern in several other contexts, his participation in the August 9, 2008, ordination of Roman Catholic woman priest Janice Sevre-Duszynska generated a swift and stern response from Vatican officials. Cardinal William

Levada, Prefect of the Congregation for the Doctrine of the Faith under Pope Benedict XVI, told Bourgeois that he had "caused grave scandal" and gave him thirty days to recant.[32] Bourgeois refused to do so in a November 7, 2008, letter to Levada and instead appealed to the primacy of conscience and the call of Archbishop Romero: "Let those who have a voice, speak out for the voiceless."[33]

When Bourgeois was asked later in the month to speak to the ISN Teach-In, something he had done every year since its inception, the ISN organizers pushed him to disclose what he would say. Bourgeois recalls that he responded, "We've got a problem here. As a speaker, . . . I've never been told what I can say and can't say. . . . And I just said, 'It might be better for you to disinvite me, and I will understand. But I will not let you know what I will say and I will not say.'"[34] Unsurprisingly, Bourgeois did speak about women's ordination at the Teach-In, and for him as well as many others in the SOA Watch movement, it was what caused the Jesuits' departure.

The ISN's executive director at the time, Ann Magovern, however, attributed the ISN's departure from its coalition with the SOA Watch to two driving factors. First was the maturation of the ISN as an independent organization with its own programming and goals. The organization, which started as a literal big tent rented by Holstein, had professionalized with a staff, a board, and an independent mission. The second factor was a question of political effectiveness.

Program director Mike Schloss summed up the internal discernment of the ISN: "I heard two questions happening simultaneously. One was an identity or mission question about ISN: What is our mission? And the second is a theory of change question: How can we be effective politically? On both of those, there was a similar answer to the two separate questions, which was, our relationship with SOA Watch is not necessarily facilitating either of these."[35]

Magovern and Schloss had discerned that the SOA Watch's organizing was no longer politically effective. Magovern reflected that the annual vigil "was becoming more and more of a witness. It was an action without any reaction. And it was really becoming more of a witness to, you know, an atrocity, which we all agreed needed to be rectified. But, there wasn't a lot of action."[36] This lack of clear political change led Magovern, who was trained as a community organizer, to push the ISN away from a direct action activism model and toward a skill-building organizing model. Rather than discomfort over the issue of women's ordination, Magovern and Schloss saw the split as one that grew out of the maturation of the ISN and its desire for a different model of organizing based in a different theory of change.

The first phase of SOA Watch organizing was characterized by the mobilization of extant constituencies. While we may be tempted to think that the differences between identity groups would be the primary challenge, in the story of the SOA Watch's relationship to the ISN we see the way that differences internal to progressive Catholicism—that is, differences of issue and organizing style—served to challenge and fracture the coalition. There was not one reason for the split, but the parting of ways displays some of the challenges for building movement coalitions. If the first phase of the organizational life of the anti-SOA movement was one of base-building coalitions, the second phase was one of internal critique generated by an influx of new analysis and viewpoints.

Internal Critique (2000–2012)

In addition to the training and mobilization of Jesuit students, another development that caused the SOA Watch's numbers to swell in the early 2000s was the arrival of the Global Justice Movement (GJM). These activists were radicalized in the wake of the Battle of Seattle in 1999 and the following protests against corporate globalization. Anarchist young people associated with Food Not Bombs, the Bread and Puppet Theater, and other radical collectives began to show up at the annual vigil and contribute to the SOA Watch's year-round organizing. Whereas the ISN parted ways with the SOA Watch, at least in part, over issues of organizing style, the GJM activists were attracted to the movement for the same reasons: its penchant for direct action and its diffuse grassroots organizing. According to one student activist, the Washington, DC–based anarchist and now scholar Michael Loadenthal, "One of the things that kind of anchored [our] annual activist calendar, in that era of having a kind of actual annual activist calendar, was a trip to Fort Benning."[37] Loadenthal and other members of the GJM found in the SOA Watch a space to network with other activists and movements, to initiate and train new recruits, and to focus their energies on a concrete target within the structure of a global system of economic and military violence.

Though this influx of new energy and analysis was a boon for the SOA Watch, it also introduced new tensions. Gill explained the tensions principally in religious terms, suggesting that "not all the newcomers identified with the movement's religious orientation, and some found it cloying, constraining, and exclusivist."[38] Loadenthal, raised "secular but Jewish," echoed this sentiment:

> Because we were organizing under a religious banner, and because we were attending an event which was kind of associated with, you know, nonviolent-pacifistic-nuns, much more so than, you know, atheist-window-smashing-anarchists, I think that general vibe, the multigenerational, multiethnic, multireligious but spiritually centric vibe was one of the

things that had people, for instance, not raise a stink and not, say, call the organizers reformists or, you know, the peace police. Or use this kind of rhetoric which you use against other entities that are telling you to be calm and, in a sense, do what we say.[39]

The religious and nonviolent identity of the movement did constrain the types of tactics that seemed appropriate to Loadenthal and his colleagues. But rather than experiencing this negatively, a major part of Loadenthal's submission to the constraint was his respect for the organizers, an opinion I heard from several GJM participants.

Gigi Burkhalter, a queer anarchist member of the radical drum corps Cakalak Thunder, shared a similar attitude. From her perspective, the SOA Watch was always "a Catholic-based thing."[40] Yet, in the context of the SOA Watch, Burkhalter found her voice as an activist and was "smitten" by the leadership. "Being at SOA, being in Georgia, felt really nice because it felt really loving and inviting. And also really smart and really radical . . . and also, like, creative. All those things really spoke to me."

That the religious and nonviolent identity served as a constraint on the tactics of GJM newcomers was not accidental. Bourgeois reflected, "After a while we had a few people coming in, they wanted to throw rocks, and, I don't know, they wanted to beat up on some of the police here or something, because they were treating us a little rough at times."[41] Bourgeois and the organizers of the annual vigil responded to the presence of more militant participants by training peacekeepers and using a "Statement of Nonviolent Discipline," read liturgically, to commit movement participants to nonviolence. The following is the statement from the 2000 vigil:

> Our goal is to expose and close the US Army's School of the Americas.
> We will act with full respect for our Latin American sisters and brothers, both living and dead.
> We will use our anger at injustice as a Nonviolent force for change.[42]
> We will act with full respect for the Nonviolent tradition that SOA Watch embodies. Accordingly at today's Vigil Action:
>
> - We will carry no weapons.
> - We will not vandalize.
> - We will not use or carry alcohol or illegal drugs.
> - We will not swear or use insulting language.
> - We will not run in public or otherwise make threatening motions.
> - We will not assault—either verbally or physically—those who oppose or disagree with us . . . *even if they assault us.* We will protect those who oppose us from insult or attack.

- We will honor the directions of the designated coordinators. In the event of serious disagreement, we will remove ourselves from the Vigil Action.
- Our attitude as conveyed through words, symbols and actions will be one of respect toward all—including police officers, military personnel, members of the larger community, and all vigilers and members of the SOA Watch family.
- If arrested, we will participate in the judicial process. Where possible, we will use it to put the SOA itself on trial.
- We know this Vigil is part of an ongoing, protracted campaign. We will return to our community and renew our work to close the SOA.[43]

Nonviolence served to discipline the vigilers, drawing out of a pluralism of identities and values their common commitment to participate in the vigil with respect and non-retaliation. By inviting all participants to read the commitments aloud, organizers expressed these commitments liturgically, granting religious authority to the commitments and soliciting—if not forcing—compliance through social pressure.

While Loadenthal experienced the constraint that resulted from the religious identity of the movement as largely unproblematic, others told me of their frustrations. Nicole Tilson, for example, reported that the Catholic commitments of her colleagues in a local SOA Watch group created "a bit of a problem." She continued,

> It [has] kind of created a challenge because when we have an event . . . we have it at one of two churches. Usually it's Catholic folks . . . that are in the church [who] show up to it. And we have a really hard time getting new people. So I kind of want to take what we do outside and say, "Let's bring in new people." I don't want Catholicism to be what drives people away. But then I get pushback that says, "Why are you trying to break that tradition? A really strong resource we have is that connection to the Catholic faith." And I'm like, "We can't grow if all we're doing is putting this Catholicism up as, you know, it's really something that scares people so tone it down a little bit." So that's a challenge in our own group. And I just kind of wonder . . . what tension there is because Catholicism has been the religion of the oppressor in Latin America. And so on a broader scheme I don't know what kind of tension there is between Roy and the church and this new wave of activists who are not Catholic who are coming in to kind of run things.[44]

Tilson, as with other younger GJM activists, tried to respect the religious differences within the movement. However, she was unwilling to allow religion to be a source of exclusion. And when making sense of why the

Catholic identity of her own local organizing group functioned in an exclusionary manner, she connected it to a longer history of hegemonic colonial oppression. Other activists, however, saw the Catholic identity of the movement as a strategic asset, one of the foundations of building a sustained movement to close the SOA/WHINSEC. Sociologist Christian Smith was correct to identify this as a central dilemma, and I heard it echoed across the movement.

Inasmuch as commonly articulated commitments to nonviolence were successful in organizing the annual vigil, they could not cover over the real and abiding differences that were growing within an increasingly plural movement. Global Justice Movement activists brought not only their presence but also their ideas and analysis. One aspect of their analysis that particularly influenced the shape of SOA Watch activism was an anti-oppression lens.

After the Battle of Seattle, author, activist, and scholar Elizabeth "Betita" Martínez asked, "Where was the color in Seattle?"[45] Her question was not only an indictment of the largely white, middle-class denizens of the "Great Battle" but also an invitation for progressive leftist movements to do better in mainstreaming an intersectional anti-oppression analysis and commitment in their work.[46] In the early 2000s, some of the SOA Watch newcomers, including Martínez, applied this call to the movement to close the SOA/WHINSEC.

Following a January 2002 strategy meeting, SOA Watch members formed the Anti-Oppression Working Group to "create a space within the SOA Watch movement to recognize and challenge the many forms of oppression that are woven into our activism, relationships and communities."[47] Working group member Jackie Downing explained that "historically, SOA Watch groups have been composed primarily of people with race, class and gender privilege operating in a society defined by white supremacy, economic inequality, sexism, homophobia and other forms of oppression."[48] The aim of the working group, then, was to understand why these dynamics endured in the movement and to identify ways "to dismantle systems and behaviors that perpetuate oppression and inequality" both inside and outside the movement.

Working group members had their work cut out for them. While the desire to build a broad-based mass movement for political change required welcoming all comers, the previous decade of organizing had been characterized by mobilizing the power latent within existing identities and networks, not critiquing that power.[49] Working group members thus took aim at the dynamics of power internal to the movement itself. SOA Watch activist Gail Taylor called out the patriarchy of the movement, saying, "SOA Watch leadership is a boys' club."[50] Though women (for example, Vicky Imerman and Carol Richardson) had been involved in the SOA Watch from the beginning, their work of research, office management, note-taking, and day-to-day movement building was too often ignored. The highly gendered division of labor led to visibility for the men's work and invisibility for the women's work.[51]

For Philadelphia-based activist Darren Parker, the dynamics of race privilege led to self-righteousness on the part of *prisoners of conscience*, movement shorthand for those arrested for civil disobedience. Noting the disproportionate national imprisonment of people of color, Parker argued that being able to enter and exit jail for reasons of conscience with a pro bono legal team and a community of support was a privilege. He chided SOA Watch activists: "Don't wear your jail time like a fucking badge. . . . Be happy that you don't have to live your life scared shitless of the system so they won't find a reason to chew you up and spit you out."[52]

The Anti-Oppression Working Group highlighted how differences of race, class, gender, sexuality, and ability functioned to legitimize some voices while excluding others. They argued that doing the work of internal critique was necessary to build a sustained and successful movement for political change. In Martínez's analysis, the working group was largely successful in mainstreaming an anti-oppression lens into the SOA Watch's organizing practice. This commitment of the SOA Watch to confronting violence through solidarity opened the movement to internal critique. As Martínez noted, "Since the organization's goal is to abolish a powerful instrument of monstrous oppression, SOAW realized it had to look at any oppressiveness within its own policies and action. It had to develop an institutional analysis rather than just focusing on individual behavior."[53]

The need for an intersectional anti-oppression analysis emerged first from the principles of nonviolence and solidarity that the movement professed. Faithfulness to these commitments required the mainstreaming of an anti-oppression lens. Not only faithfulness to the movement's founding vision and aims but its effectiveness also depended on building a plural anti-oppressive movement. Martínez observed, "Failure to do so would prevent [the] evolution of an anti-oppressive organizing practice. That, in turn, would not only be a violation of the commitment to social justice but also a strategic error, undermining the alliance building so vital to victory."[54]

Mainstreaming anti-oppression analysis and practice required not only internal critique but also structural change. At the annual vigil in 2004, the Anti-Oppression Working Group made its work a major theme of the weekend. During that time, Martínez reported, "Participants raised many problems such as arrogant leadership, favoritism toward those who had done SOA jail time, women of color saying they felt marginalized, people of color wanting respect for different communication styles, and frequent disagreement about SOAW's strict nonviolence guidelines."[55] The critiques led to changes in the modes of SOA Watch organizing. For example, efforts were made to make the vigil, the newsletter, and the ongoing organizing work bilingual (English/Spanish); to carve out separate caucuses for underrepresented voices; and to create more space within decision-making processes for those voices.

If the first phase of the movement can be characterized by welcoming and mobilizing the power of diverse constituencies, the second phase was characterized by listening more deeply to the communities beyond the largely white, largely Catholic core and by mainstreaming a critique of the way that power functioned within the movement. Even the moral authority of the prisoners of conscience and the nonviolence guidelines were questioned. While solidarity and nonviolence opened the movement to receptivity to an anti-oppression critique, those commitments had to develop. In the end, they would lead to a third phase of movement organizing that one activist described as the "turn to the Global South."[56]

Accountable Solidarity (2006–16)

Together, the mass convergence mobilizing that animated the first phase and the mainstreaming of an anti-oppression lens that animated the second opened the SOA Watch to respond to and follow the leadership of those directly impacted by the militarism that the movement opposed. The third phase of coalition building involved a transnational dynamic of forging alliances with partners in both Southern and Northern Hemispheres. In each case, the SOA Watch looked for leadership and accountability from those most proximate to the violence of the US–Latin American military system. As one SOA Watch intern expressed, the work was responding to the leadership of the "people who are directly impacted and amplifying that."[57]

At the People of Color Caucus during the 2004 vigil, one of the recommendations made was that the SOA Watch should "build closer relations with organizations in Latin America."[58] In 2006 the SOA Watch pursued this proposal in earnest by opening an office in Venezuela under the direction of former Maryknoll lay missioner Lisa Sullivan. Before 2006 the Latin America Project had consisted principally of delegations to Latin American countries. These delegations had two goals for SOA Watch activists: to build transnational connections with human rights organizations, grassroots activists, and community organizers, and to demand that governmental and military officials stop sending their soldiers for training by the US military.[59] While relatively successful in achieving the second goal of receiving commitments from some sympathetic Latin American leaders, the SOA Watch aimed to deepen its commitment to the first and "strengthen [its] cooperation with human rights organizations in Latin America."[60]

But there were significant power imbalances between staff in the Northern Hemisphere and staff in the south. In spite of some successes, including meeting with President Hugo Chávez in Venezuela and gaining his commitment to no longer send troops to the SOA/WHINSEC, there was "a lot of pushback initially with the Latin America initiative."[61] Lisa Sullivan saw this as a struggle between those who controlled the movement and those who maintained the base. While a small cohort managed the money and decision-making power, it was "globally focused . . . anti-oppression groups that said, 'Yes! This is the way to go!'"[62] As a result and with the support of Bourgeois, Sullivan began to build up the capacity of the Latin American Project, eventually scrapping the name (which was aimed at North American audiences) and calling it Equipo Sur, or Team South. After a delegation to Chile, Chilean torture survivor and activist Pablo Ruiz came on staff, and together Ruiz and Sullivan organized an *encuentro*, or "conference," in Latin America in 2010 to connect anti-militarism leaders from eighteen countries.

Back in the United States, the SOA Watch's connections in Latin America led to actions focused on current US foreign policy. When SOA graduate Romeo Vásquez Velásquez and others broke into the home of Honduran president Manuel Zelaya and forced him out of the country in June 2009, the SOA Watch was one of the anchor organizations that catalyzed activism to restore democracy to Honduras. The active presence of the SOA Watch on this emerging issue also attracted immigration lawyer and human rights activist Arturo Viscarra to the organization. An immigrant himself from El Salvador, Viscarra began writing about and then organizing around the Honduran coup in 2009. He explained, "We were organizing protests and online actions and events and fundraisers and hosting people from Honduras. . . . And through that work, that's how I became familiar with SOA Watch."[63] The SOA Watch hired Viscarra in 2013 as an advocacy coordinator. Viscarra was the first of a cohort of young activists—including field organizer María Luisa Rosal, who led the roll call at the outset of this section— that the SOA Watch hired who were in different ways directly impacted by the violence that resulted from US military training. These new staff members brought their analyses not only of US militarism but also of how that militarism was among the root causes of emigration from Latin America.

Developments in Georgia also facilitated a focus on the connection between the US military and US immigration policy. Since 2007 LaGrange activist Anton Flores-Maisonet, introduced in this chapter's opening vignette, began organizing a vigil at Stewart Detention Center—an expansive, privately owned immigrant detention center in Lumpkin, Georgia. Recognizing the opportunity to bring national attention to local immigrant rights organizing, Flores planned a mobilization the same weekend as the SOA Watch's annual vigil. Trained as a social worker, Flores had long worked on issues of immigration and militarism.[64] Alterna, the intentional Christian community he helped found, worked closely with undocumented immigrants by offering rent assistance, accompaniment with local services, and advocacy in immigration proceedings. Through their work with immigrants in LaGrange, Flores and other LaGrange activists learned about the Stewart Detention Center. They bought a house in Lumpkin and started offering hospitality to the families of detainees, some of whom traveled hundreds of miles to see their loved ones. Using the SOA Watch's annual vigil as a platform, Flores brought national attention to the work against Stewart. What began as an entrepreneurial effort on Flores's part grew into a partnership. The SOA Watch began officially cosponsoring the Shut Down Stewart vigil in 2013.

Together these coalitions, both south and north, have generated arguably the most significant shift in the SOA Watch's organizing since its inception—that is, moving its annual vigil from Fort Benning to the US-Mexico border. In October 2016, the SOA Watch held its annual mobilization in Nogales, allowing for a transnational demonstration.[65] It is beyond the scope of this study to judge the impact of this shift; however, one can see how the dynamics that I have been tracing led to this result. For Viscarra, the move to the border emerged from the connections solidified by the Shut Down Stewart vigil:

> You know it's a misnomer to call it a border vigil; it's a border–root causes vigil—border and root causes of migration. So, basically, it would be to replicate the model from Fort Benning and Lumpkin, . . . the Stewart Detention Vigil, and replicate it somewhere else. So in all the places that we looked at, . . . you're looking at border militarization, but you're also looking at the immigration issue and US military training. So I think Stewart really played a big role in that genesis.[66]

In his advocacy of the move to the US-Mexico border, former SOA Watch staff member Nico Udu-Gama also connected the move to the work of anti-oppression.

> The movement to close the SOA, just as the movement to end border militarization or the Black Lives Matter movement, must be a movement to end white supremacy. White supremacy founded this country, and has allowed our particular form of capitalism to thrive and benefit the 1%. So when we go to the border or to Fort Benning, or our local police stations we must keep this mentality at the forefront, recognize the privileges we have or don't have, and work together to reconstruct the idea of US democracy. So let's take the vigil to the border with humility and conscientiousness, as well as that perseverance and fight that has characterized our movement.[67]

While these most recent developments are still emergent, I would argue that the dynamics I have been tracing take us some distance in interpreting these significant shifts. The move to the border responds to the long discernment of the movement regarding the demands of solidarity and commitments to nonviolence. And these principles themselves are shaped by the presence of the crucified people. As one staff organizer put the question, "What would the six Jesuits who were massacred in El Salvador say today?"[68]

The argument of this chapter is that the pluralism of the movement to close the SOA/WHINSEC has served as both a challenge and a resource as it has discerned these questions. As chapter 2 showed, the solidarity between the living and the dead generated by and performed in the *¡presente!* litany did not produce a clear path of action, but it created the need for practical reasoning. Here we see that practical reasoning in action. Activists have had to weigh considerations of faithfulness to the dead alongside their sense of vocation to effective political action in solidarity with the living. A common commitment to nonviolence has operated as one of the tools for unifying this plural constituency. But is nonviolence merely a tactic, or is it a more all-embracing principle to embody? To answer this question requires engaging recent scholarly literature on strategic nonviolence and civil resistance.

STRATEGIC NONVIOLENCE AND THE ECLIPSE OF ETHICS

Suggesting that contested commitments to nonviolence could be a point of consensus across pluralistic differences, as I found within the SOA Watch, presents a question: Which account of nonviolence? Scholars have tended to divide accounts into two camps: principled and pragmatic. And since the early 2000s, analysts of nonviolence have largely focused their attention on pragmatic nonviolence. Rather than examining the ethical dynamics of a commitment to nonviolence, analysts have studied "what works." And scholars have discovered that nonviolence is working. So shifting attention from the moral justification for and religious sources of nonviolent action, scholars have explored questions of the strategy and effectiveness of nonviolent civil resistance. They have asked what components of nonviolent struggle seem to produce positive outcomes. I argue, however, that the recent turn by analysts of nonviolence to a narrow focus on "what works" is a mistake. The evasion of the ethical task fails us in multiple ways, limiting our capacity both to adequately describe the shape of nonviolent action and to form future nonviolent actors.

The State of the Field of the Study of Nonviolence

The emphasis on the strategic quality of nonviolent struggle emerges from a number of sources. Gene Sharp's crucial interventions into the theory and practice of nonviolence have been key to this emergent focus, but credit is also due to activist and public intellectual Barbara Deming and her *Revolution & Equilibrium*.[69] Following Sharp and Deming, other scholars such as Peter Ackerman, Christopher Kruegler, Stephen Zunes, Kurt Schock, Erica Chenoweth, and Maria Stephan have all argued that what is important about nonviolent resistance is not that it is good or right, that it preserves the moral integrity of the nonviolent actor or of his or her opponent, or that it integrates means and ends.[70] What is important is that it works as a method of social and political change.

The contemporary conceptualization of nonviolence in largely instrumental terms is the product of nearly a century of academic study of nonviolence. Sharon Erickson Nepstad has narrated the development of the field in three waves.[71] The first wave tracks, roughly, the proliferation of a Gandhian approach to nonviolence. Early studies blended Gandhi's emphasis on the tactics of nonviolent change with ethical and religious reflections on the inextricability of ends and means. Scholars usually characterize the commitment to nonviolence during this wave as "principled nonviolence" in which nonviolent actors work out an ethical commitment to non-harm in the political arena.

A second wave of nonviolence research followed Gene Sharp's intervention.[72] Though initially Gandhian in his approach, Sharp shifted focus to the strategic quality of nonviolence.[73] Gaining a reputation as the "Clausewitz of nonviolent warfare," Sharp developed a theory of power that enabled him to explain how nonviolence worked: it removed the pillars of support to governing authorities, stripping their legitimacy and forcing change. Key to Sharp's intervention in the field was disaggregating nonviolence from its association with pacifism.[74] By advocating nonviolence as a tactic, rather than a way of life, Sharp hoped that "large numbers of people who would *never* believe in ethical or religious nonviolence could use nonviolent struggle for pragmatic reasons."[75]

Most recently, the third wave of nonviolence research has built on Sharp's insights but given them an empirical foundation through comparative and large-N studies of nonviolent civil resistance campaigns. Moving beyond Sharp's apologetic posture, these studies have sought to analyze why nonviolent movements fail, as well as succeed, and how to make them more strategically adept. Chenoweth and Stephan, as well as Schock and Nepstad, have combined a wide-angled, comparative lens with in-depth case studies to identify some of the key causal factors that lead to the success of nonviolent campaigns.[76] Why engage in nonviolent action? For these scholars, you engage because it works, and we can show it works through empirical verification.

This most recent strategic turn in the study of nonviolent resistance has two salient features. First, scholars have emphasized the empirical effectiveness of nonviolence as a rhetorical strategy to wrest reality from the realists. Nonviolence works, they argue, and they can show it works by mustering evidence from empirical data. With interlocutors in security and strategic studies, scholars of strategic nonviolence have accepted the methodological presuppositions of the evidential discourse of the natural sciences. Evidence constructs our knowledge of what is real. Rhetorically, this works to undermine the tendency of some realists to claim that violence or the threat of violence is the most effective, albeit sometimes tragic, mode of achieving political change. Instead, for example, as Chenoweth and Stephan persuasively demonstrate, nonviolent civil resistance has historically been more likely than violent insurrections to attain even the most difficult political aims.

A second feature of the strategic turn is that nonviolence is working not only in statistically verified ways but also in diverse settings among diverse actors. In part due to the comparative methodology employed by these scholars, they have noted the abiding pluralism among actors who take up nonviolent methods. Just in the course of the last decade, nonviolent methods have animated campaigns for democratization across North Africa and Western Asia in the Arab Spring, against police violence and mass incarceration through the Black Lives Matter movement in the United States, and for accountability against corruption and impunity in Guatemala. No single unifying moral or religious vision holds these diverse movements together, yet each has deployed nonviolent methods in its efforts to achieve political change.

Peace studies scholar David Cortright has accounted for this abiding pluralism by telling a story of gradual secularization of the theory and practice of nonviolence. As with Nepstad's narration of the development of the field, Cortright argues that we have moved from "principled" Gandhian nonviolence to a "pragmatic" focus on the causal dynamics of political change. As such, he argues, "the essential considerations become tactical and strategic rather than philosophical. The emphasis shifts to a pragmatic calculation of the most effective ways to divide the loyalties of the opponent's constituency and to win the sympathy and support of bystanders."[77] Because these considerations are strategic, philosophical, ethical, or religious considerations are no longer necessary. In other words, one does not have to believe in Jesus, practice satyagraha, or interpret the Islamic principle of *ihsan* in a particular way to utilize nonviolent methods. This allows for a proliferation of the practice of nonviolent resistance, purportedly without the baggage of what political philosopher John Rawls famously identified as "comprehensive visions."[78]

Taking stock of the state of the field, we have witnessed a strategic turn in which scholars have focused, first, on the effective quality of nonviolent resistance that, second, enables the methods of nonviolent social change to be taken up in a menagerie of contexts. Interestingly for my purposes, these shifts in scholarship on nonviolence track in important ways with the developments in SOA Watch organizing. Yet, in both cases, I wish to argue that pluralization need not be equated with secularization and that continued attention to the ethics of nonviolence is warranted. More pointedly, I wish to argue that a reductive focus on "what works" is a mistake. Let me explain why.

Why the Eclipse of Ethics Is a Mistake

Though scholars such as Nepstad, Chenoweth, Stephan, and Cortright have emphasized the effective quality of nonviolence for good reason, they have purchased this focus on strategy at the price of attention to the ethics of nonviolent action. Of course, the eclipse of ethics in the academic analysis of nonviolence is understandable. The flip side of the proliferation of nonviolent methods across a pluralistic backdrop is that the variety has become a bedeviling problem. There is a real and abiding ethical difference that makes a focus on "what we do" to the exclusion of "why we do it" a tempting option. However, the evasion of the ethical task does not serve us in the end. In fact, the evasion generates its own problems.

First, descriptively, a narrow focus on effectiveness fails to adequately account for the reasons that nonviolent actors act. Chenoweth and Stephan, for example, attribute the success of nonviolent civil resistance principally to what they identify as a "participation advantage."[79] Lower barriers to entry allow more participants, and that in turn correlates strongly with movement success. Chenoweth and Stephan admit that moral considerations do play a role here, given most persons' moral aversion to killing, but they do not explore what that role is and how it operates. While admitting the function of moral motivations, they ignore the morally complex deliberations that actors engage in while deciding when, where, why, and how to engage in political action. On their own account, morals are operative. Yet when it comes time to give a description of the significant causal dynamics, morality is sidelined. Thus, a focus on effectiveness to the exclusion of ethical considerations fails as an adequate description.

Second, in addition to this descriptive failure, the strategic turn limits our constructive, normative capacity. Without an adequate description of the ethical dynamics of the politics of nonviolent action, we cannot constructively engage the processes that lead to social change.[80] The evasion of ethics deprives us of much-needed pedagogical tools that would enable the conditions for the formation of nonviolent actors in the future.

Both of these mistakes, one descriptive and one normative, are at root inextricably linked to a heuristic failure. The tendency of scholars of strategic nonviolence, repeated across multiple works, has been to categorize practitioners of nonviolence as either principled or pragmatic.[81] Memorable though these alliterative ascriptions may be, they fail to adequately describe what we are talking about. Both are predicated on false conceptions of basic terms. First, regarding principles, the operative assumption here is that *principles* are basically static commitments that are formed outside the realm of politics and applied unidirectionally. As my research shows, principles are embodied, performed, and developed through iterative practice. For the SOA Watch, commitments to solidarity are both expressed and formed by the *¡presente!* litany, and commitments to nonviolence are drawn from exemplars and precedence as well as disciplined by the recitation of those commitments publicly. It is not as though there is a static repository of moral principles in culture, religion, or moral tradition that can be stably deployed. Rather, traditions of moral reasoning themselves are constantly in development, and the artifacts of those traditions change and develop over time.[82] So ethical principles are certainly at work in nonviolent action, including action motivated by a desire for the responsible practice of effective politics.[83] The principles at work, however, may be more flexible and embodied than a static conceptualization of absolutist principled action may allow.

Second, regarding pragmatism, the thought of classical pragmatists John Dewey and William James, as well as more recent scholars such as Jeffrey Stout, Cornel West, and Jason Springs, need not be construed as a rejection of ethical reflection.[84] Dewey gave significant attention to the relation of means and ends and to their reciprocal determination. James considered *pragmatism* a philosophical tool for moderating religious and moral values with claims of scientific fact.[85] Moreover, both of these classical pragmatists considered the focus on what works itself a value-laden moral exercise. In this sense, Gandhi's nonviolence was certainly pragmatic: he cared deeply about the practical implications of his theories and was committed to working them out through experimental application. Moreover, SOA Watch actors who turn principally to questions of effectiveness do so in many cases not out of a rejection of morality but because they view the political impact of their organizing as morally significant. To use the phrase *pragmatic nonviolence* to indicate a solely instrumental orientation to nonviolence and a rejection of moral consideration is simply a terminological failure. The facile opposition of pragmatism and principle fails to describe the actual operation of moral reasoning at work within nonviolent resistance.[86]

We separate considerations of responsible effectiveness from those of moral faithfulness and considerations of principle from those of pragmatics to our detriment, both descriptively and normatively. SOA Watch actors are but one case in which effectiveness and faithfulness are irreducibly imbricating; we can think immediately of Gandhi's liberation struggle in India or the Black Freedom Movement in the United States. Instead, we have the coincidence of two principles of action. Analysts of nonviolence face the challenge of integrating those principles in a description of ethical and political practice that can account for the abiding pluralism of nonviolent actors. Thus, pluralism is not a legitimate reason for eschewing an analysis of the moral dynamics of nonviolent action.

In summarizing my argument so far, the first section treated the interstices of difference in the movement to close the SOA/WHINSEC. Against a simple subtraction story, I demonstrated that the SOA Watch movement went through seasons of pluralization, a pluralization that was aided and even obligated by the movement's commitments to solidarity. One contested principle that held the movement together was a commitment to nonviolence. A question surfaced, however, regarding whether nonviolence is merely a tactical commitment or an embodied principle. Getting clear on what is at stake in this question took us through the recent scholarly literature on nonviolence that has made a strong strategic turn. One impetus for this strategic turn in academic discourse is the pluralism among nonviolent actors. We cannot assume that nonviolent actors are motivated by a common moral vision. Yet rather than recoiling into a purely instrumental analysis of the effectiveness of nonviolent action, I argued that the need for moral analysis still remains. This chapter next examines the role that nonviolence actually plays within the pluralistic SOA Watch coalition.

NONVIOLENT POWER AND THE CONDITIONS
FOR DEEP PLURALISM

Within a means-ends schema, the recent literature on nonviolence presents a question: Is nonviolence a means to some other end, or is nonviolence itself an end? If nonviolence is merely a means, a tactic of change, then it can be used to achieve all sorts of ends, praiseworthy or nefarious, and discarded when it ceases to be useful. But if nonviolence is an end in itself, then it presumes a wider collection of associated principles, whether an affirmation of the dignity of the other, a commitment to non-harm, or the aspiration to justpeace. A society that organizes itself nonviolently requires mechanisms of redress and conflict transformation. A movement that organizes itself nonviolently requires not only nonviolent tactics of political action but the tools of internal critique and accountable solidarity as well. This section takes up the role that nonviolence plays within the SOA Watch movement. In doing so, I extend my argument that the messianism of the movement does not devolve into particularism but collaborates with a pluralism that serves as both a challenge and a resource. Commitment to the principle of nonviolence serves as one mechanism of drawing collaboration out of plurality, but it works at minimalist, mean, and maximalist registers. In the SOA Watch nonviolence functions as a discipline, as a tactic, and as an embodied principle.

Nonviolence as a Discipline

The most obvious and minimalist role that the principle of nonviolence has played within the movement to close the SOA/WHINSEC has been as a disciplinary tool of constraint and formation. The affirmation of nonviolence has operated as a way of prohibiting (and encouraging) certain behaviors, groups, and people in the movement. Faithfulness to nonviolence has required that constituencies that may have used violence as a tactic, whether punching a cop or throwing a rock or taking up arms against the state, either restrain their violent tactics or abstain from participation. Recall the "Statement of Nonviolent Discipline," where vigilers pledged that they "will not assault—either verbally or physically—those who oppose or disagree with us" and, furthermore, "will honor the directions of designated coordinators." In the event of any disagreement, the participants also pledged to remove themselves from the vigil action.[87] In this way, the commitment to nonviolence has served as a disciplinary boundary-making tool. If the participants could affirm a commitment to nonviolence, they were welcome to participate. If they could not, organizers asked that they please stay home.

The "Statement of Nonviolent Discipline" has been one of a host of technologies the organizers have used to ensure participants' adherence to nonviolence. While the statement was the most ubiquitous mechanism of discipline, as it was printed in programs and read aloud several times during the annual vigil weekend, there were many others. The peacekeeper teams, commissioned in the late 1990s as the numbers at the annual vigil began to swell, were another visible representation of nonviolent discipline. In their distinctive red baseball caps, peacekeepers have served as "guides" for the vigil participants. Peacekeeper roles have changed over the years, but in 2015, peacemaker responsibilities included

Maintaining by their own demeanor, a nonviolent presence among the participants.

Establishing a mode of conduct that is purposeful, positive, and instru-
mental in contributing to the general spirit of the vigil and action.
Helping apply de-escalation strategies in the event of a potentially violent
situation.
Offering help with communication in the event of a medical emergency.
Assisting as "guides" for the Sunday Solemn Funeral Procession.[88]

Peacekeepers have been the visible enforcers of the movement's commitment
to nonviolence. They are trained to deescalate situations of violence, whether
as a result of interactions with law enforcement or between participants.

In addition to the "Statement of Nonviolent Discipline" and the peacekeepers, SOA Watch organizers sponsor an annual Nonviolent Direct Action
Workshop to educate participants on the history of nonviolence in the movement and to encourage newcomers to take up an active nonviolent political
praxis. More than simply restraining, these workshops intend to call forth
participants into nonviolent confrontation as part of the vigil, and they are a
primary mode of recruiting new prisoners of conscience.

All these technologies of nonviolent discipline have served to exclude
some tactics, groups, and people for the sake of the legitimacy of the movement. Bourgeois, for example, recognized that any violence—particularly if
any of the Jesuit students were hurt or killed—would mean the end of the
movement. "I knew damn well if there was a college student hurt or killed, it
was over. I mean, college students wouldn't come back."[89] Thus, nonviolence
functioned not merely as a common ground but also as a tool for boundary
making. This constraining role for nonviolence is especially important in a
movement that is oriented by messianism such as the SOA Watch. Messianic
movements can, but by no means must, deploy violent means to achieve
their ends. The potent combination of a latent antinomianism, in which normal ethical constraints on violence are suspended, and a zealous desire to
enact the messianic age, if necessary with violence, haunts political messianisms. This temptation to violence is especially acute when accompanied
by a rejection of pluralism and when adherents see political, religious, or
ideological others as enemies to the messianic age. While I take up this
temptation to violence more fully in chapter 4, it is important to note here
that a commitment to nonviolence serves as a brake on messianic violence.
In this way, as well as others, the endurance of the movement has required
nonviolent discipline.

Nonviolence as a Tactic

The principle of nonviolence has operated not only as a formative, disciplinary constraint but also as an enabler of movement actions. Advocates

of nonviolence have long pointed out that nonviolence is not a passive stance toward injustice; rather, it is active and contentious, providing a host of tactics for disrupting business as usual. Gene Sharp identified 198 tactics of "nonviolent warfare."[90] While no movement uses all of these tactics, the principle of nonviolence generates a palette of possibilities from guerrilla theater to pamphleting to civil disobedience. Of the tactics that Sharp identified, the SOA Watch has used nearly 40. Each of the dilemmas taken up in this book correspond to the tactics that Sharp identified: the *¡presente!* litany examined in chapter 2 is what Sharp called a mock funeral; the coalitions explored in this chapter entailed formal declarations of support from organizations as well as group mobilization; chapter 4 takes up legal repertoires of civil disobedience and lobbying; and the fifth chapter examines exemplary lives and their representation in banners, portraits, and speeches.[91]

For some, as for the advocates of strategic nonviolence, these tactics can stand alone for deployment at key moments without having to subscribe to an absolute commitment to nonviolence. Elements of this type of calculation are present in the movement as some activists discern that nonviolence makes sense at one moment but might not in another context. When I asked Bourgeois what was key about nonviolence for him, he remembered the question of a reporter from the *Columbus Ledger*: "Are you going to resort to violence?" Bourgeois rightly found the question humorous and said, "I remember just being comical about it to bring out the absurdity of it. I said, 'Well, we are contemplating overrunning Fort Benning perhaps.'" One need not be an absolute pacifist to recognize that violently storming the gates of Fort Benning would be imprudent. Yet the fit between nonviolent tactics and the movement's context requires the deployment of practical reasoning that involves, but also moves beyond, concerns of effect.

As we saw in the case of the Ignatian Solidarity Network and its emergence within and departure from the SOA Watch coalition, a common commitment to nonviolent tactics is not enough to hold a plural movement together. Activists must also take into account considerations of theory of change and issue salience. Some tactics fit better with particular organizational identities than with others. The ISN and the SOA Watch shared commitments to nonviolent tactics. Though growing up together, they operated with different sets of organizational identities and theories of change. The SOA Watch was intentionally plural, drawing on diverse leftist constituencies and rooted in a theory of change that centered on nonviolent direct action, while the ISN was oriented specifically to Jesuit institutions of higher education and wanted to grow toward a model of broad-based community organizing. At issue for the ISN was whether the coalition supported its mission and was effective. On both, it discerned, the answer was no.

This conclusion raises the quandary, though, of how to determine what tactics within a nonviolent movement are effective. Notions of effectiveness are always, already symbolically freighted.[92] SOA Watch actors have identified a politics of accountable solidarity as effective. Together solidarity and nonviolence generate a political practice that takes into account the leadership of those directly impacted by the violence that results from US military training and US foreign policy. More than merely a tactic, the commitment to nonviolence has required SOA Watch activists to engage nonviolence as an embodied principle.

Nonviolence as an Embodied Principle

Throughout this chapter, I have suggested that nonviolence operates as an embodied principle of political action. In identifying nonviolence this way, I argue that nonviolence is more than a mere tactic; it indicates something about the mode of life for some, but not all, SOA Watch actors. It is *embodied* insofar as it is displayed through the bodies of its adherents, not merely as an idea but as a principle that enables specific forms of action. It is a *principle* insofar as it organizes action in a coherent way, connecting a host of disparate actions into a common movement.

But what is nonviolence? Is it an absolute commitment to non-harm? Is it an effective mode of political action? Against either the principled or pragmatist accounts, I would argue that *nonviolence* is a tradition of moral praxis.[93] Explaining the movement's commitment to nonviolence, Bourgeois told me, "Early on, we realized our movement must, must be rooted in nonviolence. And that's when we really started drawing on the experience, the wisdom of Ghandi, Dr. King, Dorothy Day, Cesar Chavez, and others. Their way was going to be our way, the way of nonviolence."[94] Rather than expressing a principled pacifism or a pragmatic and instrumental use of nonviolent tactics, Bourgeois named a tradition of moral reasoning, of practical wisdom. Nonviolence, as with humanitarianism, democracy, or natural law, is a discursive tradition that has its own internal logic, exemplars, and standards of reasonable justification.[95] As a tradition of thought and practice it is not uniform, but as moral philosopher Alasdair MacIntyre famously suggested, traditions are "an argument extended through time in which certain fundamental agreements are defined and redefined."[96]

Naming nonviolence as a tradition of moral praxis does not do away with its internal plurality.[97] For some, their commitment to nonviolence emerges most proximately from a desire to follow in the nonviolent way of Jesus. The historic peace churches have, since the Reformation, commended a return to Jesus and the early church as exemplars of nonviolence.[98] Radical Catholics and social gospel mainliners all make use of the example of Jesus as a paradigm of confrontational nonviolent action as well. It would be a mistake, however, to suggest that this is the only or exclusive moral source animating the SOA Watch's nonviolent practice. Think, for example, of the Buddhist peace pilgrims at the outset of this chapter. Their commitments to nonviolence emerge from their contemplative practices and prayer of the daimoku, which aims to reduce the suffering that results from negative karmic punishments. Others defend their commitments to nonviolence as a critique of imperialism: deconstructing the legalized violence of the US–Latin American military system requires using the tools of nonviolence. As poet and critic Audre Lorde argued, "The master's tools will never dismantle the master's house."[99] These commitments to nonviolence are not uniform, nor do they merely present an overlapping consensus on certain tactics. Rather, they are an internally plural set of standards of reasoning and deliberation that activists use to come to collective decisions.

A primary example of the workings of this internally plural discursive tradition is the organizational history surveyed in the first section of this chapter. It was SOA Watch activists' commitments to nonviolence that made them susceptible to newcomers' critiques that the movement was unsophisticated when it came to issues of race, class, gender, and sexuality, and, indeed, was propagating structural and cultural violence by ignoring these issues. As SOA Watch activist Chris Inserra stated, "The kind of organizing that we were challenged and summoned to do [led us to confront] our own racism in the movement in terms of white privilege, and just being a very white-led, Catholic, originally organizing movement. It became more diverse because people allowed themselves to be challenged by younger and more diverse voices and also folks across the border."[100] These transformations were successful because they relied on authorities and postulates native to a commitment to nonviolence. Oppression was articulated and understood as a form of structural and cultural violence, an expression of the same forces of empire and domination that produced the direct violence that the movement opposed. Nonviolence as an embodied principle, rather than merely a tactic, is imbricated with the commitments to solidarity that are formed in and expressed by the ¡presente! litany and the commitments to anti-oppression that entered the movement on the tails of the critiques from the Global Justice Movement. Not only the commitments to anti-oppression but also the most recent turn to accountable solidarity that amplifies the leadership of those most proximate to the violence of the US–Latin American military system should be understood as enabled by and as expressing the principle of nonviolence.

This plural but discursively coherent commitment to nonviolence within the SOA Watch movement is held together by what political theorist William Connolly has identified as a "bicameral orientation." In his book *Pluralism*, Connolly builds on his earlier work *Why I Am Not a Secularist* to make a constructive case for deep, multidimensional pluralism. Key to this case is a bicameral orientation to political life in which all of us affirm the importance of our own creeds, sensibilities, and practices while also recognizing their contestability.[101] This bicameral orientation is an expression of a commitment not to harm the other—that is, to respect the integrity of other persons' difference by both remaining true to one's own commitments and being open to convergences with others' commitments. The prayer service reviewed at the chapter's outset is an example of just this kind of orientation. Praying in the same space with very different practices, understandings, and commitments at play entails not a flattening of difference; rather, it requires a deep respect for difference with an openness to the contestability of respective positions.

The power of nonviolence in the movement to close the SOA/WHINSEC is made most manifest in its operation as an embodied principle of political practice. As an embodied principle, it does not require a static or absolutist commitment. I have argued that nonviolence operates as a tradition of moral praxis that allows the warp and woof of a pluralistic movement to turn the challenge of difference into an effective political practice.

CONCLUSION: METHODS FOR MORAL ANALYSIS IN CONTEXTS OF PLURALISM

Pluralism, rather than an obstacle to be overcome in either theory or practice, is a critical asset to the development of a broad-based movement for social and political change. An effective movement cannot depend on merely activating the identities and convictions of insiders; instead, it must figure out mechanisms to include allies through internal critique and accountable solidarity. The twenty-five-year history of the SOA Watch allows us a vantage point to witness its changing partnerships over time. To understand this history, we must pay attention to the demands of solidarity and nonviolence. Rather than reading the shift from a largely Catholic movement to a more religiously (and nonreligiously) diverse movement as secularization, I argue that it is better understood as pluralization. And rather than understanding pluralism as a reason for evading attention to moral dynamics, I show that continued attention to the ethical dimensions of nonviolent action can illuminate our understanding of why people engage in such movements.

The turn to strategic nonviolence has generated exciting new avenues of research that are worth celebrating. For analyses of peacebuilding, it offers rigorous and empirically verifiable reasons to support nonviolent civil resistance as a mode of political change and draws attention to when and why it fails. It cuts across the debates within international relations between realists and constructivists by arguing that nonviolence, strategically deployed, is not merely utopian even in the face of the most repressive regimes. For Christian ethics, it offers a way through the long, and often stale, debate between pacifists and just war theorists.[102] Effective nonviolent action can be a responsible expression of the obligation to love one's neighbor that is at the heart of the debate.

These contributions, however, will be muted if they are purchased at the price of normative analysis. As I argue throughout this chapter, a commitment to effective action need not mean a solely instrumental orientation to nonviolence; it can be understood as another moral framework (not pacifism narrowly understood). As with the *¡presente!* litany examined in chapter 2, this moral framework draws on a mixed heritage. It cannot be claimed by Christian, religious, or secular traditions alone as it is a mezcla tradition. Yet, to gain an understanding of this tradition and the norms at work within it, we need to employ methodologies that allow us to access those norms. Statistical analysis, though indispensable in identifying patterns of probability over time, cannot get at the fine-grained moral dynamics at play in nonviolent movements. Particularly in a context of pluralism, which includes not one or two but many interstices of difference, an interpretive methodology is needed.

In this chapter, and in the book as a whole, I use the extended case study method as a way to round out the epistemological blind spots of the turn to strategic nonviolence.[103] As a Christian theologian and ethicist, my aim is to elicit the norms that are operative in the context of this nonviolent movement, to make them explicit through critical juxtaposition with systematic scholarly treatment of those norms, and to demonstrate how they function. More than this, I also aim to render judgments about the adequacy of the movement's embodiment of these principles. Are SOA Watch members faithful to the bonds of solidarity formed and expressed in the *¡presente!* litany? Do they responsibly act out their commitments to nonviolence through effective political action? Moreover, I also develop a theological argument about the impact of the anamnestic presence of the dead. The messianic political theology I construct here refuses to allow our analysis to remain captured by an immanent frame. This work, as I argued in chapter 1, is at once descriptive, evaluative, and constructive.

The performance of a messianic political theology of the resurrection of the crucified people manifests obligations to solidarity and nonviolence. But what are the demands of solidarity and nonviolence? How do activists discern those demands? And how do they translate into political action? To display the kind of rich moral reasoning that is operating within this pluralistic context, we now turn to the ways in which SOA Watch actors justify their civil disobedience. What we find there is a plural but coherent account of the politics of the higher law, one that coordinates a wide range of legal repertoires and justifies the commission of acts of civil disobedience.

NOTES

1. Unpublished field notes, November 19, 2015.

2. On November 13, 2015, six days prior to the gathering reviewed here, representatives of Daesh, also known as the Islamic State of Iraq and the Levant, attacked several locations in Paris, France. The attacks renewed calls for limiting the flow of refugees given security concerns in Europe and the United States. See, for example, Adam Taylor, "The Islamic State Wants You to Hate Refugees," *Washington Post*, November 16, 2015, https://www.washingtonpost.com/news/worldviews/wp/2015/11/16/the-islamic-state-wants-you-to-hate-refugees/.

3. Alterna, "Our Mission."

4. Rawls, *Theory of Justice*, 388; and Rawls, *Political Liberalism*. See also Bilgrami, *Secularism, Identity, and Enchantment*.

5. Connolly, *Why I Am Not a Secularist*; and Connolly, *Pluralism*.

6. Bandy and Smith, *Coalitions across Borders*; and Van Dyke and McCammon, *Strategic Alliances*.

7. Audi and Wolterstorff, *Religion*; Habermas, "Religion"; Casanova, "Rethinking Public Religions," in Shah, Stepan, and Toft, *Rethinking Religion*; and Goodman, *Religious Pluralism*.

8. Asad, *Genealogies of Religion*; Asad, *Formations of the Secular*; Hurd, *Politics of Secularism*; and Mahmood, *Politics of Piety*. For an important critique of these positions, see Omer, "Modernists despite Themselves."

9. Sharp, *Politics of Nonviolent Action*; and Chenoweth and Stephan, *Why Civil Resistance Works*.

10. Arendt, *On Violence*, 44.

11. Lambelet, "Nonviolence as a Tradition of Moral Praxis."

12. Charles Taylor defined *subtraction stories* as "stories of modernity in general, and secularity in particular, which explain them by human beings having lost, or sloughed off, or liberated themselves from certain earlier, confining horizons, or illusions, or limitations of knowledge." See Taylor, *Secular Age*, 22.

13. I take up the relationship between messianism and nonviolence more fully in chapter 4.

14. Unpublished field notes, November 21, 2014.

15. Smith, *Resisting Reagan*, 219.

16. Unpublished field notes, April 30, 2016.

17. Unpublished field notes, November 23, 2014.

18. Taylor, *Secular Age*, 22.

19. Taylor identifies three prominent accounts of secularity: the first configures the secular as public spaces and institutions in which God and God-talk are inconsequential; a second conceptualizes secularity as the decline of religious belief and practice; and a third (Taylor's preferred account) imagines the secular as a space of

fragelization and pluralization in which belief and unbelief cohabitate. Taken in this third sense, the SOA Watch's development could be understood of a kind of secularization. However, it cannot be understood as secularization according to the first or second account.

20. Hodge and Cooper, *Disturbing the Peace*, 134.

21. Gill, *School of the Americas*, 202.

22. For more information, see Leadership Conference of Women Religious, "Assembly Resolutions."

23. SOA Watch, "Three Hundred Religious Leaders."

24. Pax Christi USA, "Teachers of Peace."

25. The NAACP passed a resolution of support for Rep. Joseph Kennedy's efforts to close the SOA in 1997. NAACP, *NAACP Policy Handbook*, 193.

26. As longtime coordinator of the labor caucus Rebecca Kanner remarked, "Hearing from our brothers and sisters in Latin America has been the most meaningful part and there have been real connections made." Kanner, personal correspondence, May 13, 2016.

27. Triggs, "Globalizing SOA Watch," in Prokosch and Raymond, *Global Activist's Manual*, 52–53; and AFL-CIO Executive Council, "Closing the School."

28. Hodge and Cooper, *Disturbing the Peace*, 183.

29. Rubin, "Geography of Protest."

30. Interview with former Jesuit volunteer, Notre Dame, IN, November 4, 2014.

31. "Priest Barred after Women Join in Conducting Mass: Twin Cities Archdiocese Considers Further Punishment," *Washington Post*, September 1, 1990.

32. Bourgeois, *My Journey*, 21.

33. Bourgeois, 24.

34. Interview with Roy Bourgeois, phone, October 21, 2015.

35. Interview with Mike Schloss, phone, June 5, 2015.

36. Interview with Ann Magovern, phone, September 2, 2015.

37. Interview with Michael Loadenthal, phone, November 11, 2015.

38. Gill, *School of the Americas*, 230.

39. Loadenthal continued, "You know, I think we close our eyes and imagine who's behind the scenes organizing the SOA [Watch], regardless of the accuracy of it, it's a sixty-year-old woman who is a devout Catholic, or Jesuit, and does it out of a sense of obligation and great conviction. Who wants to attend a demonstration that she organized and punch a cop in the face and get a demonstration called chaotic. You know, we would disappoint this little old lady who kind of has this plan for the demonstration." Loadenthal, interview.

40. Interview with Gigi Burkhalter, Skype, September 29, 2015.

41. Bourgeois, interview.

42. In 1997, the wording was, "We will harbor no anger, but suffer the anger of the opponent."

43. SOA Watch, "Vigil and Witness." SOA Watch borrowed these guidelines initially from the Nonviolence Guidelines from the Nevada Desert Experience's Hiroshima and Nagasaki Interfaith Peace Witness Nonviolent Direct Action Strategy Workshop of August 1987. They developed over the years, however, and the developments

reveal some of the changes in the disposition of the movement. See SOA Watch, "Memorial Service Bulletin."

44. Interview with Nicole Tilson, phone, June 8, 2015.

45. Elizabeth "Betita" Martínez, "Where Was the Color in Seattle? Looking for Reasons Why the Great Battle Was So White," *Colorlines*, March 10, 2000, http://www.colorlines.com/articles/where-was-color-seattlelooking-reasons-why-great-battle-was-so-white.

46. On intersectionality, see Kimberle Crenshaw's groundbreaking works "Demarginalizing the Intersection" and "Mapping the Margins."

47. SOA Watch Anti-Oppression Working Group, *Compilation of Anti-Oppression Resources*.

48. SOA Watch Anti-Oppression Working Group.

49. Again, Jackie Downing: "Imperialism, war and oppression are spreading. To stop them, we must build a massive grassroots, democratic movement in this country that is allied with oppressed communities here and around the world. A broad-based, diverse movement is the only type that can win real and lasting victories." SOA Watch Anti-Oppression Working Group.

50. Taylor, "Gender Equity in SOAW," in SOA Watch Anti-Oppression Working Group.

51. These gendered divisions of labor are by no means unique to the SOA Watch. See, for just one example, the treatment of Ella Baker and other women activists by leaders of the Southern Christian Leadership Conference. Ransby, *Ella Baker*, 170–208.

52. Parker, "Black Man's Look," in SOA Watch Anti-Oppression Working Group, *Compilation of Anti-Oppression Resources*.

53. Martínez, "Combating Oppression," in Martínez, Meyer, and Carter, *We Have Not Been Moved*, 75.

54. Martínez, 75.

55. Martínez, 75.

56. Unpublished field notes, November 21, 2014.

57. Interview with SOA Watch staff member A, phone, June 16, 2015.

58. Martínez, "Combating Oppression," 77.

59. Peace studies scholars refer to these as track three and track two diplomacy. For more, see chapter 4.

60. SOA Watch, "Latin America Project."

61. Interview with Lisa Sullivan, phone, May 30, 2016.

62. Sullivan, interview.

63. Interview with Arturo Viscarra, phone, September 9, 2015.

64. See Lambelet, "Sanctuary."

65. I include some discussion of the deliberation that led to this shift in chapter 6.

66. Viscarra, interview.

67. SOA Watch, "Moving 2016 November Vigil? "

68. Unpublished field notes, April 26, 2016. I take up this question again explicitly in chapter 5.

69. Sharp, *Politics of Nonviolent Action*; and Deming, *Revolution & Equilibrium*.

70. Ackerman and Kruegler, *Strategic Nonviolent Conflict*; Zunes, "Unarmed Insurrections"; Schock, *Unarmed Insurrections*; Schock, *Civil Resistance Today*; and Chenoweth and Stephan, *Why Civil Resistance Works*.

71. Nepstad, *Nonviolent Struggle*, x–xii.

72. Sharp, *Politics of Nonviolent Action*.

73. See Weber, "Nonviolence Is Who?" Sharp based his strategic turn at least in part on a misreading of Max Weber's distinction between the ethics of conviction and the ethics of responsibility. See Weber, "Politics as a Vocation"; Sharp, "Ethics and Responsibility"; and Lambelet, "Nonviolent Struggle."

74. Sharp evidences a very low view of pacifists who work from a philosophical or religious perspective across his works. See, for example, Sharp's denigration of pacifism as a philosophical system and his unsubstantiated claim that nonviolent campaigns have usually been led by "nonpacifists." Sharp, *Politics of Nonviolent Action*, 68.

75. Quoted in Engler, "Machiavelli of Nonviolence."

76. Chenoweth and Stephan, *Why Civil Resistance Works*; Schock, *Unarmed Insurrections*; Schock, *Civil Resistance Today*; Nepstad, *Nonviolent Revolutions*; and Nepstad, *Nonviolent Struggle*.

77. Cortright, *Peace*, 226–27.

78. Rawls, *Theory of Justice*; and Rawls, *Political Liberalism*.

79. Chenoweth and Stephan, *Why Civil Resistance Works*, chap. 2.

80. In a second example, in agreement with Chenoweth and Stephan, Nepstad has argued that a key causal factor historically in the success of nonviolent movements has been military defections. When she describes the process of military defection in detail, however, the principled dimensions of the effectiveness of nonviolent action show forth despite her empirical framework. Focusing on the case of the Philippines, Nepstad reported that when women, children, and vowed religious knelt down before the tanks, the soldiers believed eternal consequences trumped any punishment they might receive from President Ferdinand Marcos. If we wanted to repeat the success of Nepstad's case, we would need to know something about the moral dynamics that moved the soldiers to disobey orders. This knowledge would allow constructive insights into strategies of formation for both nonviolent actors and engagement with opponents.

81. Schock, *Unarmed Insurrections*, xvii; Cortright, *Peace*, 211–32; and Nepstad, *Nonviolent Struggle*, 4–12.

82. See, for example, Ann Swidler's "Culture in Action" for a critique of Parson's rather static conceptualization of culture as the depository of principles.

83. This claim deserves empirical verification, just as does Chenoweth and Cunningham's statement of the opposite: "In most cases, people who wage nonviolent struggle are doing so instrumentally, rather than because of a moral commitment to avoid arms." See Chenoweth and Cunningham, "Understanding Nonviolent Resistance," 273.

84. Dewey, *Essential Dewey*; James, *Pragmatism*; Stout, *Democracy and Tradition*; West, *American Evasion of Philosophy*; and Springs, *Healthy Conflict*.

85. James, *Pragmatism*.

86. Nepstad, *Nonviolent Struggle*, 11–12.

87. SOA Watch, "Vigil and Witness."

88. SOA Watch, "Become a Peacemaker."

89. Bourgeois, interview.

90. Sharp, *Politics of Nonviolent Action*, 117–448.

91. See Sharp for mock funerals, 157–63; organizations' support, 121; group mobilization, 132; legal repertoires, 315–20, 368, 420; banners, 125–26; portraits, 143; and speeches, 163.

92. For example, Francesca Polletta shows that activists' perception of what counts as strategic is culturally constructed and symbolically freighted with connotations such as professionalism, radicalism, or racial identity. See Polletta, *Freedom*.

93. I explicate this claim more fully in the essay "Nonviolence as a Tradition of Moral Praxis."

94. Bourgeois, interview. I examine more closely the role of exemplars in the generation of movement participation in chapter 5.

95. See, for example, Jeffrey Stout's defense of democracy as a tradition. Stout, *Democracy and Tradition*.

96. MacIntyre, *Whose Justice?*, 12.

97. Cathleen Kaveny rightly critiques MacIntyre for his inability to account adequately for the internal plurality of the religious traditions he wishes to recover, as well as his inability to admit the hybridity of these traditions and the ways that they have borrowed from secular and coreligionist sources. Kaveny, *Prophecy without Contempt*, 15–45.

98. For an example of this type of argument in the SOA Watch context, see Hamm, Ferrell, and Greer, "Provocateur for Justice."

99. Lorde, "Master's Tools," in *Sister Outsider*.

100. Inserra, interview.

101. Connolly, *Pluralism*, 2–5.

102. In my judgment, nonviolence offers a more promising avenue of convergence for these two traditions than does Glen Stassen's bid for just peacemaking. Stassen, *Just Peacemaking*.

103. Burawoy, *Ethnography Unbound*; and Burawoy, *Extended Case Method*. See also Bretherton, "Coming to Judgment"; and Bretherton, *Resurrecting Democracy*.

4

DIVINE OBEDIENCE
A Messianic Political Theology
of the Higher Law

Seven of us circled chairs in the Country Inn's lounge in Columbus, Georgia.[1] This was the last of a very long day of meetings. At 10:30 p.m., the dimly lit hotel lobby was empty but for a few staff. The space wouldn't be busy again until the free continental breakfast was served the next morning. "We should probably take the batteries out of our phones and put them on the table over there," suggested Tina, a representative of the SOA Watch Legal Collective.[2] Once we had removed our phone batteries and assembled, Carlos began the meeting with some very brief framing remarks, the primary import of which was to restate his own intention not to commit civil disobedience this year and signal his desire that those who were willing to "cross the line" should take the lead on directing the action.

We had gathered to discern the shape of a nonviolent direct action at Stewart Detention Center that was to be held in two days. Albert was the first to respond to Carlos's invitation, saying, "I want to do the action, but I wish I could do it without getting arrested." He wanted to create a situation where there could be a mass crossing with many others participating. Everyone liked this idea in principle; it evoked the memory of SOA Watch activism before September 11, 2001, when hundreds crossed the line onto Fort Benning. Yet immediately we were presented with a dilemma: how could we get lots of folks involved and not simultaneously tip off the authorities? To do a mass crossing, we would have to transgress, at least, a police tape line and, possibly, a human chain of officers. Given the nonviolent commitments of the movement, this seemed difficult at best.

Whereas Albert expressed some ambivalence, Brian was quite clear. Having crossed last year, he was ready to do it again to "shut down Stewart." Brian's question, however, was whether nonviolent direct action was an effective mode of social change. He confessed evolving opinions about nonviolent civil disobedience over the years and wondered aloud whether it was the best way to achieve the group's aims of not only closing Stewart, the second-largest privately owned immigrant detention center in the United States, but also fundamentally changing US immigration policy. In spite of these reservations, he saw how his action the year prior brought attention to the plight of Stewart's detainees.

Responding to Brian's concern, SOA Watch staff member Rosa shared her own struggles with the efficacy of civil disobedience. Long conversations with other SOA Watch members convinced her there were times in a movement's life cycle in which civil disobedience made more sense than others. Right now, for Stewart, Rosa suggested, it made a lot of sense. She felt that it was a good moment and that civil disobedience could be an effective tool.

With the potential effectiveness of this particular act of civil disobedience established, we then circled back to a logistical discussion of how to organize a mass crossing without tipping off the police. Albert wondered, if by informing people of potential consequences, "are we doing the work of the state?" For Carlos, the question was somewhat different: "Can we move people?" And what's the opportune moment to do that? Discussion ensued about how we could get people across the line and what we had to disclose to them.

Carlos remembered there was a lot of energy at the front of the march last year when the people turned onto CCA Road and marched to the gate. From the stage, Carlos felt "like I had an untamed horse." And the question, then, was, "How do we harness that?" Supporting Albert's desire for a mass crossing, Carlos was trying to figure out how to use the energy of the moment to encourage crossers.

The suggestion was made to just keep marching, to just keep moving across the line. However, Rosa raised the concern that this would displace the people who normally lead the march, those directly impacted by immigrant detention, some of whom could not risk arrest. The capacity to get arrested, she suggested, was a privilege, a luxury that some people just couldn't take on. There would be people without papers, people with other responsibilities. Because of that, it would be too much to expect that people directly impacted by immigrant detention would remain at the front of the line and be the first to risk arrest. The alternative, however, was that they would be removed from their place of honor at the head of the march. She argued that this would be a real mistake.

Brian strongly agreed with Rosa's caution. To displace directly impacted folks from leadership was a violation of one of his fundamental reasons for supporting the campaign to shut down Stewart. His discomfort was such that he indicated he might not cross if that was the bargain. It was strange

*for me hearing such an about-face from Brian. Earlier he had been so
resolute in his commitment to cross. Yet when Rosa raised the issue of the
leadership of directly impacted people, Brian had nearly a total change of
position.*

*All of the conversation circled around these questions: What is the goal?
Why cross the line? Albert was clear that crossing the line simply to get
arrested was not sufficient as a goal. Why are we crossing? These questions
were accompanied by others: How do we honor the leadership of directly
impacted people? What are the demands of our solidarity with them?*

*We left the planning meeting with open questions and a commitment
to return to them after the following evening's plenary.*

† † †

The planning meeting described here took place two days before the annual
vigil at the Stewart Detention Center in November 2015. As introduced in
chapter 3, the campaign to bring attention to and call for the closure of the
immigration detention center emerged alongside the SOA Watch's annual
action at Fort Benning as local immigrant rights activists saw an opportunity
to bring international awareness to an issue they had been working on in
relative obscurity. The first annual Shut Down Stewart vigil was held in
2007, and beginning in 2013, the SOA Watch officially supported this effort.
In 2015 when our planning meeting took place, the two campaigns were
significantly integrated such that members of the SOA Watch Legal Collective and staff were present at the planning meeting for the Shut Down Stewart action.

While our conversation was inflected with the singularity of the event—
its personalities, timing, and context—the patterns of practical reasoning
that I have been tracking throughout this book were right on the surface.
Principled commitments to nonviolence, such as those that Brian voiced and
questioned, were challenged by concerns of effectiveness. Simultaneously,
concerns for effective policy change were rooted in a commitment to faithful
solidarity with "directly impacted persons." The deliberation displayed in
the planning meeting fluidly moved from questions of faithfulness to questions of effectiveness and back again. This tension, in turn, was fundamentally shaped by the bonds of solidarity between the living and the dead. I saw
these patterns of deliberation repeated across the movement in training
sessions, planning meetings, communiqués, and interviews.

This chapter continues to develop a messianic political theology by taking
up a persistent dilemma of SOA Watch organizing—how to relate to the law.
From its earliest days, the movement to close the US Army's School of the
Americas has been rooted in nonviolent direct action that included civil

disobedience. Recounting the action on the first anniversary of the UCA massacre, Roy Bourgeois said that the group's intention was "to try and call attention [to the crimes of graduates] through nonviolent civil disobedience. We're going to break the law, hopefully go to prison, to cast a light on this issue that's kind of hidden."[3] Yet the movement has also utilized a number of other legal repertoires. Subsequent to civil disobedience, SOA Watch activists have used the courts as theaters of moral redress, they have targeted congressional legislators through advocacy days and constituent mobilizations, they have engaged in direct diplomacy (or track-two diplomacy) to appeal to Latin American heads of state to stop sending their soldiers to the SOA/WHINSEC, and they have made use of the discourse of higher law— variously construed as divine law, human rights, or international law—to coordinate these divergent strategies.

I argue that activists' coordination of these diverse legal repertoires— transgression, appropriation, and affirmation—requires responsive discernment, or practical reason, under a messianism of the higher law. By making plain the practical reasoning that undergirds this discernment, I aim to undermine the worry that I exposed in chapter 1 that messianic political theologies necessarily devolve into opportunistic and violent political forms by devaluing the politics of this world. Rather than viewing activists' improvisation with legal repertoires as merely opportunistic, I suggest they might be rendered coherent as a response to the activity of God in which higher law enables the free use of legal forms that cause death for the purpose of flourishing life. SOA Watch activists have transgressed specific laws while committing civil disobedience, or what Anton Flores-Maisonet calls divine obedience,[4] to dramatize their resistance; they have appropriated legal repertoires of redress through legal advocacy and lobbying as well as direct diplomacy; and they have rendered these seemingly contradictory moves— transgression and appropriation—coherent by affirming a higher law that critiques all laws by their adequacy in the service of human flourishing. In this way SOA Watch activists make use of a radical, messianic politics. To be clear, this is not the only way SOA Watch activists make sense of their activism. As noted in chapter 3, the movement is plural in multiple ways, including in its justifications for the work of social change. Yet I argue that recourse to a messianic political theology of higher law offers a compelling way to make sense of the range of SOA Watch activities.

I make my argument in three steps. First, I set the legal repertoires deployed by the SOA Watch alongside the background of legalized violence in which the SOA/WHINSEC is but one part. The improvisational use of the law must be understood against a background of legal violence in which activists hope to intervene. SOA Watch participants have to decide whether and how to use the law to interrupt and transform a system of legal violence that is hemispheric in scope. SOA Watch activists must discern where the key points of intervention lie and how to place their bodies in that breach. As such, a diverse set of legal repertoires are necessary: transgression, appropriation, and affirmation of the law.

Second, I render the improvisational coordination of these repertoires theologically coherent by examining the theo-politics of the higher law. SOA Watch activists make plural appeals to the higher law to justify their activism. The messianic content that unites these appeals is the presence of the dead, a presence that obligates weak, improvisational legal actions. Through recourse to the Pauline tradition, I argue that the late modern reclamation of Saint Paul's account of the law illuminates the shape of SOA Watch activists' nonviolent use of legal repertoires. I bring these activists' own accounts into critical juxtaposition with the messianic political theologies of Walter Benjamin, Jacob Taubes, and Giorgio Agamben. These thinkers, Jewish and secular, have thematized Paul's messianism in ways that are particularly useful for describing and evaluating the SOA Watch's political practice.

Third, I conclude by demonstrating how these legal repertoires operate in a hope for a law delivered from violence and require the exercise of a messianically conditioned practical reason. While the discourse of the higher law is a plural one in the SOA Watch, indicating a constellation of affirmations and negations, it consistently expresses commitments to relationships of solidarity that hope to transcend the asymmetries of hegemonic power. This hope is messianic not only in its affirmation of the resurrected presence of the crucified people but also in that it imagines the possibility that "the wolf shall live with the lamb, the leopard shall lie down with the kid, the calf and the lion and the fatling together, and a little child shall lead them" (Isaiah 11:6). Rather than being a cause for alarm because of the connection between messianism and violence, I argue the messianism invoked by the discourse of the higher law can generate the practical reasoning that includes both concerns of faithfulness and effectiveness. I conclude by lifting up two perennial problems regarding the ethics of civil disobedience across cases and suggest the ways that the constructive account of a messianic political theology that I am developing here offers moral guidance.

LEGAL REPERTOIRES AND LEGALIZED VIOLENCE

In an interview with two longtime SOA Watch supporters, Mary Anne Perrone and Rebecca Kanner, I asked about the kinds of deliberations in which SOA Watch activists engaged in moments of impasse. I had in mind, in particular, the 2000–2001 closure of the SOA and the opening of WHINSEC; the shift in political opportunity following the attacks on September 11,

2001; the departure of the Ignatian Solidarity Network in 2009; and the 2015–16 deliberations about moving the annual vigil to the border. As we talked, Perrone and Kanner noted challenges within the movement, particularly when it came to different theories of change. Kanner, a labor organizer and environmental activist, observed,

> [One] dynamic that I've noticed being involved in this movement is that there are people, and some of them are our staff people, who were more of the anarchist, maybe Catholic Worker [type]—I remember having discussions with some of them—who don't believe in voting. And here a big arm of our thing is [that] there are a few ways that the school can be closed: by Congress, by the president, by the military. And some of our staffers didn't believe in that thing. It is a dynamic that is still with the organization.[5]

I asked the two activists what theory of change did those who were suspicious of legislative processes propose as an alternative. Perrone responded,

> Good question! They didn't believe in voting for people, going and casting your vote. But any of the above would have worked. It was about people power, grassroots in the streets. You know, do enough, yell enough, be creative enough, that's what we all also think. . . . What if we do it this way! What if we do it that way! What if we have puppets! What if we . . . oh, we'll do a die in! We'll have civil disobedience! Then they will know, [then] change will happen. And that [public witness] is a huge part of change. We all believe that.[6]

Perrone and Kanner highlighted a split in the movement, one that has analogies with the internal divisions explored in chapter 3. While everyone in the SOA Watch movement could agree on the importance of grassroots mobilizing and nonviolent direct action, there was greater ambivalence toward legal processes.

My conversation with Perrone and Kanner elicited challenges that many movements for political change face: given an analysis that the injustice we seek to correct is not a mere aberration but built into the very structures that organize our societies, how do we pursue lasting change?[7] This old question of leftist politics often pits reformers and revolutionaries against each other.[8] At times, activists use this opposition in tactical squabbles to identify detractors as idealistic or sellouts. The tactics are used metonymically to stand in for identities in internal power struggles.[9] Yet we can put the question as one of means and ends: can piecemeal change through means of reform be used in the service of the end of broader societal transformation? The answer is clearly yes; reform and revolution need not be necessarily construed as oppositional. But these questions point to the depth of the problem: if the law enables the forms of violence that we seek to resist, is the law itself not corrupted past the point of use?[10]

The context for these questions is the system of US–Latin American militarism, which is a system of legalized violence that inheres within legal codes, domestic and international.[11] I argue that this legalized violence is best understood as a structure of US–Latin American militarism that enables the production of violence on a massive scale without centralized direction. This system of legalized violence aids and abets the production of what Ignacio Ellacuría poignantly identified as the "crucified people," or that class of poor that is ground up by the gears of civilizational progress.[12] US military training is one of the key transmission belts along which violence travels from the structure of militarism to the direct violence perpetrated on Latin American civilians.[13] This background is essential to understanding the challenge that SOA Watch activists face in determining how they can disrupt and transform the legal structure of US–Latin American militarism.

A Background of Legalized Violence

In her study of the US Army's School of the Americas, anthropologist Lesley Gill travels the pathways of migration in which money, munitions, and (mostly) men move to and from the SOA/WHINSEC.[14] Interviewing not only SOA Watch activists but also school graduates, trainers, and administrators, as well as Bolivian campesinos and human rights workers, Gill describes the SOA as one site within a wider structure of imperialist impunity. Gill grants that "language of empire" can generate, at times, too much polemical heat.[15] But it is the correct term to describe a system of military patronage by which the training and arming of soldiers, the deposition of democratically elected governments, and the systematic repression of dissent all produce US dominance and enable the pursuit of US economic interests.[16]

Key to the maintenance of this system are the relationships between the SOA/WHINSEC graduates and their hosts (and by extension the US military). Friendly relations established at the SOA/WHINSEC provide the foundation for later influence. Such relations allow the alignment of Latin American aims for advancement and US interests in hemispheric soft control. Regardless of their relative location in the military hierarchy, the technical aspects of training are less important than the students' initiation into a system of legal order and its attendant relationships of patrimony. The system itself operates so smoothly, so normally as to evade notice. But its bitter fruits are tragic and predictable violence against persons unrecognized as objects of moral or political concern: campesinos, labor organizers, dissident priests, and indigenous populations, among others. Gill demonstrates a troubling

correlation between the number of graduates of SOA/WHINSEC training
from specific countries and coup d'états in the same states in the following
years.[17]

Gill's more focused analysis of the SOA/WHINSEC as a specific case
coheres with studies of the wider structure of US militarism in Latin America. Sociologists Cecilia Menjívar and Néstor Rodríguez have argued that the
use of terror by modern Latin American states is neither an aberration nor a
remnant of a colonial past, but a part of a rational bureaucratic structure of
administration and control.[18] Menjívar and Rodríguez rightly argue that
state terror is rationally calculated within a bureaucratically organized system of power that serves to protect the economic and political interests of
the Latin American elite and their US patrons. Such rational structuring of
violence requires training within a bureaucratic structure, and within the
US–Latin American military system, this training is often provided by the US
military.

Martha K. Huggins's study of "violence workers" in Brazil confirms the
overall pattern identified by Gill, Menjívar, and Rodríguez.[19] Huggins critiques US foreign police training programs by pointing out that despite a
congressional ban from 1973, these programs serve US national security
and economic interests. Moreover, they often lead to significant human
rights abuses in contradiction to the official ideology of professionalization
and the rule of law. At cross purposes with the rhetoric of democratization
and human rights, Huggins and her colleagues Mika Haritos-Fatouros and
Philip G. Zimbardo have shown that the professionalization process itself
serves to insulate police and military officers from those they are to protect
while also placing them in dependent relationships with the training state.

Together, the focused analyses of Gill and Huggins and the wider analysis of Menjívar and Rodríguez sketch a background of legalized violence in
which US economic and political interests are served by relationships of
patronage developed through training programs such as that carried out at
the SOA/WHINSEC.[20] As Gill summarizes, "Military bases, weapons, and
strategic alliances with local security forces constitute the cutting edge of
the U.S. empire in which the American state rules less through the control
of territory than through the penetration and manipulation of subordinate
states that retain considerable political independence."[21] This system of
empire is accurately described as legalized violence. Through US military
training, Latin American officers are initiated into relationships of patronage in which their allegiances shift from their conationals to their patron.
While the curriculum is not insubstantial—as the torture manuals that
I introduce in the next section show—the technical aspects of military
training are but one aspect of a much larger system of patronage, violence,
and impunity. And when the six Jesuits and two women were killed on

November 16, 1989, this complex system began to come into view for SOA Watch activists.

(Il)legal Repertoires of Intervention

Against a background of legalized violence, the challenge for SOA Watch activists was to identify points of intervention that could begin to unravel the reinforcing structures of international legal contracts, protectionist ideologies, military cultures of patronage, and mechanisms of state terror. Of course, intervening in a system as sprawling and stable as this would confound even the most well-resourced movement. To bring the wider problem into view while focusing their limited energies, the ragtag group assembled in Columbus, Georgia, identified one potent and seemingly manageable symbol of that system—the School of the Americas.

In its origins, the SOA Watch movement's principal mode of political engagement was nonviolent direct action. Yet nonviolent direct action, often militant and revolutionary in its associations, was never the only mode of political engagement; the movement has engaged in various forms of reformist advocacy from lobbying Congress to vote to defund the school to, beginning in 1997, engaging in direct diplomacy with Latin American countries. This advocacy was buttressed by research, analysis, and education, practices that were enabled (at times) by periods of imprisonment. Thus, three political practices—sometimes taking revolutionary exception to legal systems, sometimes working reforms internal to these same systems—have rooted the movement and recurred across its twenty-five-year history: nonviolent direct action, analysis, and advocacy.

Nonviolent Direct Action

From its start, SOA Watch activists have maintained a commitment to nonviolent direct action. Together, nonviolence *and* direct action indicate a contentious and prefigurative mode of politics that uses conflict constructively to generate change. It is commonly acknowledged that nonviolence is not inactivity or acquiescence in the face of injustice; indeed, it is active and disruptive.[22] I demonstrated in chapter 3 that nonviolence plays a critical role in holding together the pluralistic SOA Watch constituency. I argued that while nonviolence performs many functions, it is best understood as a tradition of moral praxis. Whereas nonviolence has its modern roots in Gandhi's elaboration of ahimsa, which literally means "non-harm,"[23] direct action emerges from radical leftist and anarchist political theory of the nineteenth century. The classical definition of *direct action* includes any act that is undertaken directly, without the intervention or aid of some supervening authority or government.[24] In more conventional usage, it indicates a heightened militancy of protest, more than carrying signs in a march and less than amassing AK-47s and heading to the hills.[25] Martin Luther King Jr. and the Black Freedom Movement of the 1950s and '60s popularized the combination of nonviolence and direct action in a disruptive politics rooted in moral suasion and the power of love.[26] In each of these cases, nonviolent direct action is communicative as well as disruptive, at times transgressing legal strictures to display the moral passion of participants and the injustice of legal systems.

Consonant with these antecedents, the SOA Watch's practice of nonviolent direct action has combined performative and disruptive elements. As I argued in chapter 2, the particular shape of that direct action has been liturgical, drawing on a mezcla of symbolic sources from canonical Roman Catholic litanies to Latin American leftist chants. Prophetic and demonstrative, these actions transgressed liturgical boundaries and often involved some form of civil disobedience. This performative mode of protest has aimed to achieve the goals of both internal identity formation of participants and external communication of grievances to observers, officials, and the general public. So, for example, in 1997, 601 marchers carrying coffins filled with thousands of signed petitions calling for the SOA's closure crossed onto Fort Benning. The symbolism of the Latin American dead, re-membered through the ¡presente! litany, was then combined with a representation of popular will (the petition) and the transgression of boundaries through the act of civil disobedience.

In later years, several activists reported that in their crossing, echoing Abraham Joshua Heschel, they were "praying with [their] feet."[27] Rebecca Kanner reported in her 2001 trial statement,

> The three times I crossed the line at Fort Benning, I have felt what the Jewish theologian and philosopher Rabbi Abraham Joshua Heschel felt when he marched together with Martin Luther King out of Selma. He believed that it was a day of sanctification, filled with spiritual significance, and he felt as though his legs were praying. I was praying with my feet during those holy moments as we gathered together to do *tikkun olam* [repair of the world] at Fort Benning.[28]

Naming precedents in King and Heschel, Kanner understood her civil disobedience to be a kind of prayer that, in a partial way, enacted her commitment to repair the world.

In addition to the these performative protests at Fort Benning, the historical background to the deliberation featured at the beginning of this chapter included a memory of years past in which protesters walked onto the Stewart Detention Center's property and, like Joshua and the Israelites at Jericho, marched around the facility seven times while calling for its walls to crumble.[29] These actions are expressive in the sense that they enact the "propaganda of the deed"; the action itself communicates by disruptively placing bodies on the line to perform a messianic symbolism that envisions the possibility of a repaired world.[30]

The drama of these performative protests becomes disruptive through civil disobedience. Defined simply by movement lawyer and professor of law Bill Quigley, *civil disobedience* is "conduct that intentionally risks arrest to make a political statement."[31] The civil disobedience of SOA Watch activists has typically violated strictures related to the manner and place of public assembly and speech. At Fort Benning, the vast majority of those SOA Watch activists who have committed civil disobedience have been charged with criminal trespass for entering a military base to engage in unlawful activity.[32] Similar to Martin Luther King Jr.'s violation of the anti-protest injunction in Birmingham, these acts of criminal transgression do not violate, at least directly, an unjust law; rather, they are expressive acts in the positive sense.[33] These acts are what legal scholar John Alan Cohan calls indirect civil disobedience.[34] They violate specific positive laws regulating speech and assembly to dramatize activists' rejection of the legalized violence that the SOA/WHINSEC represents.

SOA Watch prisoners of conscience make sense of this violation in different ways. Some plead guilty to the violations. As Craig Adams said in his 2004 trial statement,

> I choose to plead guilty. There is no doubt that I trespassed onto the grounds of Ft. Benning. I did this to protest the use of my tax dollars to support the U.S. Army School of the Americas / WHINSEC. I plead guilty out of respect for our country's laws, Constitution, and Bill of Rights which give me the right to stand trial before you today. I plead guilty because I feel I am acting in the tradition of nonviolent civil disobedience—following the example of Mahatma Gandhi and Martin Luther King, both of whom plead guilty for their acts of civil disobedience.[35]

On the other hand, Alice Gerard, among others, defended the legality of their actions by saying, "I do not believe that I have violated any laws. I believe that my actions were protected by the U.S. Constitution's guarantee of free speech and free assembly and these rights do not end with a fence at the end of the road."[36] Whether pleading guilty as Adams did or pleading not guilty as Gerard did, activists repeatedly appealed to higher laws to justify their decisions.

Adams's and Gerard's statements demonstrate the ways in which the dramatization of grievances that begins in the street is continued in the courtroom. Activists have used the judicial process to "put the SOA itself on trial."[37] While SOA Watch prisoners of conscience usually either plead guilty to charges or not guilty while agreeing to certain "stipulated facts," their admissions of guilt (or lack thereof) are primarily opportunities to restate their moral and political reasons for committing civil disobedience.[38] In their trial statements, prisoners of conscience such as retired health care worker Louise Lynch often challenge the legality of the SOA/WHINSEC itself: "I stand before you to witness to the sacredness of civil disobedience, and 'moral obedience.'. . . We are here today to challenge the very morality and LEGALITY of the SOA/WHINSEC."[39] These activists use criminal proceedings as an opportunity to indict the legality of the SOA/WHINSEC.

In justifying their transgressions, prisoners of conscience repeatedly appeal to personal experiences of interactions with the people of Central and South America who are victims of US military training. Sister Cynthia Brinkman, with particularly apocalyptic imagery, spoke in her trial statement of a "river of blood flowing from the United States through Central America and covering South America." Brinkman worked with her order, the School Sisters of Notre Dame (SSND), in Honduras and met refugees who had fled from El Salvador. Listening to the women's stories of loved ones who attempted to flee across the Rio Sumpul but were killed by troops with US-funded weapons and training, Brinkman reported that "the unexpressed question in my sisters' eyes on that day was 'Why does your government want us dead?'"[40] Holding a fabric globe during her trial statement, Brinkman dramatically revealed a river of red fabric flowing from North to South America.

Brinkman justified her action with appeals to multiple, overlapping authorities. Her statement continued: "As a citizen of this country and a lover of God, God's creation and God's law, I say a resounding NO! Not in my name will my government further the interests of the corporate elite of this hemisphere by exploiting human beings as cheap labor and silencing their demands for justice with disappearances, torture and death—carried out by military trained at WHINSEC/SOA and paid for by tax dollars of US citizens."[41] Brinkman appealed to her responsibilities before country, creation, and God, responsibilities that together motivated her action. In her appeal to God's law, Brinkman sounded a theme that recurs in many statements by prisoners of conscience. Variously construed as "God's law," the "law of 'Love Thy Neighbor,'" "faithfulness to the God of love and justice," or "gospel obedience," these appeals purport to relativize the authority of the judge, the court, and positive law itself and place it under a higher law. I take up this motif of messianic political theologies more fully in the next section.

While the courtroom has provided a theater of redress, imprisonment has also generated a platform for amplifying the messages of the movement. Roy

Bourgeois recognized in his first actions of civil disobedience that prison time was a "great opportunity."

> That's one thing we learned about going to prison, you can't be silenced. And it really was a unique opportunity to educate people on the issue. We had to educated ourselves, and now was the moment to educate others about the basics . . . what we knew about the SOA, its history, its graduates, the atrocities that we knew about, there were many more to be discovered. So we, from prison, each of us [Charlie Liteky, Patrick Liteky, and Bourgeois], wrote, I mean it was hard work, hundreds and hundreds of letters, hand written. And from that came, I will never forget, lots of invitations: "when you get out of prison, could you please come to our college, our church, our peace group to speak about this issue?" So it was a great opportunity.[42]

Rebecca Kanner was less convinced about the efficacy of civil disobedience and prison time when she first got involved with the SOA Watch. "This whole prison thing," she observed, "it seemed like it elevated the people." It seemed to Kanner that prison time made movement celebrities but not much else. But she saw how powerful it was when a group from Minnesota showed up in Washington, DC, with pins on their shirts commemorating Sister Rita who was then doing time as a prisoner of conscience. "We were sitting on the Capitol steps, and I remember that the whole Minnesota [congressional] delegation came out to meet with the Minnesota people, and they took a picture. The whole congressional delegation was supporting those folks. . . . That was pretty powerful."[43] This experience, along with her own time in prison, convinced Kanner that "the most effective times for doing outreach are those times between the trial and going to prison."[44]

In 2018, the SOA Watch reported

> 328 acts of civil disobedience that drew sentences
> 300 different people sentenced for CD [civil disobedience]
> Over 101.5 years of prison time sentenced
> 53.5 years of probation and home confinement time sentenced
> $223,150 of fines issued
> 6,900+ community service hours sentenced
> 274 prison sentences served by 245 different individuals
> 51 probation sentences served by 51 different individuals
> 4 home confinement sentences served by 4 different individuals[45]

Prisoners of conscience generate public attention. If a religious sister, a Jesuit priest, a hospice coordinator, and a retired schoolteacher (to name just a few) are willing to spend months in prison and face stiff fines, then it seems as though we should at least learn something about their cause. I take up the way that exemplarity functions motivationally more fully in chapter 5, but here it is sufficient to note that the prison time resulting from nonviolent direct action has effectively generated opportunities for communicating the demands and analysis of the movement that otherwise would not have been available.

Analysis Building through Research and Education

Prison time not only provided further opportunities to dramatize grievances and amplify the movement's messages but also gave leaders a break from the intensity of nonviolent direct action to conduct research, to educate themselves, and, in turn, to educate others. Analysis building can be heuristically separated into three tasks: establishing the facts, identifying paths of complicity, and developing a strategy of intervention.[46] Of course, while heuristically separable, these tasks are iteratively practiced; they do not neatly follow from one to the next. Yet there is a chronological priority as the points of strategic intervention became clearer when SOA Watch actors gained access to more information about the SOA/WHINSEC and its place within the hemispheric system of US–Latin American militarism.

The first task of building an analysis is establishing the facts. This task was aided early on by the 1990 publication of Rep. Joe Moakley's "Interim Report of the Speaker's Task Force on El Salvador."[47] The focus of the Moakley Report was the UCA massacre, and while the Speaker's Task Force on El Salvador had a limited mandate, it established a connection between the US Army's School of the Americas and the assassinations of the Jesuits.[48] The report showed that members of the Atlacatl Battalion, the military unit that carried out the raid on the UCA in 1989, were trained at the SOA, with some men having been there as recently as the year prior. As might be expected, US military leaders were resistant to the charge of complicity. Acting Assistant Secretary of Defense Carl W. Ford Jr. was careful to point out that "human rights has been a key focus of U.S. training and is an important component of training currently provided by the Salvadoran Armed Forces."[49] Thus, the mere fact they were trained by US forces did not implicate US responsibility in the Jesuits' assassination. Following the logic of Assistant Secretary Ford, Salvadoran troops needed more training, not less.

While Bourgeois was in prison in 1991 and 1992, however, SOA Watch staff member Vicky Imerman slowly compiled a database of notorious graduates. Obtaining from the National Security Archives a list of the school's fifty-five thousand graduates, Imerman compared that list with clippings from newspapers and human rights reports, including the 1993 United Nations' report of the Commission on the Truth for El Salvador.[50] What she discovered was a pattern of connections between US training and civilian targeting. Imerman learned, first, that some of the most notorious abusers of human rights—including Bolivian dictator Hugo Banzer, Argentine general Leopoldo Galtieri, and nearly all of the Nicaraguan National Guard's officer corps—were trained at the SOA. Second, she found that contrary to Ford's suggestion, the countries with the most training also had the most egregious records of human rights violations.[51] A view of the structure of complicity began to emerge as SOA Watch staff continued to file Freedom of Information Act requests and investigate the curriculum of the school at Fort Benning.

These speculative connections were brought into stark relief in 1996 when the Department of Defense released the findings of a 1992 investigation showing that the SOA had utilized training manuals advocating torture and execution. Breaking the story, *Washington Post* writer Dana Priest summarized, "U.S. Army intelligence manuals used to train Latin American military officers at an Army school from 1982 to 1991 advocated executions, torture, blackmail and other forms of coercion against insurgents."[52] Identified by the movement as "torture manuals," these revelations helped to solidify the second task of analysis building—identifying the pathways of complicity.

While it was not enough to merely assert that training at a US facility equals US responsibility for the actions of Latin American soldiers, the torture manuals gave specificity to the bitter fruits of US training. They demonstrated that the training in methods of coercion and in targeting of civilians was part of the curriculum and an outgrowth of the Ronald Reagan and George H. W. Bush administrations' strategy of low-intensity warfare. Moreover, they gave material evidence to the movement's argument that the SOA was one of the key transmission belts by which the structural violence of economic inequality and militarism were converted into direct violence aimed at Latin American civilians.[53] The movement used the publication of the manuals to great effect, arguing that they proved the connections that they had identified in previous years.

Having established the facts and identified the pathways of complicity, the movement engaged in the third task of analysis building and developed a strategy of education, action, and change. Building on the moral authority that came with serving time in prison, Bourgeois and other prisoners of conscience wrote articles and letters to the editors of various newspapers and went on speaking tours throughout the United States. They used the analysis they had built through their research to make a compelling case for closing the SOA, and they called for people to join them at the Fort Benning gates for the annual vigils in November.

The strategy that the SOA Watch identified was a combination of internal and external pressure targeted particularly at Congress. While the SOA

Watch acknowledged three potential pathways to the closure of the school—through the president, the military, and members of Congress—it discerned that Congress represented the clearest opportunity. Whereas the president was largely inaccessible to a grassroots movement, and the military could be relied on only to defend its interests in the maintenance of the school, congressional representatives could be directly targeted and accessed by SOA Watch activists. Moreover, some congressional representatives, such as Rep. Joseph Moakley, were early allies. This led to the third legal repertoire of SOA Watch's political practice—advocacy.

Advocacy

Whereas the SOA Watch movement has used nonviolent direct action to violate laws and conducted research and analysis to demonstrate the injustice of the law, it has used advocacy through lobbying and direct diplomacy to bend the legal process to pursue its own aims. SOA Watch organizers identified that one way to shut down the school would be to cut its funding from Congress. Early efforts to lobby Congress were ad hoc. Rep. Joseph Kennedy II (D-MA) added an amendment to a military budget bill in September 1993, and the SOA was debated for the first time on the House floor.[54] The amendment failed in a vote of 174 to 256. But it would be the first of several attempts to defund the school through congressional action.

In the spring of 1994, Roy Bourgeois was joined by Carol Richardson, a United Methodist minister who was working as the grassroots coordinator for Witness for Peace. Whereas Bourgeois admitted that he "would rather be in prison than lobby," Richardson was a skillful DC organizer.[55] Through her leadership, the SOA Watch designed a lobbying campaign, activating the growing network of SOA Watch supporters to call on their representatives and ask them to defund the school. In addition to its annual vigil in November, the SOA Watch began in 1997 an annual lobby day in Washington, DC. Combined with a "suits and roots" strategy session, affinity groups from across the country were organized into delegations that then visited their representatives and senators equipped with talking points developed from SOA Watch staff research.

While central to the overall strategy of the movement, effective lobbying proved elusive. After years of organizing, the SOA Watch achieved a major legislative victory on July 29, 1999. Representative Moakley proposed an amendment to cut $2 million from the school's budget, a move that would have effectively closed the training facility.[56] The amendment passed 230 to 197. But rather than close the school, Senate leaders later accepted a Defense Department proposal to rename the school and change the curriculum to have, at least on paper, a greater focus on human rights. As sociologist

Selina Gallo-Cruz has shown, the Pentagon responded to the movement by opening a "new," more public relations–savvy organization and shifting the boundaries of the debate to accept the importance of human rights while challenging the claim of the school's responsibility for human rights violations.[57] The US Army's School of the Americas closed in 2000 only to be reopened in the same location, with the same instructors, and much of the same curriculum on January 17, 2001, as the Western Hemisphere Institute for Security Cooperation.[58]

While the movement was successful in raising awareness about the SOA, it failed to convince Congress that WHINSEC continued the legacy of its predecessor. The institutional shift was further exacerbated by a significant change in the structure of political opportunity after September 11, 2001. Bourgeois remembered,

> When 9/11 happened, I'll never forget, I got a call from the commanding general the next day. I was on a speaking tour and, actually, in New York City, at Fordham, and could see the smoke from the, you know, the attack. I'll never forget, though, the general calls, and he says, "You know that everything is changed now." He said, "We are at war with the terrorists, and I'm requesting that you call off your protest, you know, in a couple of months, in November."[59]

Bourgeois and the base commander both knew that the ground had shifted beneath their feet. This change in political opportunity led to significant deliberation within the movement. Some SOA Watch constituents thought it was time to celebrate victories, cut losses, and refocus on other issues. Others, however, thought that the school's reinvention plan was merely cosmetic and committed themselves to continue working for its closure by whatever means were open to them. Though some SOA Watch activists moved on, others doubled down on their commitments to seeing the school closed. As social movement theorists have shown, closures in political opportunity are often moments of tactical innovation.[60]

In the context of this closure of political opportunity, the SOA Watch began to construct significant transnational linkages with Latin American partners. Building on the past connections of US-based actors to Latin America, SOA Watch began planning delegations to directly target Latin American heads of state and military leaders, calling on them to rescind their participation in US military training programs. Combining what peace studies scholars identify as *track two diplomacy*, in which nongovernmental actors directly appeal to governmental actors in other states, and *track three diplomacy*, in which nongovernmental actors engage directly with each other, these transnational delegations were relatively successful in achieving the noncooperation of some Latin American states.[61] They gained agreements from Venezuela, Argentina, Uruguay, Bolivia, Ecuador, and Nicaragua.

Together, the legal repertoires of nonviolent direct action, analysis, and legislative advocacy form three points of a triangle of SOA Watch activism. When the coordination of the triangle is working well, SOA Watch activists engage simultaneously inside and outside the legal system.[62] But this kind of inside-outside coordination is not easy. One way to make sense of this coordination is seeing it as the cooperation of reformers and revolutionaries. According to this analysis, activists who work within the system tend to be *reformists*. They affirm the legitimacy of legal structures and think that while they might not be living up to their fullest potential, these structures are on the whole necessary and good. Meanwhile, activists who work outside the system tend to be *revolutionaries*. They understand legal structures as principally forms of domination that cannot be resisted through mere tinkering; instead, they seek large-scale social transformation.

The plurality of the movement, as I explored in chapter 3, can explain to some extent the coherence of this inside-outside coordination. In the SOA Watch movement, reformists and revolutionaries have found common cause even if they are operating with different fundamental theories of change. Yet this can explain only so much. A neat distinction between reformists and revolutionaries fails when subjected to empirical scrutiny. Reformist and revolutionary identities are often used polemically within movements to suppress dissent and delegitimize internal opponents. The reality is that many SOA Watch activists deploy both sets of legal repertoires—reform and revolution—working within and without simultaneously. In this way, they are "in the world but not of it."[63]

PRACTICE OF THE POLITICS OF THE HIGHER LAW

The argument of this chapter is that SOA Watch activists are able to hold this "in the world but not of it" posture through a messianic practice of the politics of the higher law.[64] Appeals to the higher law, not a facile cooperation of reformers and revolutionaries, allow the coordination of these disparate legal repertoires. Such appeals will immediately trouble some readers. They have even angered the judges before whom the appeals were made, with Magistrate Stephen Hyles marching out of his own courtroom in disgust during a 2015 trial. The higher law seems to enable either any sort of illicit behavior, on the one hand, or a creeping code fetishism, on the other. I would suggest that SOA Watch activism succumbs to neither of these temptations, though it at times plays at their edges. Instead, the politics of a higher law calls up a long, if controversial, strand of messianic political theology.

SOA Watch Appeals to the Higher Law

SOA Watch prisoners of conscience have processed and publicized their civil disobedience in a number of ways. Because part of the point of committing an act of civil disobedience is performative, they have used the platforms ready at hand to amplify their messages: online, alternative media, as well as mainstream newspaper editorials and op-eds; documentaries about the SOA/WHINSEC and the activism to close it; books critiquing US foreign policy and justifying activists' decisions; or memoirs giving an account of activists' time in jail.[65] One of the sources that has documented, more than any other, the reasons that SOA Watch activists give for "crossing the line" is a series of self-published booklets that reproduce court testimonies of prisoners of conscience.

Reading these trial and sentencing statements, a number of patterns emerge. The first was that when narrating their reasons for activism, prisoners of conscience made a nearly universal rhetorical decision to start with their personal experiences of having witnessed violence in Latin America. In each of these statements, prisoners of conscience justify their civil disobedience by naming their obligations to remain faithful to the people represented in these stories. In one case, retired Lutheran pastor and prisoner of conscience Brooks Anderson was asked quite directly to work to close the SOA. He recounted,

> We were [in El Salvador] for 10 days in this village. Each day we would eat our meals at—call it a restaurant. It was kind of a cooperative cooking facility. And the pastor from our church and I were standing outside. He had a little more Spanish than I, which between us was almost none. And a young lad about 12 years old came up to us, and he wanted to tell us something. And we were getting it a little bit mostly through sign language. You want to write to a school in America? No. And then we would try it again. "You want children from a school in America to write to your school?" "No, no." We were standing by an iron gate that swings. And on one side it says "open." He swings it the other way, and points to the word "closed." "You want us to go home and write about closing the School of the Americas?" "Yes, yes, yes." And that was the message we got from that village.[66]

Stories such as Anderson's are repeated throughout the trial statements. Given the relationships with Latin Americans that they had developed through human rights delegations, missionary assignments, or work with immigrants in the United States, prisoners of conscience were compelled to call for the closure of the SOA/WHINSEC. These experiences are one component of what sociologist Sharon Erickson Nepstad calls activists' biographical availability to social change work.[67] Their personal experiences, motivated by their moral and religious commitments, entangled them in relationships of obligation that demanded their engagement against US-supported violence in Latin America.

In addition to the repeated appeals to personal experiences, activists made consistent appeals to a higher law, variously construed. It would be a mistake to describe the higher law as one thing; rather, it is a constellation of concepts, historical artifacts, and legal agreements. One set of activists made appeals to immanent authorities: the US Constitution, the Nuremberg principles, international law, and human rights. Therapist and prisoner of conscience Margaret Knapke argued in her trial statement that "some laws contradict others." She continued,

> And so I think that a conscientious citizen has to very carefully discern which laws have priority—moral if not legal priority. . . . I really don't think that I or my friends here have broken the law in any meaningful sense of the word by taking political discourse onto the base. In fact, I think that we are all being essentially obedient to a law that is very dear to me and with which I'm sure you are very familiar, the Nuremberg Principles. And as you know, the seventh principle claims that citizens are required to not cooperate with government policies which produce crimes against humanity, crimes against peace, and war crimes. And so I really believe I would be grievously disobedient if I failed to speak for the people of Latin America, particularly, those under fire in Colombia and Chiapas and other regions in southern Mexico, as directly and clearly and strongly as I have by taking our message directly onto the base where it most needs to be heard.[68]

Knapke's recourse to the Nuremberg principles echoes an argument that peace activists often deployed to justify civil disobedience, though with little judicial success.[69] The seventh Nuremberg principle reads, "Complicity in the commission of a crime against peace, a war crime, or a crime against humanity as set forth in Principle VI is a crime under international law."[70] Judges often object to the claim of complicity utilized in this defense. As legal scholar Richard Falk argues, while the "zone of legal responsibility" certainly extends beyond principal state leaders, secondary figures are judged on the basis of whether they voluntarily cooperated in the commission of a crime.[71] The extent of that voluntary cooperation is the principal legal issue.

Judge Hugh Lawson raised just this question following Knapke's invocation of the Nuremberg principles:

THE COURT: In what way have you been called to cooperate with the policy of the United States Government at the School of the Americas?

DEFENDANT KNAPKE: Well, by paying taxes for one. Also, I think, you know, that . . .

THE COURT: Well, why don't you just quit paying taxes?

DEFENDANT KNAPKE: Well, I have. But, beyond that, I believe that . . . citizens are really required, and we fail miserably if we fail to communicate our concerns. And you know, I've done that through legal means. I've written letters ad nauseam to papers and congress people and I've lobbied. And I'll continue to do all of those. They are very important. But you know, the way the system works, the way I understand it, is very, very slow, at best and people in Latin America are dying today. I mean, they are dying today as we sit here in this courtroom. And so I really believe that it's important for citizens to speak with the loudest possible volume—nonviolently, but with the loudest possible volume in order to articulate their concerns about what the School of the Americas is doing.[72]

Knapke argued that the higher law of the Nuremberg principles compelled not just the cessation of material support for criminal activity (paying taxes) but also a spate of legal repertoires of redress. Admitting the importance of lobbying and writing letters to the editor, she also identified the limits of these practices. In Knapke's account, faithfulness to the people of Latin America required her to raise her concerns "with the loudest possible volume."

While Knapke appealed exclusively to the Nuremberg principles as compelling her SOA Watch activism, other prisoners of conscience, such as microbiologist Kathleen Fisher, have been more eclectic in their invocations. Fisher began her statement with an account of her "life's journey" through several Christian traditions and organizations, saying they "informed my decision to protest against the School of the Americas."[73] Beyond this, however, her decision was "also informed by two widely recognized documents of human rights."

One of these is the United States Constitution. The First Amendment speaks about freedom of speech and the right to peaceably assemble. Article 6, paragraph 2 states that all international treaties "shall be the supreme law of the land." As a layperson I understand this to mean that any international agreement such as the UN Declaration of Human Rights, takes precedence over domestic law. The other document is the Nuremberg War Crime Tribunal International Law. . . . As a US citizen I am compelled as an individual both to speak out against crimes against peace and humanity as well as to act to prevent those crimes.

My civil disobedience at Fort Benning violated a local law in order to prevent a greater crime against the people of Latin America. Because of my understanding of the teachings of scripture, nonviolence, and the law, I responded to that of God within me by carrying a coffin in honor of the dead: men, women, and children who were victims of violence.[74]

Just as Knapke did, Fisher invoked the Nuremberg principles. In addition, however, she included the US Constitution, the UN Declaration of Human Rights, and a response to "that of God within" her. Fisher's overlapping invocations of higher law lead us to a second type—namely, appeals to transcendent authorities.

While prisoner of conscience trial statements frequently include appeals to the first type of higher law, the most common appeal is to a higher law that includes God's law, divine obedience, or tikkun olam. The rhetorical power of the appeal to God's law may be due to its use by martyred Salvadoran archbishop Óscar Romero in his final Sunday homily.[75] Preaching in the cathedral in San Salvador and widely broadcast via radio across the country, Romero addressed the Salvadoran army:

> Hermanos, son de nuestro mismo pueblo, matan a sus mismos hermanos campesinos y ante una orden de matar que dé un hombre, debe de prevalecer la Ley de Dios que dice: NO MATAR. . . . Ningún soldado está obligado a obedecer una orden contra la Ley de Dios. . . . Una ley inmoral, nadie tiene que cumplirla. . . . Ya es tiempo de que recuperen su conciencia y que obedezcan antes a su conciencia que a la orden del pecado. . . . La Iglesia, defensora de los derechos de Dios, de la Ley de Dios, de la dignidad humana, de la persona, no puede quedarse callada ante tanta abominación.[76]

Romero's appeal to *la Ley de Dios*, "the law of God," operates as an exemplar for SOA Watch activists. On the one hand, the law has objective force: the sixth commandment "You shall not murder" (Exodus 20:13 NRSV) supersedes any other authority.[77] On the other hand, the law of God has a subjective element in that it is impressed on the consciences of soldiers. These two aspects of the law of God recur throughout prisoner of conscience statements.[78]

Recall, for example, Cynthia Brinkman's and Rebecca Kanner's earlier statements. Brinkman appealed to God's law and Kanner to the task of tikkun olam as the impetus for their actions. David Corcoran, a hospital chaplain, stated in his trial statement that "I believe we are gathered here in God's name. God is our witness to the truth and validity of what we say. In fact,

God is the only just Judge, the supreme Judge of all our actions."[79] For Brinkman, Kanner, and Corcoran, God's law, while variously construed, provides a context and justification for their actions. While there is specific content to this law, it is not codified. None of these activists claim that God commanded them to cross the line. What they do claim, however, is a sense of vocation expressed in an obligation to transgressive action.

Prisoner of conscience Betsy Lamb expressed this vocation by naming her friendship with the women organizers in southwest Colombia, women she had met while on a Witness for Peace delegation to the region. After reading a letter of support from four Colombian popular organizations addressed to the court, Lamb concluded,

> As a friend of these people and as a follower of Jesus, I feel a deep obligation to call the United States government to repentance for this School. . . . I tried legislative advocacy, without success. I cried during the solemn procession on November 23, as the names of so many martyred Latin Americans were read aloud, not just the names of bishops and priests and church workers, but also of some of the hundreds of thousands of lesser-known people equally loved by God. I had to do something more. Putting my own comforts on the line is the least I could do, and it is the way I have felt called to work toward this end.
>
> Will my risking up to six months in prison change things? I do not know. I can only say, in the words of the prophet Jeremiah,
>
> You duped me, O Lord, and I let myself be duped;
> You were too strong for me, and you triumphed.
> I say to myself, I will not mention God,
> I will speak in God's name no more.
> But then it becomes like fire burning in my heart,
> imprisoned in my bones;
> I grow weary holding it in, I cannot endure it
> (Jeremiah 20:7a, 9-10, NAB).
>
> Like Jeremiah, I could not endure not speaking out. More. After much prayerful discernment I felt I must do whatever I could to close the SOA, now known as WHISC or WHINSEC. I could not do otherwise.[80]

I have quoted Lamb at length because her statement synthesizes some of the patterns that recur across prisoner of conscience statements. First, Lamb rooted the motivation for her actions in relationships of friendship and solidarity with particular people in Latin America. Second, Lamb acknowledged that these relationships were formed because of her faithfulness as a follower of Jesus. Third, together, faithfulness to friends and to Jesus generated a "deep obligation to call the United States government to repentance," a call manifest first in legislative advocacy. Fourth, recognizing the limits of legislative advocacy (its lack of "success" or effectiveness), Lamb engaged in "prayerful discernment" about how else to effectively speak out. Fifth, Lamb's discernment generated an obligation to speak out even at the cost of her own comfort through civil disobedience. In the end, she concluded, "I could not do otherwise."

Whereas appeals to the immanent authorities of a higher law express a codified moral, if not legal, obligation to responsible intervention, appeals to transcendent authorities are more opaque. These appeals are not about following a code so much as they are about discerning God's calling in a particular place, time, and station. When prisoners of conscience such as Lamb state, "I could not endure not speaking out," I do not take this as a universalizable law. Rather, this statement sounds as if it is the fruit of deliberative discernment about a vocation to faithful and responsible participation in God's work in the world.

While I find an important distinction between immanent and transcendent appeals to the higher law, what unites them is their content. Upon initially reading the trial statements, I conceptualized appeals to a higher law and the nearly universal invocation of obligations of solidarity formed through particular relationships as separable rhetorical moves. However, they are not so distinct as it first appeared. In fact, these relationships, and the hope that they might be grounded in something other than asymmetries of hegemonic power, are the *content* of the higher law. These appeals to a higher law, though irreducibly plural, are not vacuous. They gesture toward hopes for sustained relationships of responsible solidarity.

Appeals to a higher law, such as those issued by SOA Watch prisoners of conscience, grind against late modern ears. In a pluralistic democracy, such appeals raise concerns of violence and quietism, as those who invoke a higher law reject established legal conventions. One response is simply to reject higher law altogether. But that rejection would deprive us of the descriptive resources to understand these activists' invocations, not to mention the constructive possibilities of critique and evaluation. Responding to categorical rejections of the higher law, theological ethicist Ted Smith has stated, "What we need is neither an endorsement of whatever kind of higher law supports our own political projects nor a ban on higher laws that becomes ideological in its drive to exterminate ideology but critical deliberation about the nature and function of appeals to higher law. For this, we need to cultivate the capacity of reasoning together about the form of a higher law. That kind of reasoning is the work of political theology."[81] And that kind of reasoning is what I take up next.

Extremist Temptations of the Higher Law: Quietism and Violence

Nowhere are the extremist temptations of messianic political theologies more visible than in appeals to a higher law. Fears of these extremes have long disciplined the Western political tradition. At stake in these debates, especially in twentieth-century general jurisprudence, has been the question of legal authority: is there something external to the law that grants the law its obligating force? Legal positivists argue that laws ought not be justified by an appeal to anything beyond the procedures by which they were enacted; however, interpretivists, following Ronald Dworkin, and natural lawyers, following John Finnis and Robert George, agree that morality does fundamentally condition the nature of law as such.[82] The jurist Carl Schmitt, by contrast, placed the exception to legal order in the decision of the sovereign.[83] Appeals to a higher law take the recognition that legal orders require some external source, ground, or justification and ratchet up the intensity. In appeals to a higher law, not only does an external source grant authority to the law but it can also justify the violation of positive law. These appeals generate the worries often associated with messianic political theologies that I indicated in chapter 1 either by taking some particularist version of the higher law and enforcing it universally through a kind of code fetishism or by using the higher law in an antinomian register to justify violence normally constrained by the law. The former worry corresponds to the first type of appeals that I identified—immanent appeals to hierarchically ordered legal formations—and the latter worry corresponds to the second, or the transcendent appeals to the law of God.[84]

Regarding appeals to the higher law, the first worry is that it operates with a temptation toward what moral philosopher Charles Taylor calls *code fetishism*, in which all goods are reduced to legal formulations.[85] The political theological impulse animating such an appeal is not altogether misguided. It is an insight carried by the natural law tradition, which insists that there is a fundamental capacity to distinguish between good and evil, and this basic human capacity transcends cultural variation.[86] It is right to call this a temptation because natural law is best understood as a capacity or power and not as a list of legal strictures, however robust. Yet the temptation remains and can be seen in the ways that the law is used in attempts to cordon off the zone of legitimate violence. Here, violence is regulated by an ever more elaborate codification of norms. While ostensibly intended to reduce violence, it can have the unintended effect of increasing it. One merely needs to think of the weaponization of human rights through the international doctrine of the Responsibility to Protect, the legalization of torture under George W. Bush, or the extrajudicial killing under Barack

Obama. In each of these cases, legal codes were expanded to include the violent exception.[87]

Alternatively, a second worry regarding appeals to a higher law is that they seem to enable a cessation of the norms that usually constrain our daily lives in order to endorse the violent enactment of a particular moral or religious vision. Messianic appeals to a higher law are made with the urgency of necessity. As R. Scott Appleby and his collaborators with the Fundamentalism Project demonstrated, modern "fundamentalisms" often selectively retrieve the "emergency clause" embedded within various religious traditions to justify not only political action but also political violence.[88] By invoking a sense of urgency and claiming responsiveness to a higher law, fundamentalists "convince believers that they are engaged not merely in a mundane struggle for territory or political power or financial gain but in a cosmic war, a battle for the soul and for the future of humanity."[89] The cosmic nature of the battle is such that necessity allows the normal constraints on violence to be ignored, producing an antinomian disregard for the law. In short, appeals to a higher law seem to legitimate violence normally constrained by the law.

There is a close alliance between these seemingly opposing intuitions, one toward ever-increasing codification and one toward antinomian rejection. By appealing to a higher law, they both seem to legitimate a mimesis of violence. Whereas the violence associated with natural law is often assigned to the state, the violence associated with messianic law is often assigned to non-state actors. While both worries are quite appropriate, I show that they are misplaced when they fund a categorical rejection of the politics of the higher law. What is needed is not a rejection of the politics of the higher law as such but a better reasoning about what a faithful and effective invocation of the higher law entails. To make this case, however, we need to detour through the late modern retrievals of Saint Paul.

Politics of the Higher Law: A Pauline Retrieval

The apostle Paul is ground zero for political theological debates about the law. Drafting the least of the apostles into inter-ecclesial battles that have ebbed and flowed since the Protestant Reformation, Paul has been long misunderstood as an antinomian Lutheran. In this version of Paul, Christian theologians and Bible scholars emphasize his conversion, his apocalypticism, and his role as the champion of grace.[90] But Paul was no Lutheran. In fact, the recent works of biblical scholars (following E. P. Sanders, James Dunn, and N. T. Wright) have retrieved Paul's Jewishness.[91] Emphasizing Paul's theology as a Jewish messianic thinker can explain, at least in part, his appropriation by the much later Jewish messianic thinker and critical theorist Walter Benjamin and the following commentaries on Paul offered by Jacob Taubes—a student of Gershom Scholem, one of Benjamin's editors—and Giorgio Agamben, Benjamin's Italian translator. Together, this stream of reflection on Paul's messianic political theology commends three points that are critical for the account of the messianic politics of the higher law offered here: as a Jew intervening in intra-Jewish debates, (1) Paul does not reject the law but (2) understands the arrival of the Messiah as decisively fulfilling the law, thus (3) freeing the law both from its connection to violence and for its improvisational use. Let me take each in turn.

First, against some readings, messianic interpretations of Paul need not portray him as rejecting the law. Paul was a Jew, a "Hebrew born of Hebrews" (Philippians 3:5 NRSV) intervening in Jewish discourse.[92] E. P. Sanders described Paul's theology of the law as consistent with the "covenantal nomism" of Palestinian Judaism.[93] By covenantal nomism, Sanders indicated that Jewish obedience to the law is predicated not on the pretense of earning salvation but is a response to the gracious election of God. God's election precedes obedience. So when Paul took up the question of the inclusion of Gentiles in God's covenant with Israel in Romans 9–11, Paul argued that by no means could God's covenant be broken. God remains true to God's promises. According to this messianic reconstruction of Paul, under the time of the Messiah the law takes on a different meaning.

Next, Paul need not be understood as arguing that the arrival of the Messiah abrogated the law.[94] Agamben instead suggests that Paul was seeking to account for the fulfillment of the law in the time of the Messiah. Fulfillment, of course, is an ambivalent concept. It could indicate fulfillment in a more perfect code or fulfillment by means of violence. Yet Agamben has in mind neither of these when he invokes "the messianic fulfillment of the law." According to Ted Smith, "The hope that Agamben calls 'messianic' is rather for the *interruption* of this cycle of law and violence. It is the hope for something like what [Walter] Benjamin called the 'relief' (*Entsetzung*) of law, the *deliverance* of law, the deep decoupling of law and violence."[95] Messianic fulfillment of the law does not reject the law as such but transforms it by decoupling it from violence. Here we might recall the challenge initially faced by SOA Watch activists regarding how to intervene in a system of legalized violence. Agamben's Paul responds that the law under messianic time is freed from its alliance with violence, freed for use. Thus, for SOA Watch activists, the law that is implicated in a system of violence is freed for use in the service of flourishing life. This does not mean that the violence of the law, especially particular laws, no longer has force; rather, it means that those who operate in messianic time can use the law against the violence that inheres within it.

Finally, a messianic account of Paul's theology of the law then is one of improvisational use. Agamben argues, "It is obvious that for Paul grace cannot constitute a separate realm that is alongside that of obligation and law. Rather, grace entails nothing more than the ability to *use* the sphere of social determinations and services in its totality."[96] This makes sense of Paul's comments in his first letter to the Corinthians:

> To the Jews I became as a Jew, in order to win Jews. To those under the law I became as one under the law (though I myself am not under the law) so that I might win those under the law. To those outside the law I became as one outside the law (though I am not free from God's law but am under Christ's law) so that I might win those outside the law. (1 Corinthians 9:20–21 NRSV)

In decoupling the law from violence, Smith argues that Agamben also decouples the law from justice, leading to an aestheticization of the law. Smith rightly critiques Agamben on this point, arguing for continuing relations between the law and justice even as the law is freed from its alliance with violence.[97] Whereas Agamben lacks clarity on what this law, decoupled from violence, might be used for, Paul was quite clear that his messianic vocation frees him to use the law in the service of the Gospel. Thus, in the case of the SOA Watch, the higher law also does not do away with the demands of justice but calls the law out of its relation with violence and to serve the flourishing of life.

In summarizing these three points, we can retrieve from Paul a messianic account of the law in which it is released from its alliance with violence and freed for its use in the service of justice. Building on the messianisms of Benjamin and Taubes, Agamben offers an analysis of Paul that gives an account of ethics under the messianic age that requires the practices of discernment instead of an easy rejection of norms or a generally applicable moral code. Smith adds an important corrective to Agamben's aestheticization of the law by insisting on the continued relationship between the law and justice even within messianic time. To be clear, this is not a historical-critical account of Paul's original intent. Yet in this retrieval of a Pauline account of the law, I find the improvisational use of the law as deployed by SOA Watch activists—who at times transgress and at times appropriate particular laws under the vocation established by a higher law—is warranted. Warrant, however, is not the same as justification. Enacting this messianic account of the law requires ongoing discernment. Thus, this chapter next renders an evaluation of the SOA Watch's discernment under a higher law.

PRACTICAL REASON UNDER A HIGHER LAW

Having journeyed through an exposition of the legal repertoires used by the SOA Watch activists, their coordination under appeals to the higher law (or higher laws), and a brief, though necessary, detour through recent retrievals of Paul's political theology, we can now return to the ethnographic vignette previewed at the chapter's outset. Recall the deliberation related to the effectiveness of civil disobedience, the justification of violating strictures of speech and assembly, and the privilege and cost of committing such actions. If my argument has been convincing, you can see in these questions an implicit discernment about the politics of the higher law. Grafting the argument of this chapter into the book as a whole, we can see how the obligations between the living and the dead that are formed by the dead's presence generate a higher law, though this higher law underdetermines what the living ought to do. Activists thus must consider and debate the most faithful and effective way to interrupt and transform a system of legalized violence.

Bringing the resources just explored into critical juxtaposition with the SOA Watch's political practice, a deliberative question arises: How might we evaluate the SOA Watch's use of the law? In keeping with the account of messianically conditioned practical reasoning, my evaluation includes the separable but dialectically related demands of faithfulness and effectiveness, and proceeds in two steps. First, using the Pauline detour as a diagnostic, I analyze the role that the politics of the higher law plays within the SOA Watch movement. Second, distilling these observations, I demonstrate how such a politics can balance the demands of faithfulness and effectiveness.

What Does the Politics of the Higher Law Do?

I have suggested that the politics of the higher law as practiced by SOA Watch activists does not fall victim to the antinomian rejection of the law or the ever-expanding code fetishism that are the Scylla and Charybdis that a politics of the higher law must navigate between. Rather, SOA Watch activists' appeals to a higher law serve three significant roles, whose functions follow directly from and develop the Pauline detour featured earlier: they relativize but do not outright reject lower laws, they express obligations of responsibility that transcend current legal orders, and they free the law for use in the pursuit of justice through a diverse set of legal repertoires. Insofar as they perform these roles, appeals to a higher law avoid both pitfalls. Let me take each role in turn.

First, by appealing to the higher law, SOA Watch activists critique the legitimacy of the positive laws that aid and abet the system of legalized violence that has meant death for thousands of Latin Americans. Importantly, as with Pauline retrievals, this petition is not a rejection of the law as such, but it removes the law from its determinative alliance with violence, giving it a different meaning. This act of relativization often involves, as with Louise Lynch's previous statement, questioning the legality of the SOA/WHINSEC itself. In this case, the law is used against the legal endurance of violence. Beyond questioning the legal status of the SOA/WHINSEC and US military training, SOA Watch activists question the legitimacy of seemingly arbitrary strictures on assembly and speech. As with Adams and Gerard, this class of relativization questions whether such strictures on procedure can be given legal force when they are out of line with a substantive account of justice. This leads to a final class of relativization in which activists call on the court and the judge to be executors of justice rather than (simply) defenders of the law. Questioning the legality of the SOA/WHINSEC does not require the invocation of a higher law, but such appeals to justice move us into different territory. If the law responds to a moral coherence that transcends it, then we cannot assume that obedience to the rule of law completes our moral obligations.

Second, appeals to a higher law express obligations of responsibility that transcend current legal orders. Such appeals call the law to its fulfillment in the service of obligations to solidarity and justice. As I have argued, these appeals are not uniform; they involve both immanent appeals, such as to the Nuremberg principles, and transcendent appeals, such as to divine obedience. Yet, immanent or transcendent, they perform similar roles in indicating moral obligations. The higher law that stands behind these invocations of abstract principle is the obligation formed between the living and the dead, or the crucified people who are presente. For Margaret Knapke, invoking the Nuremberg principles was a way of indicating her own responsibility to these dead for her intervening in what she identified as a structure of complicity in violence against civilians. For Anton Flores-Maisonet, divine obedience describes a responsiveness to the demands of solidarity that are made through particular relationships as "love crosses borders."[98] For others, the binding law of conscience obliges actions that violate positive law.[99] In each case, these appeals to a higher law give specificity to the shape of the conflict between obligations. These obligations to relationships of just solidarity take priority over the procedural demands of positive law.

It is worth noting here one way in which the SOA Watch appeals to the higher law can go wrong. These appeals can slip into a code fetishism when civil disobedience is made into an absolute obligation regardless of an activist's life station. Here, immanent appeals to the Nuremberg principles are more troubling, in my view, than transcendent appeals, for they seem to suggest a universality that is inappropriate to the moral demand. Recall, in particular, Rosa's caution to Albert in the opening scene: civil disobedience is a luxury that would be irresponsible or unwise for some people to assume. The cost of civil disobedience would demand too much of those who depend on such activists for sustenance (such as the children or elderly who are under their care) as well as of those already in precarious positions due to the criminal injustice system (such as people of color or undocumented immigrants). And for others, their actions could inadvertently discredit the movement.[100] While I suspect that some SOA Watch prisoners of conscience would express these moral obligations in a universalizing way, I did not hear them expressed explicitly. Appeals to the higher law avoid code fetishism not by manifesting universal and absolute obligations but by generating practical reasoning.

Third, as appeals to higher law relativize positive law and indicate obligations that transcend it, they neither do away with the law completely nor indicate absolute obligations. Instead, as Agamben argues regarding Paul's account of the law, the law is freed for use, which is determined by ongoing and improvisational discernment. Thus, prisoners of conscience use the punitive force of the law to perform a politics of penance. Prisoners of conscience take into their own bodies the consequences of disobedience and in doing so enter into a ritual of purgation and cleansing. Importantly, they affirm the validity of positive law, however relativized, by their submission to punishment.[101] They perform their solidarity with the tortured and killed, in an analogous but in no sense identical way, by taking the violence of the law on themselves.

But penance is not their only mode of engagement.[102] SOA Watch activists also perform a politics of piecemeal repair. Using the courtroom as a theater of moral redress to raise awareness feeds the work of lobbying congressional representatives as well as delegations of direct diplomacy with Latin American heads of state. These diverse modes of engagement are coordinated by appeals to a higher law that free legal repertoires for diverse use. Such freedom, however, requires discernment. Higher law is neither a list of demands nor a stable code; rather, it is a law formed through relationships of solidarity between the living and the dead. As such, it requires phronesis, or practical reason.

Practical Reasoning about the Politics of the Higher Law

In returning to the questions of faithfulness and effectiveness, we can now ask: Is this improvisational use of the law faithful to the obligations of solidarity to others and of fidelity to God? Is it effective in pursuing substantive change in the structure of legalized violence that the SOA/WHINSEC is but one part? Recalling my earlier elaboration, the overlapping and at times contradictory dynamic of these competing demands have been present at each dilemma I have examined. Rather than resolving that tension, as earlier thinkers have often done, I have argued that their ongoing dialectical relation makes for a richer account of the moral life. This thesis is confirmed again if we apply this rubric to the dilemma of this chapter—the use of the law.

To begin with, the structure of legalized violence allows no vantage point of complete and effective control. Control over the means of violence is not possible, for violence has inhered within the very structures of imperialist patronage that enable military training with correlates in economics, the law, and diplomatic culture. Put plainly, effective intervention in such a system evades human capacity.

Yet participants in the SOA Watch movement over time have developed relationships of solidarity with both the living and the dead that require that intervention. Faithfulness to the "dangerous memories" of the crucified people—memories of those who were meant to be forgotten, such as the villagers of El Mozote, or those who were meant to be silenced, such as Óscar Romero and Ignacio Ellacuría—demands not only memory but resistance.[103] As Jon Sobrino, the colleague of Ellacuría's who survived the UCA massacre, has argued, the task that remains is to take the crucified people down from their crosses.[104] This work of removing the crucified people from their crosses requires intervention, even if it seems beyond human capacity. It calls forth action to disrupt and transform the systems of violence that have produced death.

Faithfulness to the memory of the dead who are presente generates relationships of solidarity with the living. As SOA Watch activists, the vast majority of whom have been US based, have come into contact with people directly impacted by the military training of the SOA/WHINSEC, those relationships have demanded response. Over the years, it has meant attentively building an analysis of how US military training not only has dealt death in the past but also is a present cause of the deadly nexus of Latin American violence, Latin American immigration to the United States, and US immigrant detention. Faithfulness to the precarity of the living also requires a responsive (and responsible) politics of engagement. This is the contents of the higher law.

So while the structure of violence resists intervention, relationships of solidarity with the dead and the living demand it. How can SOA Watch activists traverse the impasse of these moral demands and structural constraints? As seen in this chapter, one way SOA Watch activists have made sense of their interventions has been through their faithfulness to a higher law. I have argued that these higher laws ought to be understood as neither a stable code nor an endorsement of "anything goes." Rather, as a messianically oriented politics, these appeals generate discernment regarding the call of God in this particular place and time. Vocation, with its attention to the singularities of status, role, and gift, illuminates which actions might be appropriate for which persons. Thus, faithfulness to relationships of solidarity are mediated by a vocation that indicates modes of intervention.

It would be a mistake to assume, however, that at this point SOA Watch activists terminate discernment and say, "Here I stand; I can do no other."[105] Rather, a vocation of memory and resistance opens into ongoing discernment about how to effectively disrupt and transform an intransigent structure of violence. One response that has been effective at times for the SOA Watch has been civil disobedience. It is effective, in part, because it performs a costly solidarity. When bystanders see that friends, priests, helping professionals, and other normal folks are willing to put their own comforts on the line, they conclude that these people's concerns must be worth paying attention to.[106] But civil disobedience alone can be just a form of an "ethics of ultimate conviction" in which, as Max Weber charged, activists leave the rest up to God. If civil disobedience is *merely* a practice oriented to the expression of moral outrage, it can too easily devolve into self-righteous grandstanding.

Preventing this outcome, however, SOA Watch activists engage in a politics of piecemeal repair. Lobbying, constituent mobilization, grassroots education, analysis building, and direct diplomacy—all of these practices build on the witness of prisoners of conscience and feed their success. These modes of activism—inside and outside conventional systems of representation and the law—are coordinated by appeals to a higher law. Rather than mere opportunism, the higher law allows activists to render coherent both the transgression and the appropriation of the law by its relationship to a messianic fulfillment of the law. When to use which legal repertoire is not immediately clear but requires ongoing discernment, both personally and collectively, about what SOA Watch activists should do. This work is the stuff of practical reason. To reduce those considerations to either faithfulness or effectiveness alone is to impoverish our understanding of the dilemmas that activists face. Moreover, to collapse the deliberation to one principle or the other constrains constructive possibilities for generating faithful new forms of effective political intervention.

CONCLUSION: POLITICS OF HIGHER LAW
AND ETHICS OF CIVIL DISOBEDIENCE

In this chapter I argue that the improvisational use of the law practiced by the SOA Watch movement is best understood not as mere opportunism but as a manifestation of a politics of the higher law that can be understood as a retrieval of a messianic, Pauline political theology. To be clear, some participants in SOA Watch activism construe this differently either by tending to express their account of the higher law in terms of immanent legal forms of international law or human rights or by eschewing the politics of the higher law (or the law as such) altogether. But in my judgment, understanding the SOA Watch's appeals to the higher law as messianic not only makes descriptive sense of the shape of SOA Watch activism but also offers a theologically satisfying account of the challenge of responding to the demands of faithfulness to the dead, the presence of the living, and the call of God in contexts of intractable legalized violence.

Higher law is best understood not as a stable code or as an emergency clause that allows any number of actions. Rather, its weak obligations open into discernment, or practical reasoning, about the demands of the higher law and how they issue forth into concrete political actions. Thus, the demands of the higher law generate an improvisational vocation that must be faithfully discerned rather than a codified norm that must be obeyed.[107] Because of this weak obligation, two final generic issues related to the ethics of civil disobedience remain open to deliberation.

First is the question of to what extent positive law is binding. Recall Adams's and Gerard's different responses to the question of whether they violated a law and thus whether their punishment was warranted. Adams pleaded guilty and invoked the tradition of Gandhi and King to justify his actions, while Gerard pleaded not guilty and invoked the US Constitution's First Amendment. Given the account of a higher law considered in this chapter, who is right? Under a messianic politics of the higher law, do positive laws still obligate submission to punishment, if not obedience?

Agamben's account of Paul's political theology is helpful at this point. As noted earlier, Paul was not an antinomian. He did not reject the law outright.[108] Rather, Paul called for those under the law to be "as if not."[109] Agamben has argued,

> What does it actually mean to remain a slave in the form of the *as not*? Here the juridical factical condition invested by the messianic vocation is not negated with regard to juridical consequences that would in turn validate a different or even opposite legal effect in its place, as does the *fictio legis*. Rather, in the *as not*, the juridical-factical condition is taken up again and is transposed, while remaining juridically unchanged, to a zone that is neither factual nor juridical, but is subtracted from the law and remains as a place of pure praxis. Of simple "use" ("use it rather!").[110]

Agamben proposes a theology of law's use that does not negate the juridical consequences of the law. Instead, even the punishment that the law intends to be a discouragement of disobedience is transposed. A messianic politics of the higher law would support Adams's conclusion: yes, he is guilty of violating positive law, but, no, the punishment does not mean what the court intends for it to mean. Rather, the repression of dissent only redounds to the credit of the dissenters.[111] Thus, on this account, submission to punishment is morally praiseworthy not, principally, because it evinces fidelity to the rule of law.[112] Instead, submission to punishment here is transposed into an askesis of solidarity.

This leads to a second issue pertaining to the ethics of civil disobedience regarding the extent of complicity. Recall, in this case, Knapke's discussion with Judge Lawson. Knapke's appeal to the Nuremberg principles prompted Lawson to ask in what ways the defendant had cooperated with US foreign policy. Just below the surface of these questions is the challenging but applicable principle of responsibility: how far does the responsibility for the deaths of civilians in Latin America extend?

I have argued that the SOA and its institutional successor, WHINSEC, are one of the transmission belts by which the legalized violence of militarism is transferred into direct violence in Latin America. In my judgment, the US military, which directs the training at the WHINSEC, and US policymakers are responsible at one degree of remove from the direct violence that Latin American militaries have exercised on civilians in their countries. Using the highly technical but instructive language of Catholic moral theology, the US military and foreign policymakers at times have offered formal cooperation—that is, intending the targeting of civilians—and at times have offered immediate material cooperation, which did not intend these killings but gave essential aid to enable their actions.

But beyond the US Departments of State and Defense, what about US citizens? Are we also complicit? Furthermore, is there a generic responsibility to intervention, as Knapke seems to suggest, by appealing to the Nuremberg principles? These difficult questions go beyond the scope of this chapter. However, provisionally, I would argue that rather than looking for a generic or universal responsibility, the obligations that require a response are particular. Remember my observation that nearly every prisoner of conscience statement began with an account of the activist's personal engagement with particular persons who were victimized by the impact of US militarism in Latin America. These personal relationships of solidarity with the living and the dead are the obligations that require a response (responsibility) and not a generic attribution of complicity.

As with the first problem, the messianic obligations of solidarity are weak and thus require ongoing discernment. I have indicated ways to include considerations of both effectiveness and faithfulness in that deliberation. But weak obligations leave SOA Watch activists with a motivational problem. How can they call people into the movement? If they cannot motivate people with a strong account of responsibility, how can they project visions of activist identity that galvanize movement members and draw in new supporters? One of the ways the SOA Watch has approached this task is by mobilizing the memory of the martyrs as exemplars of movement activism. It is to the promise and problems of the dilemma of exemplarity that I now turn.

NOTES

1. I participated in this scene in Columbus, Georgia, as an observer. I have changed names and details to protect the anonymity of other participants. Because I recollected the details after the fact from jottings, most of the following is a paraphrase, but direct quotations are exact. Unpublished field notes, November 19, 2015.

2. Such concerns about surveillance were not mere paranoia. Through a Freedom of Information Act request filed by Washington, DC–based lawyer Mara Verheyden-Hilliard, SOA Watch organizers confirmed their suspicions of government surveillance in 2015. The 429 pages of documents reveal the coordination of a network of governmental agencies, including the Counterterrorism Division of the Federal Bureau of Investigation (FBI), to monitor SOA Watch activities. See Patrick O'Neill, "Report: FBI Infiltrated Nonviolent Protest outside Georgia Army Base," *National Catholic Reporter*, November 12, 2015, http://ncronline.org/news/peace -justice/report-fbi-infiltrated-nonvoilent-protest-outside-georgia-army-base.

3. Interview with Roy Bourgeois, phone, October 21, 2015.

4. Unpublished field notes, November 21, 2014.

5. Interview with Mary Anne Perrone and Rebecca Kanner, Ann Arbor, MI, January 15, 2016.

6. Perrone and Kanner, interview.

7. For example, we can see two different takes on the use of institutional apparatus to challenge or undermine those very institutions in Audre Lorde and Michel de Certeau. See Lorde, "Master's Tools," in *Sister Outsider*; and Certeau, "Walking in the City," in *Practice of Everyday Life*. Whereas Lorde would commend a rejection of the master's tools in the work of deep change, Certeau sees possibilities for subversion and resistance within structures of power.

8. The opposition of revolution and reform is a long-standing feature of debate in leftist political thought. See, for example, Eduard Bernstein's classic formulation in *Preconditions of Socialism*. See also Rosa Luxemburg's response in *Reform or Revolution*.

9. See, for example, the rise and fall of "participatory democracy" as an animating practice and value of the Student Nonviolent Coordinating Committee. Polletta, *Freedom*, chap. 4.

10. These questions are related to what peace studies pioneer Johan Galtung identified as structural violence. Galtung defines structural violence by analogy to direct violence. Whereas *direct violence* has an act, an actor, and an actee (one acted on), *structural violence* has an act and an actee but no actor. He summarized, "Violence without this relation [between actor, act, and actee] is structural, built into

structure. Thus, when one husband beats his wife there is a clear case of personal violence, but when one million husbands keep one million wives in ignorance there is structural violence." Galtung, "Violence, Peace," 169. To be clear, Galtung does not wish to suggest that structures are agents in themselves. Rather, he argues there are situations where laws, economic policy, cultural mores, topographical formations so constrain and deform human flourishing that such constraints are best understood as a form of violence. For a helpful elaboration of this concept, see Paul Farmer's account of structural violence and health care in *Pathologies of Power*, especially chap. 1. Helpful as Galtung's intervention has been, he was not the first to suggest that evil can come to reside in societal forms. That idea is a much older one, and it has its roots in Christian formulations of the doctrine of sin. See Moe-Lobeda, "Structural Violence," in *Resisting Structural Evil*.

11. Jack Nelson-Pallmeyer identifies this structure with the rather clunky phrase *military-industrial-congressional complex*. See Nelson-Pallmeyer, *School of Assassins*, xv. I have chosen to identify the structure as merely militarism, in keeping with the Kingian tradition of naming militarism, alongside racism and materialism, as structural evil that requires attention and revolutionary redress. See King, "Time to Break Silence," in *Testament of Hope*, 240.

12. Ellacuría, "Crucified People," in *Ignacio Ellacuría*.

13. Uvin, "Global Dreams," in Tétreault, Denemark, Thomas, and Burch, *Rethinking Global Political Economy*.

14. Gill, *School of the Americas*.

15. Gill, 233–34.

16. While each Latin American country has its own history, for just one example see Schlesinger and Kinzer's *Bitter Fruit* for their account of the overthrow of the "democratic spring" in Guatemala.

17. Gill, *School of the Americas*, 78–89.

18. Menjívar and Rodríguez, *When States Kill*.

19. Huggins, *Political Policing*; and Huggins, Haritos-Fatouros, and Zimbardo, *Violence Workers*.

20. Recent investigative journalism has shown evidence for US military training not only in Latin America but also across the globe. See Douglas Gillison, Nick Turse, and Moiz Syed, "The Network: Leaked Data Reveals How the U.S. Trains Vast Numbers of Foreign Soldiers and Police with Little Oversight," *The Intercept*, July 13, 2016, https://theintercept.com/2016/07/13/training/.

21. Gill, *School of the Americas*, 3.

22. This claim is often made by distinguishing nonviolence from pacifism by suggesting that pacifism is passive and nonviolence is active. This characterization is itself dubious, however, as David Cortright demonstrates in his history of the peace movement. Pacifism as an identifier emerged to encompass the peace movement as a whole at the beginning of the twentieth century. During World War I, it became identified more narrowly with absolute pacifists, or those who rejected military violence in every situation, rather than a more capacious encapsulation of a social movement. See Cortright, *Peace*, 8–11.

23. Gandhi, *All Men Are Brothers*, 77–97. See also Cortright, *Peace*, 211–15. While Gandhi is undisputedly the source of the political practice of nonviolence in

recent history, as both concept and practice nonviolence has a longer legacy. See, for example, Mark Kurlansky's history, *Nonviolence*, where he identifies the praxis of nonviolence in multiple ancient sources.

24. For example, see de Cleyre, "Direct Action." "Every person who ever thought he had a right to assert, and went boldly and asserted it, himself, or jointly with others that shared his convictions, was a direct actionist. . . . Every person who ever had a plan to do anything, and went and did it, or who laid his plan before others, and won their co-operation to do it with him, without going to external authorities to please do the thing for them, was a direct actionist" (221).

25. See Graeber, *Direct Action*, 201–11. Graeber's particular focus is on the protests against the Summit of the Americas in Québec City in 2001, and he entertains an objection to the claim that these types of protests are direct actions. They do not create a new system of economic relations but were aimed, at least symbolically, at disrupting and dismantling the systems of hemispheric economic coordination and domination. According to the classical definition, such protest does not seem to qualify as direct action because it is still targeted at elite figures. Yet both those involved and external observers would have identified these protests as direct action, not only because they proposed a different mode of economic relation, but also because they modeled, however incipiently, an alternative mode of self-organization by deploying affinity groups, consensus building, and confrontational politics directed at elites.

26. See, for example, King, "Negro Is Your Brother."

27. Clemens, interview. See also Held, *Abraham Joshua Heschel*, 23.

28. Kanner, "Why Civil Disobedience?," 21.

29. See Joshua 6.

30. For a classic exposition of the propaganda of the deed, see Mikhail Bakunin's "Letter to a Frenchman" (in *Bakunin on Anarchy*, 195–96): "From this very moment we must spread our principles, not with words but with deeds, for this is the most popular, the most potent, and the most irresistible form of propaganda."

31. Quigley, "Advice for Lawyers."

32. Activists have been charged with state as well as federal violations. For the former, see "Criminal Trespass," Off. Code of Georgia Ann. § 16-7-21; and for the latter, see "Entering Military, Naval, or Coast Guard Property," 18 U.S.C. § 1382 (1948). Quigley, personal correspondence, January 26, 2016.

33. Bass, *Blessed Are the Peacemakers*, 107–8.

34. Cohan, "Civil Disobedience."

35. Craig Adams, "Trial Statement" in Lamb, *Voices of Courage*, 21.

36. Alice Gerard, "Trial Statement" in Lamb, 27.

37. SOA Watch, "Vigil and Witness." See also chapter 2.

38. William Quigley counsels fellow lawyers that "people who engage in CD [civil disobedience] often have goals that do not prioritize a finding of not guilty. They are often more interested in having their say and telling the truth than having their case dismissed. Some want court over as soon as possible and want to minimize the consequences. Others do not." See Quigley, "Advice for Lawyers."

39. Louise Lynch, "Statement in Court," in Lamb, *Voices of Courage*, 30.

40. Cynthia Brinkman, "Statement," in Lamb, 22.

41. Brinkman, 22.

42. Bourgeois, interview.

43. Perrone and Kanner, interview.

44. Perrone and Kanner, interview.

45. SOA Watch, "Prisoners of Conscience."

46. This way of organizing the activities of analysis building has affinity with the "see, judge, act" method of Joseph Cardijn. See Zotti, "Young Christian Workers."

47. Moakley, "Interim Report."

48. Moakley summarized, "Those who pulled the trigger and committed this heinous crime included men trained with American money, by American servicemen, on American soil. We all must bare [sic] some responsibility for this crime—in much the same way we must bare [sic] some responsibility for the war and the refugees that war has created." Moakley, 1.

49. Moakley, appendix D.

50. Hodge and Cooper, *Disturbing the Peace*. See also the UN's Commission on the Truth for El Salvador, "From Madness to Hope."

51. These findings cohere with Martha K. Huggins's research on the training of violence workers in Brazil. See Huggins, *Political Policing*; and Huggins, Haritos-Fatouros, and Zimbardo, *Violence Workers*.

52. Dana Priest, "U.S. Instructed Latins on Executions, Torture: Manuals Used 1982–91, Pentagon Reveals," *Washington Post*, September 21, 1996. These claims were verified by an Amnesty International investigation that showed the training manuals advocated the following: "Motivation by fear; Payment of bounties for enemy dead; False imprisonment; Use of truth serum; Torture; Execution; Extortion; Kidnapping and arresting a target's family members." Amnesty International, "Unmatched Power," 5.

53. Uvin, "Global Dreams."

54. 103 Cong. Rec. H7297–7301 (1993). See Hodge and Cooper, *Disturbing the Peace*, 151.

55. Bourgeois, interview.

56. 106 Cong. Rec. H6700–6709 (1999).

57. Gallo-Cruz, "Protest and Public Relations."

58. The extent of this change is an issue of controversy. Activists claim, "Different name, same shame." However, political scientist Ruth Blakeley argues the change in curriculum was significant and that the current courses offer the best human rights training anywhere in the US Army system. See Blakeley, "Still Training to Torture?" While she is likely correct that WHINSEC did change its curriculum and has become the site of extensive human rights training, she does not adequately deal with the role the institution plays regardless of curriculum within a wider system of patronage and impunity.

59. Bourgeois, interview.

60. Ganz, "Resources and Resourcefulness"; and McCammon, *U.S. Women's Jury Movements*.

61. Davies and Kaufman, *Second Track/Citizens' Diplomacy*; and Kraft, "Track Three Diplomacy."

62. As feminist political theorist Jo Freeman wrote, "Political change does not involve isolated efforts either within or without the system. . . . Rather it involves a

dynamic system of reciprocal influences whose effects are determined by their mutual relationships." Freeman, *Politics of Women's Liberation*, 2.

63. Social movement theorist Chris Dixon uses this vaguely biblical phrase (which draws on John 17 and Romans 12, and Dixon attributes to anarchist organizer Ashanti Alston) to describe a revolutionary strategic framework that engages in reformist struggles for the purpose of movement building. See Dixon, *Another Politics*, 125–54.

64. Part of this chapter is derived from an article published in *Political Theology*, copyright 2018, Taylor & Francis, available online: https://www.tandfonline.com /doi/full/10.1080/1462317X.2018.1467662. Published here with permission.

65. For one example of an activist using a personal blog as a platform of amplification, see Steve Clemens's blog *Mennonista*, http://www.mennonista.blogspot .com/.The number of mainstream media placements are legion, but see, for example, the human interest story regarding the treatment of Cynthia Brinkman SSND in Ron Harris, "Nun, 67, Waits for Word to Begin Prison Sentence," *St. Louis Post-Dispatch*, March 2, 2004. For documentaries, see Richter, *School of Americas*; and Uassouf, *Somos Una América*. For books, see Nelson-Pallmeyer, *School of Assassins*; Hanrahan, *Conscience & Consequence*; and Beisswenger, *Locked Up*.

66. Knapke, *Voices for the Voiceless*, 11.

67. Nepstad, *Convictions of the Soul*.

68. Knapke, *Voices for the Voiceless*, 27.

69. As lawyer Bernard Lambek argues, "While the civilly disobedient may have a strong moral claim under Nuremberg, absent special circumstances such as those in the Pentagon Papers case, vindication through the courts appears unlikely. Furthermore, even if the courts did accept that activists in the peace movement have a duty under Nuremberg to stop government crimes, defendants would still encounter the judge's reluctance to regard civil disobedience as a legitimate means of discharging that duty." Lambek, "Necessity and International Law," 491.

70. International Committee of the Red Cross, "Principles of International Law."

71. Falk, "Nuremberg Defense." Elsewhere, Falk has an expanded conception of the zone of responsibility but does not argue that such responsibility includes civil disobedience. Analyzing the Son My massacre during the Vietnam War, Falk wrote: "The issue of personal conscience is raised for everyone in the United States. It is raised more directly for anyone called upon to serve in the armed forces. It is raised in a special way for parents of minor children who are conscripted into the armed forces. It is raised for all taxpayers whose payments are used to support the cost of the war effort. It is raised for all citizens who in various ways endorse the war policies of the government. The circle of responsibility is drawn around all who have or should have knowledge of the illegal and immoral character of the war. The Son My massacre put every American on notice as to the character of the war." Falk, "Son My," 35.

72. Knapke, *Voices for the Voiceless*, 27.

73. Knapke, 36.

74. Knapke, 36.

75. Romero's final Sunday homily was also used in an early action at Fort Benning in 1983. See chapter 2 of this volume.

76. "Brothers, you are of our same people, you murder your same brother peasants. Before an order to kill a man, the Law of God ought to prevail which says: 'DON'T KILL.' . . . No soldier is obligated to obey an order contrary to the law of God. No one has to obey an immoral law. Now is the time to recover your conscience and to obey your conscience over a sinful order. The church, defender of the rights of God, of the law of God, of human dignity, of the person, cannot remain silent before such an abomination." Romero, "La iglesia." Translation mine.

77. To be clear, Romero was not a pacifist and did issue defenses of just war. In this case, he ought to be understood as calling up the long Catholic tradition of reflection on unjustified killing with particular attention to the immunity of noncombatants.

78. Appeals to conscience are best understood not as appeals to a kind of individual autonomy but rather to the higher law that resides in the individual as divine deposit. See, for example, Cajka, "Rights of Conscience."

79. Lamb, *Voices of Courage*, 23.

80. Lamb, 29. Poet-theologian Julia Esquivel draws on this same refrain in her poem "Confesión" in *Threatened with Resurrection*.

81. Smith, *Weird John Brown*, 109.

82. Dworkin, *Law's Empire*; Finnis, *Natural Law*; and George, *In Defense of Natural Law*.

83. Schmitt, *Political Theology*.

84. I develop these distinctions systematically in Lambelet, "Lovers of God's Law."

85. Taylor, *Secular Age*, 704–7.

86. Porter, *Nature as Reason*, 13. For the medieval jurists, this is what the apostle Paul had in mind in Romans 2:15 when he said that even the Gentiles have the law "written on their hearts." This capacity transcends cultural variation. As Cicero classically remarked, "There will not be one law at Rome, and another at Athens." Cicero, *On the Commonwealth*, 71.

87. Walter Benjamin identified this dynamic, in which the violent exception to the law is brought within the realm of law, as "mythic violence." See his "Critique of Violence," in Bullock and Jennings, *Selected Writings*, 248. Benjamin was engaged here in a long debate with Schmitt. For more on this conversation, see Weber, "Taking Exception to Decision"; and Agamben, *State of Exception*, 52–53. Finally, connecting mythic violence to concrete cases, see Smith, "Divine Violence."

88. Almond, Appleby, and Sivan, *Strong Religion*, 240. While the immediate figure that comes to the Western mind might be the "Islamist terrorist," it is also helpful to remember that Christian terrorist Paul Hill called on a higher law to justify his murder of two abortion providers. See Smith, *Weird John Brown*, 100–101.

89. Appleby, "Rethinking Fundamentalism," 233.

90. Westerholm, *Perspectives*; and Martyn, "Apocalyptic Antinomies," in *Theological Issues*.

91. Sanders, *Paul and Palestinian Judaism*; Dunn, *New Perspective on Paul*; and Wright, *Paul*. See also Boccaccini and Segovia, *Paul the Jew*.

92. Boccaccini, "Inner-Jewish Debate," in Barclay and Gathercole, *Divine and Human Agency*.

93. Sanders, *Paul and Palestinian Judaism*.

94. See, famously, Albert Schweitzer's account of the incompatibility of the law and eschatology in his *Mysticism*, 189.

95. Smith, *Weird John Brown*, 115.

96. Agamben, *Time That Remains*, 124.

97. See Smith, *Weird John Brown*, chap. 4. See also Brown, "Paul's Apocalyptic Cross," in Davis and Harink, *Apocalyptic*.

98. See, for example, Flores-Maisonet's response to the death of his undocumented friend in Flores-Maisonet, "Does Love Cross Borders?"

99. As retired special education teacher Mary Early reported to the judge in her trial statement, "Personally, I am here in response to a higher law than this court, and that law is a law of conscience, an informed conscience. I have done that to the best of my ability, and that is what brought me to Fort Benning in '96, '97, and, God willing, in '98." Quoted in SOA Watch, *Speaking Truth to Power*.

100. Each of these considerations came up in my fieldwork. Parents, as well as those employed in helping professions, had to discern how to balance competing obligations. When asked whether he would commit civil disobedience, a Black participant in a nonviolent direct action workshop simply stated, "I'm not trying to go to jail. We've got enough black folks in prison." Unpublished field notes, November 20, 2015. And in one case, a prisoner of conscience who had crossed the line multiple times was encouraged not to do so because his crossing again would not serve to raise greater awareness and might lead outsiders to view the movement in a negative light.

101. It would be a mistake to construe this submission to punishment as universal across SOA Watch activism or as unambiguous. Prisoners of conscience have particularly resisted exorbitant fines and have sometimes chosen not to pay them, but I know of no case where a prisoner of conscience has not submitted to imprisonment.

102. And if penance were the sole mode of engagement, I would judge the actions of prisoners of conscience as inappropriate attempts to shed guilt by facilely taking the place of the oppressed other rather than productively and effectively joining with the oppressed in struggle.

103. The connection between memory and resistance is evoked graphically by "Missed," an SOA Watch poster designed by César Maxit that depicts Ingrid Johana standing at the gates of Fort Benning. Below Johana, a banner reads "Memoria y Resistencia." Also depicted in the image are blue roses, which, Maxit explained, "symbolize reaching the unattainable: memoria y resistencia. Memory of the hundreds of thousands murdered by graduates of the School of Assassins, and resistance to militarism." César Maxit, personal correspondence, April 4, 2016. See Geglia, *Not Forgotten*. I take this up more fully in chapter 6.

104. Sobrino, *Principle of Mercy*.

105. Weber quoted this statement, which is apocryphally attributed to Martin Luther, in "Politics as a Vocation," 127.

106. I take up the ambiguities and problems of enacting such a politics of sacrifice in chapter 5.

107. Agamben argued, "Just as messianic power is realized and acts in the form of weakness, so too in this way does it have an effect on the sphere of the law and its

works, not simply by negating or annihilating them, but by de-activating them, rendering them inoperative, no-longer-at-work." Agamben, *Time That Remains*, 97.

108. This is where Agamben departs from Alain Badiou and, in my judgment, stays closer to the Paul of scripture. Compare with Badiou, *Saint Paul*.

109. See 1 Corinthians 7:29–31.

110. Agamben, *Time That Remains*, 28.

111. The danger of this line of reasoning is, of course, that it valorizes suffering. This is an important caution, but it seems to me simply descriptively true that in cases of nonviolent direct action that employ civil disobedience, punishment bestows a moral authority to the activist who receives it. I take up the problems that this produces more fully in chapter 5.

112. This is John Rawls's argument for the validity of civil disobedience. He stated, "The law is broken, but fidelity to law is expressed by the public and nonviolent nature of the act, by the willingness to accept the legal consequences of one's conduct." Rawls, *Theory of Justice*, 366.

5

FOLLOWING THE MARTYRS
Moral Exemplarity, Charismatic Leadership, and the Politics of Sacrifice

Our first attempt was a bust.[1] *The twelve of us couldn't find a table big enough at the Mediterranean restaurant where we had planned to eat in Phoenix. So we made our way down the street to a pizza and beer joint, which could accommodate our delegation and the two local organizers, Claudia and Erica, who were planning to join us. After a bit of negotiating, we discovered a way to push several tables together, find seats, and order some food.*

We were on the first full day of a weeklong delegation to the US-Mexico border. Led by SOA Watch staff and longtime volunteers, the twelve participants reflected some of the diversity of the movement in age, hometown, race, and religion. Our goals were, first, to learn about the impact of militarism on the US-Mexico borderlands and, second, to help plan the border convergence scheduled for later in the fall. To achieve both, we had scheduled meetings with local organizers to benefit from their experience and analysis, and to invite their input into the SOA Watch's process of strategic deliberation.

Claudia and Erica joined us, and we began by hearing from Claudia, who discussed her work with #Not1More, a national direct action movement that grew out of organizing in Arizona. Like the SOA Watch, #Not1More had mixed direct actions, litigation, movement building, policy-oriented advocacy, and culture work to build a sustained campaign for nonviolent social change. Claudia introduced us to the Arizona context, focusing her commentary on the failure of US immigration policy and the ways that local organizers have attempted to pull back the curtain on the militarization of the US-Mexico border. Whereas Claudia's work had been principally with directly impacted immigrants, Erica worked largely with white, middle-class Unitarian Universalists. She spoke with us about the challenge and importance of allies' supporting directly impacted people and organizations.

After sharing about their experiences in organizing, Claudia asked us, "Why did you all decide to come to Arizona?"

SOA Watch staff member Rosa responded that our work with the SOA Watch has been expanding to include immigration over the years. Particularly through partnership with Anton Flores-Maisonet and the Shutdown Stewart campaign, but also through the influx of new staff, many of whom are immigrants themselves, the SOA Watch has lately focused on the connection between state violence in Latin America and immigration in the United States. Initially, Rosa noted, our movement grew out of the murder of the six Jesuits and their housekeeper and her daughter. "But," she said, "we must ask ourselves, 'What is the call today? Where do our energies lie?'" In a way, the SOA Watch was so effective in shining light on the SOA/WHINSEC that the problem multiplied, and it's no longer just at the SOA/WHINSEC. So Rosa suggested that now we ask ourselves, "What would the six Jesuits who were massacred in El Salvador say today?"

† † †

What would the Jesuits say today? What would they do if they shared our time and place in history? I heard these questions, and alternative versions of them, repeated across the movement. Whether referring to Óscar Romero, the four North American churchwomen killed in El Salvador, the Jesuits and the two women massacred at the UCA, or more recently Rufina Amaya, the sole survivor of the massacre at El Mozote, or Berta Cáceres, the indigenous environmental activist assassinated in Honduras, SOA Watch participants look to the exemplary dead for moral and political direction. When discerning what to do, how to deepen involvement, and, ultimately, how to intervene in and transform the hemispheric system of US–Latin American militarism, SOA Watch activists and organizers have repeatedly turned to the venerated martyrs as paradigms to follow.

This move, of course, is an ancient moral practice in which practical wisdom is gained by emulating exemplars. As Aristotle argued, "Regarding practical wisdom we shall get at the truth by considering who are the persons we credit with it."[2] For Aristotle, exemplars functioned epistemically: they revealed the virtuous mean that is the object of an excellent life. As SOA Watch actors have discerned how to intervene in the US–Latin American military system, the exemplary dead have served epistemically as pedagogues.

In addition to the Aristotelian insight that exemplars demonstrate a life of virtue, as exemplary *dead* these martyrs also reveal the injustice of the system. Martyrs—literally witnesses[3]—are exemplars both by giving an example of an excellent life and by demonstrating the failure and injustice of the US–Latin American military system. The praiseworthiness of their lives intensifies the injustice of their deaths. For many SOA Watch activists, their encounters with the life of a martyr are what pushed them over key motivational obstacles to their involvement in the movement.

Exemplars are not merely self-evident but also created through rituals of memory, mourning, and veneration. The SOA Watch, as with many other movement organizations, has become quite adept at focusing participants' attention on common exemplars, framing the actions of those exemplars in particular ways, and mobilizing those framed memories to support movement activity. These are what I call technologies of iconography—the *¡presente!* litany, puppetista constructions, essays on the anniversaries of martyrs' deaths, pilgrimages to sacred locations in the lives of these saints—that serve to focus participants' moral attention, generating admiration of these exemplars and holding them up as persons to emulate.

Not only do exemplars serve as moral pedagogues but also movement leaders promote their own authority by drawing on the legacies of the exemplary dead. By narrating their own lives in connection with those of the martyrs and by showing how they are faithful to the martyrs' legacy, leaders authorize their voice and station within the movement. This authorization becomes problematic, however, when we remember that exemplars are pedagogues both in their modeling of an excellent life and in their revealing the injustice of the US–Latin American military system. Thus, as activists desire to faithfully follow the martyrs, they must ask, Faithfully follow them in what way?

Even when exemplars do not serve to reveal injustice, they cannot function as blueprints. We must, inevitably, discern for ourselves what aspects of an exemplary life are worthy of emulation. There is a persistent gap between the life of the exemplar and the life of the follower that requires the exercise of practical reasoning (even as the exemplar reveals the workings of practical reason). This discernment becomes particularly fraught at two points. First, the emulation of exemplars is dangerous when the exemplars have suffered directly at the hands of the US–Latin American military system. Is sacrificial suffering to be emulated? Second, when leaders draw on a messianic politics of sacrifice, we rightly worry that such politics tends to generate a messiah complex. Can the gap that requires practical reasoning be sustained in the presence of charismatic authority?

This chapter takes up the dilemmas that emerge from the interlocking dynamics of moral exemplarity, charismatic leadership, and the politics of sacrifice. While I demonstrate that the production of exemplarity has played a critical role in motivating solidarity activists to engage in activism, I argue that the results are ambivalent. Moral exemplarity authorizes not only acts of courage and compassion but also cults of personality as movement leaders use exemplars to cultivate their own power. Moreover, it plays into a dangerous valorization of suffering that has deep roots in the Christian theological imagination. Though I worry about the authoritarian tendencies present in this valorization, I do not wish to do away with the politics of sacrifice altogether. Rather, my thesis is that by attending to the moral demands of faithfulness and effectiveness, the messianic politics of sacrifice can be rightly used to undermine and transform oppressive systems that generate suffering in the first place.

In making my argument, I first examine the technologies of iconography that focus the moral attention of SOA Watch participants on exemplars. Engaging in ritual, art, affective, and symbolic work enables the movement to frame martyrs as both models for emulation and examples that reveal injustice. I show how the emotion of admiration, an affect moral philosopher Linda Zagzebski argues is fundamental to the moral structure of exemplarity, is formed through these technologies. Next, I demonstrate how movement leaders draw on these technologies to instantiate their own charismatic authority. Here, in conversation with Max Weber, I examine the paradox that charismatic leaders both attract disciples who wish to follow in their way and yet hold them at bay through their magical status. Basic to this is the politics of sacrifice and the ambiguities that attend it. I take this up in the third section, drawing first on womanist Delores Williams's critique of redemptive, vicarious suffering and then on Black liberation theologian James Cone's response. I argue for a chastened engagement in the politics of sacrifice and conclude by showing how keeping in play a practical reasoning that engages both the demands of faithfulness to the martyrs and effective political action with the living allows for the right use of that messianic politics.

TECHNOLOGIES OF ICONOGRAPHY

Although Aristotle might be cited as the source for classical accounts of exemplarity, there is a distinctively late modern mode in which exemplars function within the SOA Watch movement. This mode has a deep genealogy, one that draws on the late antique emergence of the cult of the saints as much as on the modern fixation on "representative men" and the contemporary dynamics of celebrity.[4] The martyr-exemplars of the SOA Watch are "friends of God" in the late antique sense: as they are venerated and emulated, "the *praesentia* of the saints" is made available to followers.[5] While not Thomas Carlyle's "great men," the SOA Watch's exemplars do play a representative role as their biographies tell the story of the movement and point to the values it holds most dear.[6] Even as the operation of exemplarity in the SOA Watch draws on these earlier sources, so too it makes use of the late modern dynamics of celebrity. The SOA Watch has become a cause célèbre through the participation of famous actors, such as Martin Sheen and Susan Sarandon; musicians, such as the Indigo Girls, Rebel Diaz, and Pete Seeger; and Catholic left luminaries, such as Liz McAlister, Sister Helen Prejean, and Jon Sobrino. Thus, *icon* has a multivalent meaning, both in the traditional Christian sense of an image of devotion that directs the viewer beyond the saint to God and in the contemporary sense of a figure of public adulation and fame.

Technologies

Each of these senses, however, has a consistent theme: exemplars are not self-evident but are created through technologies of iconography. As anthropologist June Macklin argues, in the creation of the story of a saint, there are three narrators: the saint, the saint's devotees, and those with the power to authorize the saint. Macklin notes, "Of this storytelling triad, the aspiring saint is the least important."[7] Consequently, we must attend to the ways in which martyr-exemplars are generated, framed, and sustained. What technologies construct exemplars as objects of moral admiration?

Liturgy

The most obvious way in which the dead are produced as exemplary, as objects of moral attention and admiration, is the *¡presente!* litany itself. As I argue in chapter 2, this litany focuses the moral attention of SOA Watch participants on the dead as persons to whom obligations of solidarity are owed. Reducing this experience to ethics alone, however, limits the power of what happens in the litany. Like the late antique Christians for whom saints' days were filled both with the *praesentia* of the holy and the *potentia* for the miraculous, these annual litanies are powerful moments in the life of the movement and effective in generating motivation and in renewing commitment. Their power is not merely in reminding participants of the moral obligations of solidarity, although that is part of it. Their power, as Peter Brown observed in his study of the cult of the saints, is also in bringing heaven near to earth. While the late antique venerators of the saints hoped for miraculous healing, provision, and protection, SOA Watch participants look to the saints to provide power in political effect. When we claim that the dead are presente we are making a messianic claim that the impenetrable wall of death is cracking and that we all are "threatened with resurrection."[8] The mechanism for harnessing the magical power of this claim is the politics of sacrifice, an issue I take up more fully shortly.

But what is the connection between the litany and the dynamics of exemplarity? One way to get at this question is to look at who gets included. According to John Wright-Rios, the Catholic liturgist who wrote the tune for the improvised litany of the saints, there was heated debate in the late days of the Central American Solidarity Movement about who met the criteria of martyr and hero. He explained,

> I from the very beginning wanted [the litany] to be focused on martyrs, people who especially . . . maybe not, it didn't have to be somebody who's Christian. It could be Mahatma Gandhi, and I used Gandhi's name in this and Ken Saro-Wiwa and Stephen Biko, and I don't know what Biko's religious affiliation was. But that it had . . . there was a sense of a religious faith-based association. But also I really wanted to focus it on nonviolent struggle.[9]

While religious affiliation was not essential for inclusion, according to Wright-Rios, a commitment to nonviolence was. But others in the CASM wanted to include guerrillas and liberation fighters in the litanies. Wright-Rios argued that these figures were not exemplary in the same way; we may call them heroes, but they were not martyrs. Calling their names in a litany of the saints thus would be inappropriate.

As practiced at the SOA Watch's annual mobilization, the planners of the litany have been less selective in their inclusion. Organizer Chris Inserra, who has kept the list of names since the late 1990s, has included anyone who is thought to have died at the hands of the graduates of the SOA/WHINSEC. She explained,

> The list of names has gotten bigger and bigger over the years. I am the keeper of a lot of those names. People send me names, you know, the Colombia massacres and the El Mozote massacre; I've got all that. The Ayotzinapa 43, I've got those names. I've got the [names of those killed after the coup] in Honduras. . . . I've got people killed on the border, particularly as we've focused on border militarization. I've got those names. People who walk on to the stage who are survivors of torture will hand me little slips of paper, and I keep adding those names. So it grows every year.[10]

Yet, consistently, it is the six Jesuits, their cook, and her daughter massacred at the UCA; Óscar Romero; and the four churchwomen killed in El Salvador who are named first in the litany, thereby giving them a place of honor that amplifies their exemplary status. Pride of place is given to those figures who in their lives and deaths serve as paragons of the values of the movement: solidarity, nonviolence, and justice seeking.

Imagery

Organizers have framed key figures as exemplary not only in the litany but also in images, banners, and other movement propaganda. From the mid-2000s to 2015, the stage team has hung a banner prominently over the speakers' platform that reads, "'Those who have a voice must speak for the voiceless'—Óscar Romero / ¡No Mas! Close the School of Assassins!" Romero's statement has been used as a slogan and framing device for the movement.[11] Cofounder Roy Bourgeois is particularly fond of the phrase, using it to justify the actions of the movement: "Romero said it best when he said that we who have a voice must speak for the voiceless. Those of us who live in the US can speak without fear of being disappeared or tortured or assassinated and therefore we have a responsibility to do so [to speak]."[12] While Romero may not have objected to this use of his words, he wrote them (quoting from Proverbs 31) in his fourth pastoral letter in a discourse on the importance of the church's role in "defending the rights of the poor."[13] For those SOA Watch participants who are attentive to the life of Romero and the context of these words, they call to mind an ecclesial commitment to the poor. For others less familiar with Romero's legacy, however, these words still invoke the demands of solidarity yet without any ecclesial overtones. What is important to note here is merely that the words have come to obtain a moral status independent of their context. As a slogan emblazoned on a banner, they are invested with an excess of ambivalent meanings while carrying the moral weight of the exemplar.

Beyond words, the images of key figures also serve as icons to the movement. Whether on shirts, on placards, or in the form of enormous twenty-foot-high cardboard puppets, the likeness of the Salvadoran martyrs, as well as others, are ubiquitous. Since her death in 2007, a banner remembering Rufina Amaya, the sole survivor of the El Mozote massacre, has hung next to the Romero quote on stage right during the annual vigil. Those at the front of the *¡presente!* litany procession also often carry placards depicting the faces of the victims of the UCA massacre. Also at the annual vigil, longtime Central American solidarity activist Shirley Tung sells shirts to raise funds for delegations and Latin American human rights organizations. The shirts feature the words and images of movement luminaries, including the rendering of Óscar Romero by Robert Lenz.[14]

One of the most striking aspects of the aesthetics of SOA Watch actions is the use of giant puppets. Puppetistas depict Mary of Guadalupe and Romero in his classic brow-line glasses alongside more abstract figures such as the "blue madre," portraying a mother mourning the loss of her child, or images of maize growing from military helmets turned upside down. Started by Catholic Workers who had experience in the anti-globalization movements of the early 2000s, the puppetistas have drawn on the radical, countercultural puppetry tradition developed by Bread and Puppet Theater and its founder Peter Schumann.[15] As puppetista Nicole Tilson explained, organizers affectionately call the process of developing the puppets for the annual vigil *cardboard chaos*. Participants bring ideas and images, and over a week they organically construct a common story that becomes a puppetista parade following the *¡presente!* litany on Sunday morning. The narrative has changed each year, responding to current events, but a through line has remained consistent. Tilson explained,

> All the years that I've been down there, it's been like, "Let's have something that represents all the corporations in one structure," which kind of ends up just turning into this kind of comical baddy character. And then forces of good . . . and the hopeful bird, flower, and trees rise up out of it [laughter] and the elements of hippiedom circle around it. That's what ends up happening as the result of the creative process of trying to, you know, bring together everyone's creative ideas and make them homogenous. That's what ends up happening.[16]

In depicting an apocalyptic scene that associates evil with economic and military structures, it is the exemplars and their allies who beat back the forces of oppression with the power of nonviolence, justice, and peace.

In addition to these prominent figures, the iconography of the movement includes less recognizable persons. The names of the victims of SOA/WHIN-SEC graduates are written on the crosses that participants hold during the litany, often a name that is previously unknown to its carrier. Other names were lifted up in a 2014 banner campaign. Under large, red stenciled lettering stating "greatly MISSED," a graphic artist placed images of Victor Jara, the Chilean musician killed in the 1979 coup; Isis Obed Murillo, a nineteen-year-old protester who was killed by Honduran soldiers in the wake of the 2009 coup; and Celina Maricet Ramos, the daughter of the Jesuits' housekeeper killed in 1989. SOA Watch activists have wheatpasted these posters, along with graphics developed by artist César Maxit, on walls in Washington, DC and Columbus, Georgia.[17]

Narrative

What is significant about both the puppets and the posters is not only their aesthetic quality but also their capacity to shape a story, a narrative that tells watchers and participants about the failures of the US–Latin American military system and the economic neoliberalism that accompanies it. While it is conventional to call stories of the saints hagiographies, the term has a negative connotation and fails to convey what is occurring in the narrative intervention that exemplars actually make in the movement.[18] By their stories, they construct a master narrative of critique and hope. This master narrative has room for many others, but it is effective in clarifying the context, characters, conflict, and content of the work of the SOA Watch. The historical context is the hemispheric system of militarism, its economic drivers, and its colonialism that is manifest today in the practices of military training. That context is driven home by the physical, geographical context at the gates of Fort Benning or, after 2015, on the US-Mexico border. The characters are targets, such as the SOA/WHINSEC, the multinational corporations, and the US political class, on the one hand, and heroes, such as the martyrs, directly impacted people, and solidarity activists, on the other. The conflict between the two groups is put in apocalyptic terms, thus inviting, if not forcing, participants to choose a side. The content, then, is the gradual transformation of a system that produces death into one that brings life.

While each year's puppetista pageant tells a slightly different story, the 2015 performance was particularly noteworthy and representative.

Following the vigil, the puppetistas began their annual ritual, a pageant telling the story of repression and resistance in the Americas.

The musicians' collective started it off singing "De Colores." As the musicians sang, children and adults carrying cornstalks danced in the middle of a circle in front of the stage.

A large cardboard monkey entered the scene. In the middle, there was a group of six indigenous men, farmers who were planting seeds. The music shifted to a more sinister tone as musicians beat rain barrels and scraped tin cans. Vultures entered the scene, flying around the indigenous farmers. In the center, the farmers mounted a powerful resistance, but they couldn't beat back the forces of evil: the monkey and vultures, as well as a woman on stilts dressed as the Statue of Liberty.

Then the mosquitoes entered, buzzing loudly, with labels on their wings like [General] Ríos Montt, Plan Colombia, World Bank, Big Oil, CIA [Central Intelligence Agency], and the SOA. Meanwhile, the monkey stole export crops, mainly bananas, while the mosquitoes harassed the farmers.

With whirling vacuum hoses, a twenty-five-foot-high calaca, or skeleton, crawled in and raised up in the smoke of incense. Participants wiggled their fingers at the calaca, which wiggled its fingers back. The calaca and the Statue of Liberty had a showdown, and the calaca emerged victorious.

Finally the defeated Liberty was resurrected as the Virgin of Guadalupe, and the music became upbeat again. Together, musicians and the gathered crowds chanted, "¡Todos somos Americanos!" (We are all Americans!)[19]

Narratives such as the one told in the puppetistas pageant help participants focus and make meaning of what they are doing together. Which side are they on? With whom do they identify—Lady Liberty or the Virgin of Guadalupe?

The same is true of the martyr stories that are told in the movement through speeches, email blasts, and articles. For example, on the thirty-fifth anniversary of the rape and murder of the four North American church-women in El Salvador, SOA Watch supporters Jean Stokan and Scott Wright remembered these martyrs and called for actions faithful to their legacy in an article published on the SOA Watch's website. Stokan and Wright encouraged readers by reminding them that "throughout these years, you have kept the memory of the martyrs alive, and have asked: What do they require of us today? . . . What would they be doing today, if they were living in our times? And what ought we to be doing?"[20] Drawing on the stories of these four church workers, evaluative questions invite speculation not only about the possible positions of the martyrs today but, more significantly, about the responsibilities of those who seek to remember and emulate them. Stokan and Wright used an ancient Christian affirmation that the martyrs are the "seeds of the church" to argue that the martyrs plant seeds of memory, hope, and responsibility that come to fruition in the lives of those who follow them.[21]

This was the case for Steve Clemens, who committed civil disobedience at the 2005 annual vigil. Clemens had long been involved in CASM activism, first as a member of the Koinonia Community in Americus, Georgia, and later through the SOA Watch. In 2005 he traveled to El Salvador with the Center for Global Education at Augsburg College and participated in the commemoration of the twenty-fifth anniversary of Romero's assassination. While on pilgrimage in El Salvador, Clemens decided to cross the line at Fort Benning later that year. A number of circumstances aligned to guide Clemens toward his decision: his children had moved away, his spouse was supportive, and Christian peacemaker teams in Iraq reported that US soldiers were using the torture techniques that the SOA Watch had exposed and denounced on Iraqi detainees.[22] While Clemens's decision to commit civil disobedience at the gates of Fort Benning was made for particular personal and contextual reasons, the point of motivational clarity came during his pilgrimage to El Salvador. Clemens explained, "It made such a close connection to what the School of the Americas was teaching in South and Central America that I felt it was an appropriate time to kind of take that risk and cross the line again."[23] As with Stokan and Wright, Clemens connected his current experience to that of Romero's and analyzed the decisions before him in light of the martyr's life story.

Thus, similar to icons, the stories of the martyrs both reflect and point beyond the actual lives of the martyrs. The narrative becomes a script by which SOA Watch activists narrate and make sense of their own lives and context. Asking what the martyrs would do discloses responsibilities for SOA Watch activists in the present.

Dynamics of Exemplarity

What role do these various technologies of iconography play in shaping the strategic deliberation of the movement? What moral and political work do they do?

Moral philosopher Linda Zagzebski has argued that the foundation of moral exemplarity is the emotion of admiration.[24] Relying on social psychologists' accounts of exemplarity, Zagzebski posits that admiration is a pretheoretical emotion that we learn to trust upon reflection, particularly reflection within a community of others. Admiration has two aspects that are important to the moral structure of exemplarity: it elevates the exemplar as a person of excellence, and in doing so it identifies that person as a paradigm of imitation. Zagzebski remains agnostic on the internal reasons for the connection between elevation and emulation, but the two aspects come together in the emotion of admiration.[25] While Zagzebski is certainly right to identify admiration as foundational to the moral structure of exemplarity, it is important to note that the process of reflection whereby admiration is refined more often resembles the symbolic, embodied, and ritual framing that I have described in the previous section than the deliberation of a seminar classroom. That critique aside, however, once admiration is established, Zagzebski helpfully identifies a number of moral functions that it performs. Those who admire the exemplars, through their admiration, apprentice themselves to the exemplar. Similar to novitiates under a superior, admirers look to the exemplar as a teacher and a guide who motivates their discernment in spite of complexity and authorizes their action in spite of difficulty.

Thus, applying Zagzebski's insights to the SOA Watch, exemplary martyrs perform three distinct functions in the movement: they *teach* through their lives a way of excellence and through their deaths the injustice of the military system. As a result of their teaching, they *motivate* action on issues of contemporary concern. And by their model, they *authorize* that action, giving it a sure precedent.

The first and most venerable function of exemplars is their pedagogical role. This was Aristotle's insight: the excellent person serves epistemically to grant onlookers a concrete vision of the good life. Exemplars serve as pedagogues by revealing a life of excellence. Thus, by learning about the lives of the martyrs of El Salvador, movement participants gain concrete manifestations of the principles of solidarity, justice, and nonviolence. By rendering such principles as specific and historical, admirers begin to imagine the ways in which they too might embody such principles. Sociologist Sharon Erickson Nepstad explains, "Movement stories . . . offer a model of action, as the narrative's heroes reveal methods of exercising agency that the audience can emulate."[26]

In the SOA Watch, exemplars serve as more than merely models for action; they also work as lenses through which to view the systems, actors, and actions that produce death. This has obvious affinity with the Christian affirmation that not only is Jesus the "exemplar of all exemplars" but also his life, passion, crucifixion, and resurrection reveal God's judgment of death itself.[27] For some early SOA Watch participants, the stories of the Salvadoran martyrs were their first exposure to the US–Latin American military system. While the killing of unnamed civilians may have been lamentable, the assaults became real and relatable when priests and vowed religious were killed. The "moral shock" of these deaths became a lens through which to understand the violence of US foreign and military policy across Latin America.[28] That the assassinations of people with positional privilege such as an archbishop, North American and European missionaries, and other clergy occasion moral shock and not the killings of largely anonymous campesinos and indigenous poor should give us pause. It indicates the ambiguity of the politics of sacrifice, an issue I explore further in this chapter. These ambiguities noted, however, both a model of the good life and a lens through which to analyze violence—direct, structural, and cultural. The two aspects are related in that the intensification of one leads to the intensification of the other: the more excellent the life, the more unjust the death.

In both aspects, the exemplary martyrs motivate movement participation. They are models to follow, paradigms for action. Óscar Romero and Ignacio Ellacuría raised prophetic voices against the unjust violence perpetrated on the poor of El Salvador. So too, then, SOA Watch participants should attempt to speak honestly and incisively about the causes and consequences of military violence in their own time and context. Ita Ford, Jean Donovan, Dorothy Kazel, and Maura Clarke left the comforts of their homes in North America to work among the poor in Central America. So too, then, SOA Watch participants should be willing to sacrifice their comforts for the work of justice and peace. In the face of multiple threats against her life, Berta Cáceres spoke clearly and loudly against the abuses of indigenous Honduran people's human rights and environmental integrity. So too, then, SOA Watch participants should speak clearly and loudly while calling for specific legislation (HR 5474, the Berta Cáceres Human Rights in Honduras Act) and supporting the SOA Watch.[29] As Cáceres's obituary on the SOA Watch website declared, "No matter how many death threats she received, no matter how many times she was followed, pursued, or threatened, Berta would not be silenced. And she must not be silenced today. Berta's voice and struggle must continue to be heard."[30]

Yet SOA Watch activists do not make decisions about their political involvement by merely following the rigid blueprint of the exemplars. As

SOA Watch staff member Rosa suggested in the Phoenix pizza parlor, the question for the movement is, "What would the six Jesuits who were massacred in El Salvador say today?" A gap persists between exemplar and admirer, between the historical exigencies that characterize the moment of martyr and those of the follower. Bridging that gap induces a problem for followers. They cannot merely do what the exemplar did. Rather, the exemplar becomes a rubric for discernment, for practical reason. The invocation of the exemplars at moments of decision, as in the pizza parlor scene conveyed earlier, shows how the rubric operates. By calling on the exemplars, a whole host of associations are brought to bear: prophetic commitments to solidarity and justice, a willingness to speak truth to power irrespective of the consequences, and an openness to the possibility of sacrifice in service to others. The exemplars evoke not only principles but also narratives that shine a light on present decisions. While there is no direct translation of the exemplar's life into that of the followers, indirectly the exemplars serve as rubrics of discernment that motivate movement involvement.

The iconography of the SOA Watch movement not only has served to facilitate a cognitive attachment to the exemplary martyrs but has accomplished the emotional work of generating affective bonds between the living and the dead as well. Through iconographic depictions, with names written on crosses and chanted, through narratives shared informally or in training sessions, and through a host of other mediums, the projection of the hopes and ideals of the movement onto these particular individuals generates what Durkheimian social theorists might call a totemic object of veneration.[31] It is not necessary to follow Durkheim's reductive account of religion to appreciate the power of his insight—that is, that the bodily copresence, shared attention, and reflexive consciousness generate collective effervescence that, in turn, motivates action.[32]

The pedagogical and motivational operations of the exemplary martyrs are possible due to the dynamics of *authority*. As shown in chapter 4, the SOA Watch as a movement has often questioned the legal authority of positive law by appealing to higher law, variously construed. In the absence of a written codification of a higher law, exemplars operate as authorities who grant moral weight to the positions staked out by activists. By framing exemplars as objects of admiration, the movement positions those exemplars as moral authorities whose words and lives operate as foundational premises for the justification of decisions. Should we speak truth to power even if it puts us in harm's way? Should we include other people of goodwill in our movement? Should we move from the annual vigil site of Fort Benning to the border? Bringing the exemplars to bear on these pivotal questions for the life of the movement authorizes activists' decisions.

But more than simply offering sources of justification, movement leaders are most effective in consolidating their own authority when they can associate themselves with exemplars. Few have been more adept at this than Roy Bourgeois, whose case I take up in the next section. In stump speeches at college campuses and progressive churches across the United States, he has honed his testimony in a way that associates his own life story with that of the martyrs. But not only Bourgeois develops his authority in this way; young leaders in the movement also generate their authority by their own proximity to the violence of the US–Latin American military system. For example, in a video chronicling the 2014 banner and wheatpasting campaign mentioned previously, young activists held up the images of those disappeared and killed in Latin America beside them. The resemblance between those killed and those carrying on the work of change is unmistakable; this symbolic association lends authority to their leadership in this solidarity movement. The authority that these movement leaders generate through their association with the exemplary martyrs, however, is ambivalent in its consequences. On the positive side, it places them within a tradition of deliberation and activism, holding them accountable to paradigms of lives lived for nonviolence, solidarity, and justice. On the negative side, it is susceptible to cults of personality and, especially, to a politics of sacrifice that can tend to valorize suffering. This specter of the messiah complex haunts any messianic political theology. It is to these potential problems that I now turn.

MOURNING THE DEAD, FOLLOWING THE LIVING

The SOA Watch is a movement founded on a messianic politics of the memory and presence of the exemplary dead. These memories, however, refuse to stay dead. The ritual, art, and narrative of the movement participates proleptically in the resurrection of the dead. In the last section I suggested that the exemplary dead, in addition to teaching and motivating movement participation, function to authorize the leadership of certain SOA Watch activists who are able to associate their own stories with the lives of the martyr-exemplars. This claim deserves further examination, one that takes us to the social theory of authority developed by Max Weber.

Exemplarity and Charisma

Charisma is a rather more familiar term than exemplarity.[33] As the sociologist of religion Martin Riesebrodt has noted, the term *charisma* is "probably one of the more popular concepts" derived from sociology.[34] It is also one of

the more misunderstood. We talk about athletes, politicians, and other public figures as being "charismatic," noting their personal charm, their ability
to lead others, and their way with words. This notion of charisma as an
inherent psychological trait of certain persons, however, is at odds with the
classical sociological usage. Rather than a personality trait, Max Weber used
the term to refer to the social dynamics of authority that groups place on
particular leaders. Weber developed a threefold typology to explain the generation of what he called legitimate domination: rational, traditional, and
charismatic.[35] *Rational authority* is generated through legal and bureaucratic systematization according to the logic of scientific and technocratic
effectiveness. *Traditional authority* is power generated from the force of
habit—this is the way it has always been, this is the way it always shall be.
Charismatic authority, in Weber's famous articulation, is grounded in "devotion to the exceptional sanctity, heroism or exemplary character of an individual person, and of the normative patterns or order revealed or ordained
by him."[36] For Weber, charismatic authority was vested in followers' belief in
the exemplarity and supernatural, miraculous capacity of the leader.

Weber's account of charismatic authority has two apparently contradictory aspects.[37] On the one hand, charismatics generate their authority through
a supernatural, miraculous, or magical power. Weber, the social scientist of
disenchantment, remained agnostic on the reality of these capacities. What
was important was not the charismatic leader's actual inherent capacity
but the leader's ability to secure certain goods for followers.[38] Inherent
capacity or not, the attribution of magical power creates a distance between
the charismatic and the follower as it reveals a special ability that the
leader has and the follower does not. On the other hand, charismatic leaders generate their authority by serving as exemplars in the sense that they
are objects of mimesis, or imitation. These two aspects, one that creates
distance between leader and follower and the other that brings them closer
together, seem contradictory.[39]

These two aspects are not actually contradictory, however, if we keep in
mind that Weber was drawing on the work of German theologian and jurist
Rudolph Sohm. Although Weber can be justly attributed as popularizing the
concept of charisma, he was not its modern originator. Sohm used the concept of charisma, which he drew from historical critical readings of the New
Testament and particularly the Pauline epistles, to explain the social organization of the church in his *Kirchenrecht*.[40] Drawing on the New Testament's
account of charisma, it makes sense to keep the grace-filled status of leaders
and their exemplarity together. This is, of course, fundamental to Christological accounts of the Christ as an exemplar.

For social theorists, the question that Weber's appropriation of Sohm's
theological concept has raised is whether the classical theorist's concept is

truly sociological or not.[41] David Norman Smith and Paul Joosse defend a social constructionist reading of Weber's theory by counterposing him to Sohm.[42] While Weber drew from Sohm and admitted his debt, he radically altered Sohm's concept, generalizing it beyond the single case of early Christianity and including morally ambiguous characters such as the berserker and the warrior priest in the category. Peter Haley agrees with this description of Weber's change but laments the loss of theology in a process of secularization.[43]

I want to propose a different tack. I think Weber was right to generalize the concept of charisma and to argue that it is principally socially constructed. Social theorists, however, tend to make their arguments by focusing on the magical quality of leaders rather than their exemplarity. Magic, more so than exemplarity, is susceptible to a disenchanting sociological analysis and critique. Magic can be disenchanted; exemplarity is more difficult to dismiss. Thus, magic, rather than exemplarity, tends to be the preoccupation of social theorists. We might remain agnostic on the question of innate quality, however, while still analyzing the mechanisms by which leaders come to gain charismatic status, and at least one of those mechanisms is the dynamics of exemplarity. Thus, a social constructionist account of charismatic leadership does not get us off the hook from doing the work of political theology. Rather than having Sohm's work stand in for theology specifically and religious analysis more generally, and thereby rejecting both, Weber invites us to consider the normative force of exemplarity and its manifestation within charismatic authority. This analysis is sociological, yes, but it requires verstehen, which when analyzing movements animated by religious sources and norms invites deploying the analytical tools of political theology. In particular, we need to analyze the normatively ambivalent role of sacrifice in the generation of charismatic authority and how it coordinates the two aspects of charisma—magic and mimesis.

Narratives of Sacrifice and the Transference of Authority

In the previous section I argued that admiration for the exemplary dead is generated through a number of technologies of iconography: liturgy, imagery, and narrative. Each of these technologies of formation, with the exemplary dead as its primary object, can be harnessed by charismatic leaders to furnish their own authority. It is easy to imagine simple and sophisticated versions of this transference. For example, liturgical transference of authority is granted to those who march at the front of the ¡presente! litany: SOA Watch staff, cofounder Roy Bourgeois, celebrities such as Martin Sheen, movement luminaries, and directly impacted people. Or iconic transference of authority is accomplished, in at least some small way, by those who wear the images of Romero or the four churchwomen on their shirts, claiming the martyrs as a brand and an expression of their aesthetic identity.

The technology that SOA Watch leaders have used to generate their own authority most effectively has been narrative, in particular the narrative synchronization of the biography of the leader with the lives of the exemplary dead. At least since the Acts of the Apostles' account of Paul's conversion on the road to Damascus, hagiographic narratives that link the protagonist to some prior authority have long been part of the Christian theological tradition. As with the functions of exemplarity enumerated earlier, these writings serve to inspire readers to piety by providing a paradigm of holiness while also giving evidence of the saints' magical status. The autobiographies of movement leaders do similar work by revealing the sacrifices of the leaders and associating them with the sanctity of the exemplary dead. These testimonies—shared in meetings, rallies, stump speeches, and pamphlets—are important mechanisms in transferring authority from the dead to the living.

Few have been more adept at generating this kind of authority than movement cofounder Roy Bourgeois. It has helped that Bourgeois is a raconteur from Lutcher, Louisiana, well formed in the storytelling traditions of Cajun country. But he developed his capacity to narrate his own life in biographical synchronization with that of the exemplary dead in college classrooms, church halls, and living rooms across the United States as he traveled to recruit participants into SOA Watch activism. In Bourgeois's narration, each plot point in the hagiographic stories of the martyrs is punctuated by his response. His stump speech, one I have heard a number of times during my research, is thrilling to hear.

The highlights of the story connect the listener to a much wider narrative about the themes and personas of the SOA Watch. Bourgeois was a navy lieutenant in Vietnam who received a Purple Heart for his service. While in the military, he grew disillusioned with the role of the United States in Southeast Asia, was mentored by a navy chaplain, and decided to join the priesthood. Following his military service, seminary, and ordination as a Maryknoll priest, he spent five years in Bolivia, where, he reports, "the poor, my teachers, introduced me to their 'theology of liberation' and a God who empowers and gives hope to the poor."[44] After becoming involved in political struggles against Bolivian dictator Hugo Banzer, who was, as Bourgeois points out, supported by the United States and trained at the SOA, he was denied reentry to Bolivia. Bourgeois then turned his attention to El Salvador, where in 1980 both Romero and the four North American churchwomen were killed. "It brought El Salvador close to us because they were our own," Bourgeois reflected.[45] In response, in 1983 Bourgeois and two conspirators climbed the tall pines outside the Fort Benning barracks where Salvadoran soldiers slept, then played a recording of Romero's last Sunday homily in which he called on the military to "¡cese la represión!" Arrested, the priest spent eighteen months in prison, with some of that time in solitary confinement.

In Bourgeois's telling, all of these background events prepared him for his later response when the six Jesuits were murdered at the UCA. Bourgeois relays his experience:

> When I read that report [from Representative Moakley's congressional investigation], it got a lot of, a lot of coverage, I decided to return to Ft. Benning to investigate the school. I went down with the support of my Maryknoll community; didn't have to convince them really because we work in Latin America and . . . know firsthand the brutality of the military. We thought it was important to investigate this School of the Americas that we knew very little about. I found this apartment right outside of the main gate that became the SOA Watch, School of the Americas Watch. We didn't have a movement back then of course; we just had a few kindred spirits coming into town. [These were] friends who I called: "Come down, we got work to do here."[46]

Building on these early intuitions, though making clear that he had "no vision of starting a movement," Bourgeois narrates the emergence of one.[47] And it was the exemplary dead, according to Bourgeois, that gave vision and direction to the group's early actions. In his 1997 trial statement he declared to the judge, "We go to prison empowered by the martyrs, the victims of the graduates of the School of the Americas, those thugs that we bring here to train. . . . We go to prison empowered by people like Jean Donovan, Dorothy Kazel, my friends, Ita Ford and Maura Clarke, missionary women from the United States who have been raped and killed by graduates of the School of the Americas."[48] Similar to the protection and healing that late antique Christians gained through their petition of the saints, Bourgeois claimed the empowerment and aid of the martyrs of El Salvador in his declaration to the judge.

At each point of Bourgeois's narrative, he highlights a dialectic between the major events of concern for SOA Watch participants and his actions: when Romero and the four churchwomen were killed, Bourgeois climbed a tree outside the barracks at Fort Benning and played Romero's final Sunday homily. When the Jesuits were assassinated, Bourgeois read the congressional report and led a motley crew of activists and friends to investigate the school. On the one-year anniversary of the Jesuits' murder, Bourgeois held the first SOA Watch action at Fort Benning. By narrating his story in this way, Bourgeois positions himself as the rightful inheritor of the moral authority of the exemplary dead.

Bourgeois is not alone in this narrative act, however. His biographers, James Hodge and Linda Cooper, also participate in this transference of moral to charismatic authority through their hagiographic portrait of Bourgeois in *Disturbing the Peace*.[49] As with his own self-narration, Hodge and Cooper situate Bourgeois as carrying on the legacy of the martyrs and weave together his own story with that of the movement.[50]

Other members of the movement participate in this transference as well. For example, retired United Methodist missionary, pastor, and army veteran Charles Butler testified at his trial for civil disobedience at Fort Benning that "Father Roy Bourgeois is the one who pretty much single-handedly in the beginning [realized] the terrible suffering of the six Jesuit priests that were killed, and so he began to protest the presence of the School of the Americas. But a movement begun with one person about 10 years ago began to grow."[51] Beyond attributing the early growth of the movement to Bourgeois, Butler suggested in his sentencing statement that Bourgeois's voice was the instrument of God's call on his life. After learning of the US involvement in human rights violations during missionary work in Central America, he became frustrated and disillusioned. Butler testified, "Amid this turmoil I heard a prophetic voice. It was the voice of Father Roy Bourgeois: 'You are called to be a voice for the voiceless.' God spoke to me at a deep, inner place of my soul."[52] According to Butler, God spoke to him through Bourgeois's invocation of Romero's call to be a "voice for the voiceless." While the point of Butler's story was not to instantiate Bourgeois's charismatic authority, his testimony (both in the legal and theological sense) reveals the transference at work.

Though Bourgeois clearly draws on the moral exemplarity of the dead to instantiate his charismatic authority, the dynamics are not without ambiguity. For example, savvy members of the SOA Watch network recognize the dangers of charismatic leadership and have made clear that Bourgeois is not that kind of leader. Bill Quigley, a law professor and one of the members of the SOA Watch Legal Collective, said of Bourgeois that "he's beaten the cult of personality. So many movements are known only by their leaders. . . . [Bourgeois] has gotten himself out of the way. It shows the breadth and strength of the movement."[53] Quigley's observation that Bourgeois has "gotten himself out of the way" was echoed by younger members of the staff collective. One told me, "Many organizations suffer from 'Founders Syndrome,' where they can't change, they can't shift focus. That's not us. Roy is very hands-off and lets us chart our course. This is a great step forward to shift focus. A lot of organizations can't do that."[54] Referring to the shift from Fort Benning to the border, the young activist expressed her sense that the SOA Watch was not unduly wedded to Bourgeois's charismatic authority in a way that prevented flexibility and change.

Yet former Equipo Sur coordinator Lisa Sullivan, among others, credits Bourgeois's prophetic leadership with the success of the movement. "I . . . think whether we like it or not . . . there's been this really brilliant, inspired person, who's Roy, who kind of gets these ideas."[55] In particular, Sullivan credited Bourgeois with the "crazy" idea that they could organize Latin American heads of state. While noting Bourgeois's charismatic creativity, Sullivan was also careful to acknowledge that he was anything but controlling. Without such bold, visionary action, Sullivan suggested that "you can get kind of just bogged down." From Sullivan and Quigley, we can see the ambiguities of charisma at work. Even those who wish to emphasize Bourgeois's evasion of the cult of personality do so in ways that only reiterate the aura of his charisma.

Bourgeois is not the only leader who draws on these dynamics. Younger leaders use similar strategies of testimony and narrative to instantiate their authority. And even at the most rudimentary level, you can see the dynamics at work in the most common question I received as a participant in SOA Watch activism: How many years have you been down here? It is a question that asks about my commitment and the legitimacy of my presence. When I respond, "I've been coming since 2005," I generally am granted some credibility. Through long-standing commitment, I show that I am not merely an activist-tourist but also a willing participant who makes the sacrifices necessary to attend the annual vigil and participate year after year.

From Bourgeois to marginal movement figures such as myself, sacrifice plays a pivotal role in the generation of legitimate authority. More pointedly, I would argue that the two aspects of Weber's theory of charisma, magic and mimesis, are held together through the politics of sacrifice. Regarding magic, movement leaders create distance between themselves and their followers through high-risk activism. As I suggested in chapter 4, not every SOA Watch participant occupies a subject position that would allow him or her to responsibly engage in such high-risk actions. Yet prisoners of conscience have a special authority in the movement because they do what others hesitate to do: they submit themselves to significant risks of legal consequences, imprisonment, fines, and violence, sometimes excessive, by law enforcement.

These risks are always qualified by the fact that they pale in comparison to the suffering endured by Latin American partners. As Shirley Way put it as she prepared for her prison sentence, "The price is very small indeed in comparison with the costs my fellow human beings have had to and continue to bear at the hands of graduates of the School of the Americas/Western Hemisphere Institute for Security Cooperation."[56] SOA Watch cofounder and antiwar activist Kathy Kelly described in detail her experience of being roughed up and hog-tied by police after she refused to be treated with disrespect. Reflecting on the experience, she said, "This morning's aches and pains, along with the memory of being hogtied, give me a glimpse into the abuses we protest by coming to Fort Benning, GA."[57] These activists' sacrifices for the cause, their submission to imprisonment and abuse at the hands of law enforcement, demonstrate their commitment and perform solidarity. They create distance between others in the movement insofar as others are unwilling to undergo such an askesis, at times for very legitimate reasons. This magical distance is not the miraculous provision of the saints, but it does operate within an economy of sacrifice in which benefits are thereby gained for followers and participants. Through dramatic acts of high-risk civil disobedience, SOA Watch prisoners of conscience have brought increased attention to the campaign to close the military training facility. I take up the theological underpinnings and dangers of this theory of change in the next section.

The magical sacrifice that prisoners of conscience perform also inspires mimesis. In a passage thick with the dynamics of exemplarity, authority, and sacrifice that I have been tracking, John Dear—priest, anti-war activist, and SOA Watch supporter—narrates the last days of the four churchwomen killed in El Salvador in 1980:

> On November 29th, as Dorothy Day died at the Catholic Worker house in New York City, Ita [Ford] and Maura [Clarke] flew to Managua, Nicaragua, for a four-day conference of Maryknollers working in Central America. On the night before their return to El Salvador, Ita shared with the group a passage from the writings of Óscar Romero: "Christ invites us not to fear persecution because, believe me, brothers and sisters, those who are committed to the poor must risk the same fate as the poor, and in El Salvador, we know what the fate of the poor signifies: to disappear, to be tortured, to be captive, and to be found dead by the side of the road."
>
> Jean [Donovan] and Dorothy [Kazel] drove out to the airport to meet Ita and Maura that evening after their flight from Managua. The four women were last seen alive driving out of the airport down the main road.[58]

Citing Ita Ford, who was quoting Romero, after the death of Dorothy Day, Dear situates the sacrifices of Ford and her colleagues within the venerable narratives of these other saints of nonviolent struggle.

But Dear's point is not merely to extol the saintliness of these missionaries; rather, it is to motivate readers to follow in the martyrs' footsteps. In the pamphlet's conclusion, Dear notes that following in the legacy of the four churchwomen killed in El Salvador, thousands have gathered annually at the gates of Fort Benning to call for the closing of the SOA and the establishment of a new foreign policy. He concludes,

The meaning of Jean [Donovan]'s life and death, as well as all the other martyrs, is not just in their sacrifices and their witness, but in their call to follow in their footsteps, to enter into the life of the poor, to struggle for justice with the poor, to stand with the poor, to defend the poor, to speak out for the poor, and to become one with them. Just as Jesus called Jean to walk the road of peace, Jean now calls us, in Jesus' name, to become God's instruments of justice and peace.[59]

Dear, just as other movement leaders, uses the sacrifices of exemplars to call other movement participants into high-risk activism. Moreover, he uses his own sacrifices in the pattern of the martyrs to generate his authority in the movement.

The dynamics of charismatic authority thus draw on moral exemplarity through the politics of sacrifice. By engaging in high-risk activism, movement leaders synchronize their own lives with the exemplars', generate their authority, and call on others to follow in their footsteps. In their high-risk activism they both attract followers for their courage and willingness to put their bodies on the line and distance themselves from followers for whom such risk is imprudent. But does solidarity require such sacrifice? I have already suggested in previous chapters some of the dangers of this line of thinking, particularly in universalizing an obligation to sacrifice to all movement participants regardless of station. Some movement participants, particularly people of color and those directly impacted by the violence of US–Latin American militarism, have critiqued movement leaders for using the politics of sacrifice to authorize their voices. Leaders, in their charisma, silence other voices sometimes explicitly through censure, critique, and marginalization but more often implicitly, simply by the amplified power of their own speech and presence.[60] To adequately grapple with the ambiguity of the politics of sacrifice, I now turn to Delores Williams's important critique of vicarious surrogate suffering in Christian theology.

THE POLITICS OF SACRIFICE

The politics of sacrifice is a key component of the moral authority of both dead exemplars and living leaders in the SOA Watch movement. The sacrifices of exemplars demonstrate the contours of an excellent life lived for others while also revealing the injustice of a system of legalized military violence that brutally takes the lives of such admirable persons. The sacrifices of leaders hold together the attraction-repellant dialectic of charisma, both inspiring followers while keeping them at arm's length. Jail time and abuse at the hands of authorities are inspirational while also keeping these forms of high-risk activism out of reach for many SOA Watch participants. In both cases, the shape of the politics of sacrifice is Christological. The politics is made intelligible by its relation to the crucifixion, death, and resurrection of Jesus Christ.

Take, for example, the oft-repeated retelling of the assassination of Óscar Romero. The day after he gave his famous last Sunday homily in which he called for the Salvadoran security forces to "¡cese la represión!" Romero was assassinated while celebrating the Eucharist. According to a letter sent by the Cooperativa Sacerdotal ARS (a priestly cooperative in El Salvador also known as COOPESA) to support the 2003 SOA Watch prisoners of conscience, the following were Romero's last words: "Que este cuerpo inmolado y esta Sangre Sacrificada por los hombres nos alimente también para dar nuestro cuerpo y nuestra sangre al sufrimiento y al dolor, como Cristo, no para sí, sino para dar conceptos de justicia y de paz a nuestro pueblo."[61] Romero's prayer, repeated by the priests of COOPESA, was that Christ's sacrifice would prepare others to sacrifice, not for the sake of suffering but to bring about peace and justice for the people. The liturgical context in which Romero was assassinated gives only more power to his words, and we cannot help but see Romero's sacrifice, his death at the order of SOA graduate Roberto D'Aubuisson, as an echo of Christ's.

While sacrifice has long been a central problematic of Christian discipleship, recent authors have rightly raised questions about the ways in which the valorization of sacrifice can legitimize violence.[62] None have made this critique as incisively as womanist theologian Delores Williams. In her essay "Black Women's Surrogacy Experience and the Christian Notion of Redemption," Williams identifies surrogacy, or the act of standing in for another, as a fundamental problem in Christian accounts of Jesus's salvific role. Beginning with the experience of African American women, Williams identifies two "faces" of surrogacy: coerced and voluntary. Coerced surrogacy was the result of chattel slavery in which Black women were forced into surrogate roles in nurturance, field labor, and sexuality, thus standing in as the matriarch in the home, standing in as the laborer in the field, and standing in as the sexual property of slave-owning white men. After the Civil War and emancipation of the slaves, surrogacy continued but was now "voluntary."[63] Why, Williams asks, would black women voluntarily submit to a program of violence and dehumanization? The answer she provides is the valorizing power of Christological accounts of atonement through surrogate suffering. The result of these forms of surrogacy is not only that Black women's roles and social identities have hardened into negative stereotypes but also that those stereotypes have been blessed by Christian theology in which Jesus is imaged as the ultimate surrogate.

Using the experience of Black women as a sociohistorical lens by which to read and critique Christian theology, Williams historicizes and rejects classical accounts of atonement. Whether *Christus Victor*, juridical, or humanist models of atonement, all portray Jesus's sacrifice on the cross as the means of redemption.[64] Jesus stands in for humanity, thus giving surrogacy "an aura of the sacred."[65] Williams asks, "If black women accept this image of redemption, can they not also passively accept the exploitation surrogacy brings?"[66] Williams concludes that Black women cannot accept this image of redemption, for, "to do so is to make their exploitation sacred. To do so is to glorify sin."[67] Williams's alternative is to focus on the liberatory aspects of Jesus's life and teaching; this, rather than surrogate suffering, is what is atoning for Black women. Williams rejects categorically that suffering should be understood as sacrifice—literally, to make (*-fice*) holy (*sacri-*). Rather, surrogate suffering is defilement, going against the intentions of God.

Williams's essay, first published in 1991, has become a touchstone in Christian theological and ethical reflection on the meaning of the cross. What does Christ's suffering and death mean for those who wish to follow Jesus of Nazareth? If Christ is the paradigm, the exemplar of exemplars, is sacrifice an essential part of discipleship? Political theologians have since wrestled with these fundamental questions of theodicy, Christology, atonement, and ethics.[68] While Black theologian James Cone accepted the power of Williams's critique—that is, the surrogate suffering of the cross can and often does underwrite the suffering of Black women—he was not willing, with Williams, to do away with the positive significance of the cross altogether. Siding with M. Shawn Copeland (among others), Cone argued that the cross, and the suffering that accompanies it, ought to remain a fundamental part of Christian theology, specifically Black liberation theology.[69] Rooted in the reality of Black people's struggle for justice, Cone concludes, "The cross is the burden we must bear in order to attain freedom."[70]

For Cone, as for Copeland, suffering is a brute fact that accompanies the struggle against unjust structures. Whereas Williams rejects attempts to make theological meaning of the cross in anything other than a negative register, Cone and Copeland see a positive possibility. Copeland, for instance, stays with Black women's testimonies not only in the experience of suffering but also in the meaning making of that suffering. In Black women's suffering, Copeland finds resources for resistance: memory, wit, sass, and courage. These resources provide an outline for a theology of suffering from a womanist perspective, a theology that remembers, resists, and redeems. While Copeland accepts Williams's rejection of redemptive suffering, she flips the script to suggest that by their resistance and endurance in the face of oppression, Black women redeem suffering. Copeland concludes, "Black women invite

God to partner with them in the redemption of Black people. They make meaning of their suffering."[71]

What does this winding path through theological reflections on the Christological significance of Christ's suffering and death mean for the dynamics of moral exemplarity and charismatic leadership in the SOA Watch movement? Williams had in mind Black women as a class and not solidarity activists, many of whom come not from the margins but the class of the masters. But this difference only amplifies the ways her concerns should lead us to interrogate the dynamics of the politics of sacrifice. On the one hand, we should be mindful of the ways in which valorizing surrogacy can justify violence against marginalized people. This violence is subtle but can occur even within the movement itself. As privileged, white North Americans encounter their complicity in systems of legalized violence, they often want to "do something." Engaging in high-risk activism in support of the aims of the SOA Watch can be one way to expiate the guilt that privileged activists feel.[72] But this can be a very paternalistic performance of solidarity, particularly insofar as their suffering serves to amplify the voices of activists who are not directly impacted by the legalized violence of the US–Latin American military system. Activists can operate with a messiah complex in which their sacrifices are the means of the salvation of the movement. Recall the activists of color featured in chapter 4 who critiqued prisoners of conscience who used their jail time as a badge of honor. Activists should be wary of equating the voluntary sacrifice that comes from a place of privilege with the coerced suffering that is imposed on Latin American peoples.

On the other hand, suffering is an expected outcome of the struggle against unjust structures. Those who resist should anticipate repression as they work for freedom. Many activists—not just privileged, white, US citizens—make heroic sacrifices in the struggle for peace and justice. As Copeland notes, suffering is a brute fact of human life, and as Cone argues, if we look to the cross of Jesus as a lynching tree, we can see sacrifice as part of the struggle for freedom against the powers of violence and death. But can the politics of sacrifice be rightly used in the service of effective political struggle? Can the exemplary dead be a moral resource by which living activists discern their call in their own place and time?

I believe the politics of sacrifice can be used without falling into the trap of valorizing suffering by universalizing the obligation to sacrifice regardless of one's state of life and subject position. Consonant with the overarching argument of this book, to make the right use of this politics requires a practical reason that balances the demands of faithfulness and effectiveness. In the final section of this chapter, I draw out the implications of this form of practical reasoning for the politics of sacrifice.

CONCLUSION: THE END OF SACRIFICE AND THE POSSIBILITY OF A POLITICS OF PENANCE AND REPAIR

The question "What would the six Jesuits who were massacred in El Salvador say today?" haunts the SOA Watch movement. In the question, the crucified and resurrected people speak by calling forth SOA Watch participants into faithful and effective political action. The shape of the question is messianic insofar as the crucified and resurrected people are speaking; it is in their persistent and disruptive *presencia* that heaven and earth are brought near. Their dangerous memories constantly invite the movement to reevaluate its actions. Have we been faithful to the legacy of the dead? Have we acted responsibly in relation to the living?

In this chapter, I have argued that the moral exemplarity of the dead teaches, motivates, and authorizes. In particular, through the dynamics of narrative synchronization, charismatic leaders draw on the moral authority of the exemplary dead to instantiate their own voices within the movement. While crucial for motivating movement involvement, this dynamic has a strong shadow side. Authoritarian tendencies, evidence of a messiah complex, lurk right below the surface. Such authoritarian charisma is especially evident when the gap that invites practical reasoning between the dead and the living collapses as leaders become the sole interpreters of the martyrs. Given this dynamic, it seems that messianism is the problem, not the solution.

I have argued throughout this book that the SOA Watch is a messianic movement. In particular, it is messianic in its insistence on the presence of the crucified people, an affirmation that lies at the heart of the *¡presente!* litany. Yet messianism has its liabilities, with a principal one being its association with leaders who claim explicitly or implicitly to be the Messiah. No such claims are explicitly made by the leaders of the SOA Watch, but there is a constant struggle regarding the role of charismatic leaders and their authority within the movement. As theologian James W. Perkinson rightly states, "The damnable real-life effects of this Western messianic complex—promising one or another version of universal salvation (whether spiritual or political or economic) and encoding an intractable presumption of supremacy—is all too evident in even a cursory survey of modern history."[73] He goes on to examine the presumptuous arrogance of imperial dominance animated by the impulses of salvation, from the "Doctrine of Discovery" and its justification of Christian domination of native peoples to the development regime that purports to save the unwashed, undeveloped masses. Perkinson invites us to unmask the soteriology, or the account of salvation, that animates these dynamics and, by extension, the soteriologies that fund even movements for progressive social change.

Attending to the messianic politics of the SOA Watch leads us to several questions: What is the account of salvation that animates this movement? Who is the actor, the Messiah, that brings about salvation? What are the means by which that salvation is achieved? One crass rendering of the soteriology of the movement seems to be that if we get enough people to suffer, we will win. If we pile up the sacrifices of prison time, fines, and probation high enough, then we can harness the magic of exemplars to bring about lasting, even eschatological change. This implicit soteriology is concerning both theologically and sociologically, as an account of God's action and as a theory of change.

Traditionally Christians have affirmed that Jesus is the Messiah and that the advent of Jesus brings an end to sacrifice. This is not to say that followers of Jesus will avoid hardships. Indeed, the Gospel of Mark remembers Jesus teaching his disciples: "If any want to become my followers, let them deny themselves and take up their cross and follow me. For those who want to save their life will lose it, and those who lose their life for my sake, and for the sake of the gospel, will save it."[74] Yet the economy of salvation is accomplished through the work of Jesus and requires no addition. If Jesus's act of salvation is sufficient, then no other sacrifices are needed to achieve salvation. In other words, Jesus—not leaders, not movements—saves.

This does not get us out of difficult problems regarding the relationship between God's salvific acts and human responses to in those acts. However, it relativizes human agency, placing it within the providence of divine agency. Jesus's inauguration of the end of sacrifice frees humans to a politics of penance and repair. Let me take each in turn.

Penance, the liturgical practice of confession and satisfaction of sins, operates within the economy of salvation. In the words of the catechism of the Catholic Church, penances "help configure us to Christ, who alone expiated our sins once for all."[75] Importantly, the acts of penance do not themselves expiate sin; rather, they orient the penitent to the Messiah, who alone expiates. In particular, for the white, North American activists who feel a compulsion to sacrifice to save themselves from their sins of complicity with the US–Latin American military system, this redirects the hope of what our activism might accomplish. Scandalously we might affirm that our sins have already been forgiven, that no further sacrifice is needed. And we might be freed, therefore, to acts of penance that do not accomplish that act of salvation but do respond to it. These acts of penance are "fruits worthy of repentance."[76] In this account, then, there is only one Messiah, only one act that satisfies for the forgiveness of sins. No action of the movement can finally roll back the sins of violence that have claimed the lives of thousands of Latin Americans. No action of the movement can raise the crucified. Yet, through acts of penance, we respond to the salvation that we could not produce.

But what are these acts of penance? This is the work of *repair*. Rather than a politics based on guilt, this is a politics based in relationships of accountability. To respond to the presence of the dead means to be in relationships of accountability with the living. SOA Watch activists cannot merely claim faithfulness to the legacy of the crucified people as justification for their actions. Their work of repair must proceed in accountability with those who continue to live under threat of the US–Latin American military system, on both sides of the hyphen/border. The evaluative question for acts of repair is not, Do they sacrifice enough and thereby bring the salvation we seek? The evaluative question should be, Do they keep faith with the relationships of accountability between movements north and south, and enable effective political change?

The messianism of the movement to close the SOA/WHINSEC and change US foreign policy in Latin America is ambiguous. While it can allow a messianic complex, I have argued that it need not and that it can be the grounds for a politics of penance and repair. In chapter 6, I probe more deeply the possibilities of a messianic political theology with martyr and theologian Ignacio Ellacuría. What, finally, do Christians mean when they make the creedal affirmation of a belief in and a hope for the resurrection of the body?

NOTES

1. The following story is based on unpublished field notes, April 26, 2016.

2. Aristotle, *Nicomachean Ethics*, sec. 4.5.

3. See Augustine, "Against Faustus," in O'Donovan and O'Donovan, *From Irenaeus to Grotius*, 118.

4. For each, see Brown, *Cult of the Saints*; Emerson, *Representative Men*; and Macklin, "Saints and Near-Saints," in Hopgood, *Making of Saints*.

5. As Peter Brown summarized in his *Cult of the Saints*, something peculiar and new emerged between the third and sixth centuries CE. Not only were the living to be emulated but also the dead were to be venerated, and in their veneration heaven and earth were brought near. See Brown, *Cult of the Saints*, 105.

6. In this sense, the exemplars are more similar to Ralph Waldo Emerson's "representative men," pointing beyond themselves and calling those who admire them to a higher greatness. See also Carlyle, *Works of Thomas Carlyle*.

7. Macklin, "Saints and Near-Saints," 2.

8. Esquivel, *Threatened with Resurrection*.

9. Interview with John Wright-Rios, Skype, November 10, 2015.

10. Interview with Chris Inserra, phone, October 7, 2015.

11. For the place of frames in social movement theory and religious ethics, see Snarr, "Waging Religious Ethics."

12. Bourgeois quoted in Nepstad, *Convictions of the Soul*, 111.

13. Notably, the biblical context of this quotation from Proverbs immediately raises concerns of paternalism and patriarchy in that the majority of the respective chapter commends a "capable wife." Also see Romero, *Voice of the Voiceless*, 138. For Spanish, see Romero, "Misión de la iglesia," para. 56.

14. Lenz OFM based his representation of Romero on the ubiquitous icon of Our Lady of Perpetual Help. Taking an icon that appears across the Roman and Eastern churches and resignifying the character is part of the iconographic method that generates admiration for the martyr-exemplars. For more, see Lenz, *Featured Icons*.

15. For a history of the latter, see Bell, "The End."

16. Interview with Nicole Tilson, phone, June 8, 2015.

17. Geglia, *Not Forgotten*.

18. "Not only do saints contest the practices and beliefs of institutions, but in a more subtle way they contest the order of narrativity itself. Their lives exhibit two types of negation: the negation of self and the lack of what is needful but absent in the life of the Other." Wyschogrod, *Saints and Postmodernism*, xxiii.

19. Unpublished field notes, November 22, 2015.

20. Wright and Stokan, "Remembering Maura."

21. Regarding "seeds of the church," see Tertullian, "Apology," in Kalantzis, *Caesar and the Lamb*, 114. Also, as Wright and Stokan wrote, "You remember the martyrs, and you remember the crucified peoples, and never let us forget our responsibility to challenge a world that institutionalizes violence and greed." See Wright and Stokan, "Remembering Maura."

22. Clemens, "Risking Arrest."

23. Interview with Steve Clemens, phone, October 5, 2015.

24. Zagzebski's aims are much more comprehensive than my own, as she seeks to construct a free-standing exemplarist moral theory. See Zagzebski, *Divine Motivation Theory*; and Zagzebski, "Moral Exemplars."

25. Regarding this connection, Zagzebski cites J. David Velleman, but René Girard's work on mimesis is pertinent here as well. See Velleman, "Motivation by Ideal," in Curren, *Philosophy of Education*. See also Girard, *Violence and the Sacred*.

26. Nepstad, *Convictions of the Soul*, 110.

27. Brown, "Saints as Exemplars," 6.

28. For more on "moral shock" in social movements, see Jasper and Poulsen, "Recruiting Strangers and Friends."

29. SOA Watch, "June 15."

30. Gynther, "Berta Cáceres, ¡Presente!"

31. Durkheim, *Elementary Forms*.

32. Collins, "Social Movements," in Goodwin, Jasper, and Polletta, *Passionate Politics*.

33. Part of this chapter is drawn from material previously published in a special issue of the *Journal of Religious Ethics*, copyright 2019, Wiley Periodicals Inc., focused on the ethics of exemplarity. See Lambelet, "Mourning the Dead." Although I read it after I had drafted this chapter, I have learned much from Vincent Lloyd's account in *In Defense of Charisma*, especially his useful distinction between authoritarian and democratic charisma.

34. Riesebrodt, "Charisma," 1.

35. As with other of Weber's ideal types, the suggestion is not that these three pure ideals adequately capture any one empirical case but rather that they are heuristics by which to understand the social phenomena of authority. Weber, of course, was quite mindful of this liability and remarked, "The usefulness of the above classification can only be judged by its results in promoting systematic analysis." And, later, "the idea that the whole of concrete historical reality can be exhausted in the conceptual scheme about to be developed is as far from the author's thoughts as anything could be." Weber, *Economy and Society*, 216. The interplay of the types is significant: we might view chapter 4's consideration of the place of the law as a struggle between the three different types of authority. My interest in this chapter, however, is Weber's third type, charismatic authority. Furthermore, we would be wise to interrogate whether any form of domination is rightly named "legitimate." Weber's much-critiqued, as well as maligned and misunderstood, advocacy of a value-free social science can mislead us on this point. In my account, authority, domination, and legitimacy are irreducibly value-laden concepts that require the tools of normative analysis. It is beyond the scope of this book to resolve the apparent contradictions in Weber's thought; I do not read him as excusing domination, although the terms of his analysis allow this interpretation.

36. Weber, 215.

37. Riesebrodt argues that these contradictory aspects—the exemplary developed more in Weber's political sociology and the magical in his sociology of religion—are not adequately systematized and are in the end problematic. I would argue, however, that Weber is more right than Riesebrodt allows and that the function of charisma and exemplarity in the SOA Watch bears this out. See Riesebrodt, "Charisma."

38. As Weber argued, "If his leadership fails to benefit his followers, it is likely that his charismatic authority will disappear." Weber, *Economy and Society*, 242.

39. Together these two aspects introduce an instability into the gap between the exemplary dead and the admiring living that demands practical reasoning. This instability can devolve into an authoritarian reduction of the gap, a problem that I treat further in this chapter.

40. Sohm, *Kirchenrecht*.

41. For a critique of these more general worries as they shape sociological discourse and a call for greater epistemic reflexivity that acknowledges the co-construction of the concepts of sociology and religion, see Vásquez, "Grappling," in Bender et al., *Religion on the Edge*.

42. Smith, "Faith, Reason, and Charisma"; and Joosse, "Becoming a God."

43. Haley, "Rudolph Sohm on Charisma."

44. Bourgeois, *My Journey*, 5.

45. Bourgeois, *Father Roy Bourgeois*.

46. Bourgeois.

47. Interview with Roy Bourgeois, phone, October 21, 2015.

48. SOA Watch, *Speaking Truth to Power*, 7–8.

49. It should be no surprise, therefore, that the foreword is penned by Catholic actor and celebrity Martin Sheen.

50. Thus, the appropriately chosen subtitle for their work is *The Story of Roy Bourgeois and the Movement to Close the School of the Americas.*

51. Knapke, *Voices for the Voiceless*, 21.

52. Knapke, 34.

53. Hodge and Cooper, *Disturbing the Peace*, 197.

54. Unpublished field notes, April 26, 2016.

55. Interview with Lisa Sullivan, phone, May 30, 2016.

56. Lamb, *Voices of Courage*, 20.

57. Lamb, 15.

58. Dear, *Jean Donovan*.

59. Dear.

60. Freeman, "Tyranny of Structurelessness."

61. "May this Body immolated and this Blood sacrificed for humanity, feed us also in order to give our body and our blood over to suffering and pain, like Christ's, not for its own sake, but in order to give concepts of [bringing about] justice and peace for our people." See Romero, "La última homilía." See also Lamb, *Voices of Courage*, iii.

62. To use the language of peace studies scholarship, the Christological valorization of suffering operates as a form of cultural violence that renders the suffering of marginalized persons natural, invisible, and justified. See Galtung, "Cultural Violence."

63. Williams is clear eyed about the power of social pressures and does not see emancipation as freedom from softer forms of coercion. However, there is a categorical difference between pre- and postbellum realities.

64. For these three models in digest, see Aulén, *Christus Victor*.

65. Williams, "Black Women's Surrogacy," in Cooey, Eakin, and McDaniel, *After Patriarchy*, 9.

66. Williams, 9.

67. Williams, 13.

68. See, for one of many possible examples, Theodore W. Jennings's recent analysis of atonement in *Transforming Atonement*, chap. 10.

69. Grant, *White Women's Christ*; Copeland, "Wading through Many Sorrows," in Townes, *Troubling in My Soul*; and Terrell, "Our Mothers' Gardens," in Trelstad, *Cross Examinations*.

70. Cone, *Cross and the Lynching Tree*, 151.

71. Copeland, "Wading through Many Sorrows," 124.

72. Historian and activist Clare Land tracks these same desires to help and the latent paternalism of the motivation among nonindigenous solidarity activists in Australia. See Land, *Decolonizing Solidarity*.

73. Perkinson, *Messianism against Christology*, xxviii.

74. Mark 8:34b–35 NRSV.

75. Catholic Church, *Catechism of the Catholic Church*, para. 1460.

76. Matthew 3:8 NRSV.

6

CONCLUSION
The Presence of the Crucified People

Checking email after lunch I noticed a new message in my SOA Watch folder. The subject line read: "Moving the 2016 November Vigil to the Border?"[1] In the message, SOA Watch staff organizer María Luisa Rosal invited feedback on a proposal that organizers had first floated at the spring strategy session held the previous April. "SOA Watch has always been a movement organization," Rosal wrote. "For this possible move to the border to be a success, we need everyone's input, energy and creativity. What do you think about the idea? Would you be interested in being part of a mobilization to the border in November 2016?" Rosal directed movement participants to an online forum to express their views on the possible move.

I had heard rumors of this potential change but hadn't been privy to the internal deliberations about moving the location of the SOA Watch's annual mobilization. Having just begun drafting some of my research analysis, this request for public deliberation couldn't have come at a more perfect time. I watched with interest as SOA Watch participants from across the globe weighed in on this central question about the life of the movement.

Reading through the comments, I saw each of the dilemmas represented in my research come up. Would the ¡presente! litany continue to play a role in the formation of the movement? How would the plural movement coalition respond to this significant change in focus? What place would civil disobedience play, and what kind of responsibilities does the movement have to continue to honor the sacrifices of those who spent time in jail? What would the martyrs call us to do today?

SOA Watch cofounder Roy Bourgeois stated simply, "The collective wisdom is moving us to respond to today's realities."[2] Without taking a definitive stand on the question at hand, he implicitly supported the move, saying, "We are called to express our solidarity with the injustices taking place on the border and the US militarization that is causing so many deaths across Latin America and causing so many of our brothers and sisters to flee to the United States."

Other participants weighed in, raising concerns about the logistics of travel and location. "I guess I want to know where on the border," stated Cally Golding. Sonia Silbert suggested that "it would be harder for people from DC to go, so we're less likely to organize a van . . . but I assume it would be much more accessible for people living in other parts of the country." Some wondered whether it would be possible to hold two vigils—one on the border and one at Fort Benning. "Cannot SOA Watch take on two issues?" asked Rael Nidess. "Continue the vigil at Ft. Benning with the 'Presente' demonstration for the victims of the SOA and hold a separate vigil, perhaps in coordination with other refugee justice organizations, . . . using the 'Presente' crosses for the victims of the border war."

While some advocated a two-site strategy, Francois Guillot argued against moving to the border at all, saying, "I understand the reasoning behind it and how the issues are related, but I think the movement should focus on the SOA, and the vigil should take place at Ft. Benning." He continued, "There are plenty of immigrant advocates and that topic is largely discussed in the media and elsewhere. . . . Moving the vigil to the border will dilute discussions and blur the focus."

This critique was voiced by a number of commenters. They felt by shifting to the border, the SOA Watch would lose its historic and unique focus on the SOA/WHINSEC. Caroline Besse Webster also advocated remaining at Fort Benning, saying, "The sacrifice made by our SOAW Prisoners of Conscience must not be forgotten."

One of the strongest voices of resistance to the change came from Chapter 27 president Dave Logsdon of Veterans for Peace. He stated,

> *To relinquish the beachhead we have at the gates of Ft. Benning, while it may sound exciting, would be a huge mistake in so many ways. This powerful two day transformative event in Columbus is an absolute gift to progressive action. The gathering of tribes, the Presente Procession, our veterans march on Sunday, this would be impossible to recreate anywhere! We have been sending a bus every year from Minnesota filled with a diverse group of people of all ages. This trip has been the beginning of many a peace activist. I know change has tremendous appeal, but you should weigh carefully this decision.*

Drawing on military metaphors, Logsdon worried that by relocating the battle, the movement would cede the war to the SOA/WHINSEC. While not categorically opposed, he strongly encouraged caution.

Yet reading through the scores of comments, a consensus in support of the move began to emerge. In particular, participants stated repeatedly that a move to the border reflected the recent developments of the movement to become "more diverse," to include young people of color as leaders, and to expand the issues of concern included in the movement. Former staff member Nico Udu-Gama stated, "It's time for the SOA Watch movement to join the efforts of many groups and people to address the immigration issue. Our analysis of US intervention in Latin America and beyond is important to understanding why people are forced to migrate. . . . Our movement is becoming more diverse, as well; we're seeing more young people of color standing at the gates and taking space within the movement." Longtime SOA Watch Labor Caucus member Jerry King stated, "Expanding our message in a border mobilization is only a natural progression."

Whether cautious or enthusiastic about the change, all seemed to agree that the ¡presente! litany would continue to be a part of whatever action they took. Ana Maria Vasquez, for example, suggested that the anniversary of the death of José Antonio Elena Rodriguez, who was shot by US Border Patrol agents while walking on the Mexican side in Nogales, might be an appropriate occasion for the gathering. The claim presente would thus be expanded to include victims of the low-intensity border war. The presence of the litany, however, didn't resolve the question of what other tactics might be used. Tawana Petty and Nico Udu-Gama emphasized that any action would need to be done in respectful coordination with directly impacted folks on the border. Paula Miller, a Catholic Worker living in Tucson, proposed a number of such partnerships and suggested that Nogales could be a site that would allow a number of tactics of resistance.

Prisoner of conscience Liz Deligio made a strong case for the move to the border by placing it in the context of the twenty-five-year history of the movement.[3] She began by calling on the martyrs and stating, "For 25 years the SOA Watch Movement has been on a journey, a journey to live into the radical hope that marked the lives of 14 year old Celina Ramos, her mother Elba, and Jesuit priest dissidents Ignacio Ellacuría, S.J., Ignacio Martín-Baró, S.J., Segundo Montes, S.J., Juan Ramón Moreno, S.J., Joaquín López y López, S.J., [and] Amando López, S.J."

Deligio continued,

> *We have seen that the infamous SOA is not just a building; it is not just a policy. The School is a mindset with roots as old as the colonization of the Americas. It is the belief that land, resources and human rights are commodities that can be bought, stolen and destroyed. In that mindset there are no ancestors, no memory, and*

no imagination. Inside that set of beliefs Celina, Elba and the six Jesuits were dangerous enough to assassinate but not human enough to have a right to live.

The SOA, according to Deligio, is not a building but an ideational system and structure of empire. For Deligio, as for others, the question remains, How can we do the impossible—namely, disrupt and transform the US–Latin American military system?

As [a] social movement organization with roots on both sides of the border, we have come to see that we too must be able to move. That we too must follow the SOA as it devastates, controls and forcibly disappears. For we carry the ancestors, the memory and the imagination as antidote to empire in our voices, our songs, our direct action, our legislation, our Vigil, our Puppetistas and our hearts.

Over the past 25 years, the SOA Watch movement has grown and evolved from a handful of people who gathered at the gates of Fort Benning, to a hemisphere wide movement. Thousands have been educated and mobilized to take a stand against empire and militarization, and against all that the SOA represents. New activists are joining long-term SOA Watch members, including many youth and students from multinational and working-class communities. Together, we can bring the antidote of the Vigil, the challenge to the SOA, to a new place.

† † †

In October 2016, the SOA Watch did, in fact, move its annual vigil to the US–Mexico border in Nogales (Arizona and Sonora). The activists' comments included here are but snippets from the long and difficult deliberation about the strategy and direction of the movement. This was practical reasoning in action. How can the movement remain faithful to Celina, Elba, Ignacio, Segundo, Juan, Joaquín, Ignacio, and Amando, among so many others, while responding to today's demands for effective political action? This was practical reasoning under a messianic sign.

For some in the SOA Watch, faithfulness demanded that the movement stay and remain committed to the politics of memory at Fort Benning. For others, effectiveness required a move that rejected a ritualized memorialization of the past and instead allowed engagement with the living. Both accounts of what the movement should do are framed by the impossibility of the task of disrupting and transforming the US–Latin American military system. Yet the obligation to tackle the impossible task is rooted in an equally impossible hope that the dead are present. A prospective imagination would

suggest that the path of mere faithfulness would likely lead to further dwin-
dling numbers and ultimately an expressive, but ineffectual, action maintained by a few die-hard activists, while the path of mere effectiveness might
terminate in an apathy of historical amnesia, resulting in a resignation to the
power of the military system. History, and the enduring presence of the dead
in history, will ultimately judge the wisdom of this move. Social movements
grow and decline, and the move to the border—a risk for the SOA Watch—
will surely mark a new chapter in this movement's life cycle. Rejecting a politics of mere faithfulness or effectiveness, I interpret the move to the border as
a productive coordination of the tensions between faithfulness and effectiveness. Faithfulness to the resurrected presence of the dead requires responsiveness to the demands of the living, a responsiveness that issues forth into
effective political action.

   This is, of course, the thesis of this book. A messianic political theology of
the crucified and resurrected people generates practical reasoning that
engages the dialectic between faithfulness and effectiveness. Though messianism and practical reason are often seen as opposing forces—messianism
tempting an antinomian rejection of practical reason, practical reason
rejecting the extremism and urgency of messianism—I have shown how the
¡presente! liturgy serves as a mediating force. The messianic affirmation of
the presence of the dead in the ¡presente! litany generates the need for practical reasoning about the obligations performed in the liturgical protest.
While the liturgical protest generates obligations of solidarity, it underdetermines the political actions that follow. Thus, the need for practical reason
remains, even as the development of that practical reason, which balances
demands of faithfulness and effectiveness, is fundamentally conditioned by
the messianism of the liturgy. Messianism, liturgy, and practical reason are
inextricably bound in the political theology that I have developed through
engagement with the SOA Watch.

   As I set out in chapter 1, developing this political theology has required
three heuristically separable but overlapping tasks: description, evaluation,
and construction. I call these tasks heuristically separable but overlapping
because any description has already been selected and framed with evaluative and constructive aims in mind. And in this work, I have curated ethnographic vignettes, historical materials, and interviews in such a way that
they develop the constructive account that I wish to make. Admitting this is
not to say that I have arranged them unreflexively; rather, through critical
juxtaposition I have hosted a conversation between a representation of the
material dynamics of SOA Watch activism and the theoretical resources
of multiple academic discourses, particularly political theology and strategic nonviolence. While my informants may not finally agree with each of
my evaluative and constructive conclusions, I hope that they will at least

recognize in my descriptions an accurate representation of themselves and their movement.

Constructively, I have argued that we should understand the *¡presente!* litany as a creedal affirmation of a hope for and belief in the resurrection. What this means has remained admittedly oracular across the book, in part because there is not a consensus about the meaning of the affirmation that the dead are presente among movement participants. What I mean by it, and what I think each chapter attests to in different ways, is that the dead are already agents in our political processes acting on, against, and through us. Whether binding us in obligations of solidarity, compelling us as a higher law to acts of transgression, or inspiring us through their examples of sacrifice, the dead refuse to stay dead. But, recalling Augustine's question, how are the dead "able to do such great things?"[4] The dead are agents not as resuscitated bodies but in the peculiar sense that Jesus the Messiah is the first fruit of the resurrection and by God's action has broken the power of death. This is the action of God irrupting in history. The dead are not mere ghosts or memories. The crucified and resurrected people are presente. And as such, the agency of the dead is wholly attributable to the agency of the God of resurrection. I join with creedal Christians to affirm that I believe in the resurrection of the body, and that belief radically orients the way we ought to practice politics.

Yet insofar as the dead are already agents, they are also not yet resurrected. The performance and invocation of the presence of the dead through the *¡presente!* litany does not enact resurrection. The powers of death built into the legalized violence of the US–Latin American military system appear to retain their hold on the lives of Latin American peoples. The military training at the SOA/WHINSEC continues apace and has spread to other sites well beyond Fort Benning. Repression in the Southern Hemisphere and xenophobic fears of immigrants in the Northern Hemisphere have stoked new calls for "border security," which means death for those making the harrowing trip across the US-Mexico border. Death still exercises its sting. We live in between the times of the already and the not yet. The cry presente is both an affirmation and a denouncement, a hope and a lament.

Here, I push the constructive task of this research further by dwelling with the messianic political theology of Ignacio Ellacuría, one of the six Jesuits whose assassination in 1989 gave rise to the SOA Watch movement. By doing so, I take seriously SOA Watch activists' question, What would the Jesuits do? In particular, I ask, What did Ellacuría do? And what might he do today?

Ellacuría was the president of the Universidad Centroamericana who gave his life with and on behalf of the Salvadoran poor. He shaped the university to be an institution in service of the poor and advocated for a peaceful settlement of the civil war. The Atlacatl Battalion, trained at the School of the Americas, sought to neutralize Ellacuría as a political force through assassination. It is, thus, worth tarrying in this final chapter with Ellacuría's liberation theology and its significance for the themes of this book.

THE MESSIANIC POLITICAL THEOLOGY
OF IGNACIO ELLACURÍA

Ellacuría's work begins and ends with the historical reality of the poor in El Salvador. Importantly, as with some of the SOA Watch activists who invoke his presence, he was not one of the poor. Though rightly identified as a martyr of El Salvador, Ellacuría was born in the Basque region of Spain in 1930. Entering Jesuit formation at seventeen years old, Ellacuría was educated in Ecuador, Austria, and Spain and was influenced especially by Karl Rahner, the German Jesuit theologian, and Xavier Zubiri, the Basque philosopher.[5] With Rahner, Ellacuría's education in the decade prior to the Second Vatican Council led him to encounter theology that acknowledged "God in all things" and rejected a strong distinction between natural and supernatural orders. With Zubiri, Ellacuría focused on *reality*, rather than being or essence, as the proper object of philosophy. Combining these two formidable figures with his emerging work in El Salvador, the young priest and scholar began to develop a liberationist philosophy that was rooted in the relationship between history and salvation, or what he termed *historical soteriology*.

The relationship between salvation and history was the dominant question animating Ellacuría's scholarship. His book *Teología política* (literally *Political Theology* but retitled *Freedom Made Flesh* when published in English) centered on the thesis that "salvation history is a salvation in history."[6] Like SOA Watch activists after him, Ellacuría rejected ahistorical spiritualizations of salvation. Rooted primarily in the doctrines of the incarnation and Trinity, he instead argued that history was the "fullest location of reality and salvation."[7] For this affirmation, Ellacuría and other liberationists were targeted by Cardinal Joseph Ratzinger, the prefect of the Congregation for the Doctrine of the Faith who later became Pope Benedict XVI. Ratzinger charged that such ideas were forms of "historicist immanentism" that conflated the reign of God with the history of class struggle.[8]

Ellacuría's response was direct and forceful. First, he argued that history, not politics, is the location of salvation. While salvation does have political implications, he claimed, the sphere of politics does not capture the fullness of integral liberation. History is itself metaphysically dense, and it is in history that God and humans "intervene conjointly" to do the work of liberation.[9] Next, Ellacuría affirmed that history is the location of salvation because God has elected for it to be so: "God has self-revealed in history."[10] The story of Israel, of the church, and of Jesus Christ are histories of God's work in history. In particular, the life, death, and resurrection of Jesus is the ultimate sign of God's historical presence. God chose to reveal God's self through this incarnation, and it is the sign through which humanity gains access to the grace of liberation. Finally, Ellacuría contended that because the triune God has chosen to incarnate Godself in history through Jesus Christ, we too should look for God's gracious activity in history in our time. The Word is made flesh in history through Jesus Christ, and Jesus Christ is made incarnate among the poor, the crucified people.

Ellacuría's historical soteriology was rooted in a trinitarian affirmation of the incarnation. The incarnation therefore grounds the messianism of his political theology. Reading Jesus in his historical context, one of Roman occupation, lent a mode of apprehending the political distinctiveness of Jesus's life, death, and resurrection. Ellacuría argued that Jesus's mission was political but was not captured by the politics of violence and oppression of his context. This ambiguity thus characterized Jesus's messianism; his reign is not of this world.[11] Yet Jesus was tempted by false messianisms of violence and triumph throughout his life and at times was justly confused for a zealot.[12] Jesus's reign, though remaining political, transcended violence even as it refused a privatized, depoliticized quietism. Ellacuría maintained, "If we see the temptation to false messianism as the key temptation in Jesus' life, we will be able to get a clear view of the political character of his mission and of the precise character of his own messianism—a messianism quite distinct and different from other messianism of the past and present."[13] Recalling the messianic temptations that I put forward in chapter 1 and have developed throughout this book, according to Ellacuría, Jesus's messianism rejected the options of depoliticized quietism and violent enactment. But what was positively distinctive about the messianism that Jesus offered?

Ellacuría answered this question from his context of working in the Salvadoran crucible of increasing military repression and outright civil war. In arguably his most famous essay, "The Crucified People: An Essay in Historical Soteriology," Ellacuría identified the crucified people as the principle of historical salvation. By *crucified people*, he meant "that collective body that, being the majority of humanity, owes its situation of crucifixion to a social order organized and maintained by a minority that exercises its dominion through a series of factors, which, taken together and given their concrete impact within history, must be regarded as sin."[14] Writing in the wake of the assassination of his Jesuit colleague Rutilio Grande in March 1977, one of 1,063 people arrested and 147 murdered by security forces that year, Ellacuría had in mind the suffering people of El Salvador. The crucified people in his own Salvadoran context were oppressed through a five-hundred-year history of exploitation specified in "the violence of the civilization of capital, which keeps the immense majority of humanity in absolutely inhuman bio-logical, cultural, social, and political conditions."[15] However, we must take into account not only this long colonial history but also the legalized violence of the US–Latin American military system—a system supported integrally by the SOA/WHINSEC—that was crucifying the people of El Salvador and others across Latin America.

Through reference to Second Isaiah's suffering servant, Ellacuría contended that the crucified people are the principle of salvation for the entire world, a recapitulation of Jesus's messianic incarnation. The steps of Ellacuría's reasoning are worth rehearsing briefly. First, he extended his call for historicizing theology by rejecting sacrifice as a metaphysical necessity. In an argument that resonates with the account of sacrifice offered in chapter 5, he instead read Jesus in his own historical context. By relating Jesus's context to that of suffering today, Ellacuría claimed that Jesus's crucifixion was a "historical" necessity—not a metaphysical one—and the result of the sin of structural violence. Establishing this connection between the crucified God and the crucified people, he then moved to a historical exegesis of the suffering servant, drawing a line of continuity between Second Isaiah, Jesus, and the crucified people as a class. Ellacuría concluded by arguing that by their identification with Jesus, the crucified people are thus revealed as a site of God's salvation. In their death they proclaim judgment; in their resurrection they enable liberation. Thus, the crucified people not only reveal sin but also are bearers of salvation in their resurrection. With Ellacuría, we might say that the crucified people are presente.

What would it mean to make this affirmation that the crucified people are presente? In his short essay, Ellacuría only gestures to the hope of resurrection. Still, it is fair to say that resurrection was a constant, but unsystematically treated, feature of Ellacuría's work. For Ellacuría, the promise of resurrection enabled the struggle for justice. In an essay written just two years before his assassination (and cited in the epigraph to this book), Ellacuría argued, "The security of the resurrection does not take away the desire to struggle but strengthens it. As a follower of Jesus, one tries to do this out of hope."[16] Ellacuría developed in his writings and his life a politics that was "threatened with resurrection."[17]

Maybe it was only after his assassination that the full implications of resurrection could come to flourish in Ellacuría's corpus. Thus, in the wake of Ellacuría's own martyrdom, his colleague at the UCA Jon Sobrino more fully developed a theology of resurrection, first in his own essay "The Crucified Peoples" and later in the second volume of his Christology, *La fe en Jesucristo: Ensayo desde las víctimas* (*Christ the Liberator: A View from the Victims*). Like Ellacuría, Sobrino claims that the crucified people bear both the light of judgment and the grace of salvation. The light of judgment is twofold, both unveiling the ideologies that justify the death and dehumanization of the crucified people and dispelling the darkness through the "light of utopia."[18] But not only this; Sobrino also identifies the crucified people as signs of salvation. In verifying salvation historically, Sobrino argues that "above all, the crucified peoples offer values that are not offered elsewhere."[19] These values have a humanizing potential by offering hope, gratuitous forgiveness, solidarity, and faith.

Though incipient in his essay, Sobrino brings this theology of the resurrection to much fuller expression in *Christ the Liberator*. The entire first part of his study treats the resurrection of Jesus from the perspective of the "victims." While Sobrino's powerful text deserves extended analysis beyond the scope of this book, here I merely wish to name the way his contributions illuminate Ellacuría's messiansim. First, the resurrection is not merely "the return of a dead body to everyday life . . . but the action of God by which the eschatological irrupts into history."[20] The resurrection is not due to the immortality of the soul or mere memory. Rather, the resurrection is the action of God in history. This hope for God's action is given first of all to the crucified in history.[21] Like Ellacuría, Sobrino insists that salvation must be historicized, and resurrection, as an integral part of God's work of redemption, must also be made historical. What would this mean? Sobrino argues these historicizations of the resurrection are partial signs that point toward a final fulfillment.[22] "Partial 'resurrections' in history are clearly not the final resurrection, but they generate hope in its being possible—and help us to understand it."[23] Such language runs the risk of aiding a standard narrative of progress in which we build the reign of God, we resurrect the dead. But if we take seriously the reality and finality of the death of these crucified people, no such progressive hope is possible. Instead, we hope in the action of God that irrupts in history, an action that we cannot produce but to which we can respond. Thus, Sobrino argues that the "praxis needed in the present [is] taking the crucified people down from the cross."[24] In this way, we respond to God's work of resurrection. "Understanding today that Jesus has been raised by God entails the hope that we can be *raised*, but it follows from what has been said that we also have to be, in some way, *raisers*."[25] To claim that the crucified people are presente is to claim both that they serve as a messianic sign of hope and that we have something at stake in taking them down from their crosses.

So, finally, how do we respond as raisers in God's work of resurrection? There is no simple answer to this question, but this was Ellacuría's life's work, not only as a scholar but also as an administrator, a priest, a Jesuit, a citizen, and a human. To answer the question required him to delve deeply into the work of discernment. For Ellacuría this work was informed by his practice of the Spiritual Exercises of Saint Ignatius, a standard part of Jesuit formation that served as a special feature of Ellacuría's conversion to the poor in El Salvador.[26] Participating in God's resurrection meant being converted to and by the poor and taking down the crucified from their crosses. This is no mere paternalism. Ellacuría shaped a university that built a holistic approach to thinking, researching, and acting to dismantle structures of violence and death that plague the poor. Furthermore, Ellacuría's conversion to the poor was a response to his own searching for God's salvific presence. "Christ is in the poor," he proclaimed. "It is not us who have to save the poor, but rather it is the poor who are going to save us."[27] Ellacuría lived out his own call to participate in this resurrection through his effective love of the poor. He argued, "There is a Jesus-project that neither reduces Jesus to a project nor concretizes into a single particular project, but has definite and operative norms: that which favors, and integrally favors, the poor, the poor as a people. It seeks to struggle and overcome all forms of domination and injustice, according to the spirit and letter of the beatitudes—all of this from personal and efficacious love."[28] Identifying how to participate in God's work of resurrection requires discernment. To connect Ellacuría's writings to the language of this book, discerning the obligations that flow from the presence of the resurrected among us leads into a practical reasoning that engages both effectiveness and faithfulness.

PRACTICAL REASON UNDER A MESSIANIC SIGN

Those who would invoke the resurrected presence of the dead, especially using Ellacuría's and Sobrino's language of "taking the crucified people down from the cross," employ a distinctive mode of practical reasoning. This is an anamnestic politics, one that is rooted in dangerous memories.[29] These memories of the crucified burst the malaise of technocratic time, which would sacrifice the poor on the altar of progress. But this is not only a politics of memory; it is also a politics of resistance that participates in the resurrection life of the triune God. The cry presente enables practical reasoning under a messianic sign. The presence of the crucified and resurrected people shapes practical reasoning in at least three ways: they judge our pretensions, they animate our hopes for resurrection, and they invoke God's action even as they call us to respond to it.

First, the presence of the crucified and resurrected people can interrupt, challenge, and judge the myths of developmental progress that we tell ourselves in our late modern milieu in which politics is more and more trusted to the technocrats and statisticians. Such myths sap the energy of political action. If progress is inevitable, then why act? Moreover, the dead tell the lie on the myth of capitalist development itself, revealing not progress but an ever-rising pile of dead bodies.[30] The haunting presence of the dead judges our political arrangements, showing them for the legalized violence that they are. As Ellacuría noted on the Latin American quincentenary, it is true today:

> The powerful nations of today say they are coming to the third world to make us "democratic." But their "generous proposals" conceal a very different political and economic project. To discover and unmask the real truth of that project, we do not need to look inside the borders of the dominant Western nations, but rather outside their borders—to the places that manifest the underlying effects of that Western project and its purposes, of which the primary representative and bearer is the United States.[31]

The presence of the dead not only sheds light on the pretensions of empire but also judges our constructive interventions, such as the SOA Watch movement, ever calling us to more faithful, more effective action. This does not undermine the possibility of remunerative and piecemeal political action. Far from it. Rather, the presence of the dead in our politics refuses any final arrangement that would seek to conceal the suffering wrought by our policies. For Ellacuría, it was the crucified people who interrupted and judged our pretensions. It is not enough for the dead to be merely remembered, as though memory is a purely cognitive process. Instead, the dead must be remembered, or put back together, such that they continue acting as agents in our political processes. For a movement such as the SOA Watch, this awareness requires ongoing discernment and deliberation. Whether to include a wider group of diverse newcomers, to expand focus to immigration, to move the annual gathering to the border, or to give thanks and turn attention elsewhere were all active considerations for movement participants. The resurrected presence of the crucified keeps us engaging the dialectic of faithfulness and effectiveness, refusing its collapse on one side or the other.

Second, the disruptive presence of the dead allows us to cultivate hopes that exceed the immanent nexus of material causation. This is, in part, what the ¡presente! litany accomplishes. It performs a remembrance of the dead, and it anamnestically re-presents the dead by calling on God to raise them up. But the liturgical protest is an act of hope, not of fulfillment. In an important sense, the dead were not raised at the gates of Fort Benning. The ¡presente! litany did not provide a fulfillment of messianic hope. Yet neither was the litany a mere reminder of the fulfillment. In the liturgical protest, messianic hope and fulfillment were inseparably related in a relation of analogy but not identity. The performance of the creedal affirmation of a belief in the resurrection of the dead and hope for the resurrection of the body invokes God's action and is the first fruit of that action. As I have argued throughout this book, the litany is but one step, and by no means the last. The *¡presente!* litany opens participants to discern a whole host of political actions that flow from it. None of these actions finally fulfill the hope for resurrection—only God can do that—but they are expressions of a hope in God's actions.

Third, the presence of the crucified and resurrected people in our politics reminds us that it is not, finally, all up to us. Because we cannot resurrect the dead, we invoke the action of the crucified God who is for the crucified people. This invocation does not mean we throw up our hands, as though because we cannot raise the dead we cannot act at all. Rather, this invocation acts in the hope that we might participate in God's promised action, both already and not yet. The SOA Watch is not bringing God's reign. But because the reign of God has come near, we are freed to participate in it. We are thereby made messengers of the Good News of God's coming justice and peace. Such a politics requires a cooperative rather than a competitive account of the relation of divine and human agency.[32] And, therefore, it requires a practical reasoning that persists in discerning effective, faithful political performance. As such, God's resurrection action is the very ground of the possibility of political action.

Practical reasoning under a messianic sign generates a politics of "radical hope." A messianic political theology need not devolve into violent enactment or apathetic resignation, but, rather, recalling Liz Deligio's earlier comments, by carrying "the ancestors, the memory and the imagination," such a theology and praxis can offer an "antidote to empire." Enacting such a politics requires discernment as it is not immediately clear what the resurrected presence of the crucified people demands from us. Thus, a move to the border after twenty-five years at the gates of Fort Benning might be the call for this time and place. However, the messianic sign reminds us that we are not the only ones active in history. The dead are being raised, and our action is but a creative participation in the resurrecting action of God.

A POLITICS THREATENED WITH RESURRECTION

How would a politics threatened with resurrection look in the face of an impossibly intractable system of legalized violence? How can we sustain creative energy and commitment to nonviolent, responsible solidarity in the face of such a system? This book has attempted to answer these questions by both celebrating and critiquing the twenty-five-year vigil of the SOA Watch at the gates of Fort Benning.

One symbol the SOA Watch used in its movement propaganda is a blue rose. Designed by graphic artist César Maxit, the blue rose was intended to represent the unattainable. Displayed under a banner reading "Memoria y Resistancia" (memory and resistance), Maxit explained that the rose evoked "memory of the victims and resistance to militarism and empire." He continued,

> Both goals seem impossible. Too many victims, too powerful a military complex. I had crossed the line onto ft Benning about 15 years ago, and that year we planted corn on the base. I heard a rose bush was used to commemorate the original soaw martyrs, so i decided to use blue corn and blue roses to represent those 2 ideas. I had read that because blue roses don't appear in nature, it is sometimes used as a symbol in literature. . . . having a blue rose is reaching the unattainable . . . having that which was thought impossible.[33]

The blue rose represents the impossible hope that the US–Latin American military system will come to an end, that the crucified people will be raised, and that in place of empire and exploitation will emerge relationships of peace with justice. The presence of the crucified and resurrected people may call us to the border and beyond. Although movements such as the SOA Watch will rise and fall, the presence of these dead will continue to challenge those who remember to persist in lament and resurrection hope. The persistence of such hopes requires a willingness to discern constantly the call of faithfully effective political action in this historical moment. Cultivating such impossible hopes of memoria y resistancia is the gift and work of those threatened with resurrection.

NOTES

1. SOA Watch, "Moving 2016 November Vigil?"
2. This and following quotations were gathered from SOA Watch, "Moving 2016 November Vigil?"
3. For more about Deligio's history in the SOA Watch movement, see Fleischer, "Too Cruel for School."
4. Augustine, *City of God*, bk. 22, chap. 9.
5. Michael Lee's helpful introduction to Ellacuría's work emphasizes these two formative influences. See Lee, "Ignacio Ellacuría," in *Ignacio Ellacuría*.
6. Ellacuría, *Freedom Made Flesh*, 15.
7. Ellacuría, "Christian Challenge," in *Ignacio Ellacuría*, 125.
8. Ratzinger, "Instruction," sec. IX.
9. Ellacuría, "On Liberation," in *Ignacio Ellacuría*, 44.
10. Ellacuría, "Christian Challenge," 126.
11. John 18:36.

12. Ellacuría, *Freedom Made Flesh*, 60.

13. Ellacuría, 56.

14. Ellacuría, "Crucified People," 208.

15. Ellacuría, "Latin American Quincentenary," 35–36.

16. Ellacuría, "Christian Challenge," 131.

17. Esquivel, "They Have Threatened Us."

18. Sobrino, "Crucified Peoples," in *Principle of Mercy*, 55.

19. Sobrino, 55.

20. Sobrino, *Christ the Liberator*.

21. Sobrino, 43.

22. It is critical to note Sobrino's care in arguing that history can provide us with partial, analogous signs of resurrection, but these manifestations do not complete or replace the eschatological significance of God's action. Sobrino is here repeating a point he made consistently in the first volume of his Christology, where he argued that liberating actions are signs of the reign of God but not of its fullness. See Sobrino, *Jesus the Liberator*.

23. Sobrino, *Christ the Liberator*, 49.

24. Sobrino, 47.

25. Sobrino, *Principle of Mercy*, 47.

26. Lassalle-Klein, *Blood and Ink*, 36–52.

27. Cited in Lassalle-Klein, 342.

28. Ellacuría, "Christian Challenge," 130.

29. Metz, *Faith in History*, chap. 5.

30. I have in mind the image evoked by Walter Benjamin in his ninth thesis on the philosophy of history in which the angel of history "sees one single catastrophe which keeps piling wreckage upon wreckage and hurls it in front of his feet." Benjamin, "On the Concept of History," 392.

31. Ellacuría, "Latin American Quincentenary," 30.

32. Tanner, *God and Creation*; and Sobrino, *Christ the Liberator*.

33. Maxit, personal correspondence.

BIBLIOGRAPHY

PRIMARY SOURCES

AFL-CIO Executive Council. "Closing the School of the Americas." AFL-CIO America's Unions, August 4, 1999. https://aflcio.org/about/leadership/statements/closing-school-americas.

Allende, Isabel. "Isabel Allende on 'Maya's Notebook,' Drug Addiction, 1973 Chilean Coup & Death of Poet Pablo Neruda." Interview by Amy Goodman. *Democracy Now!* New York, April 30, 2013. https://www.democracynow.org/2013/4/30/isabel_allende_on_mayas_notebook_drug.

Alterna. "Our Mission." http://web.archive.org/web/20160810081652/http://www.alternacommunity.com/.

Amnesty International. "Unmatched Power, Unmet Principles: The Human Rights Dimensions of US Training of Foreign Military and Police Forces." New York: Amnesty International USA Publications, 2002. http://www.amnestyusa.org/pdfs/msp.pdf.

Anonymous clergy SOA Watch participant. Interview. Phone, October 5, 2014.

Anonymous death penalty attorney. Interview. Phone, September 25, 2015.

Anonymous former Jesuit volunteer. Interview. Notre Dame, IN, November 4, 2014.

Anonymous SOA Watch staff member A. Interview. Phone, June 16, 2015.

Anonymous SOA Watch staff member B. Interview. Phone, September 8, 2015.

Anonymous SOA Watch volunteer. Interview. October 16, 2015.

Beisswenger, Donald F. *Locked Up: Letters and Papers of a Prisoner of Conscience.* Nashville: Upper Room Books, 2007.

Bourgeois, Roy. Interview. Phone, October 21, 2015.

———. *Interview with Father Roy Bourgeois, Founder of the School of the Americas Watch.* Scan Select Program, copyright by Mike McCormick. 2006. https://www.youtube.com/watch?v=jkXABRWuZJ0.

———. *My Journey from Silence to Solidarity.* Edited by Margaret Knapke. Yellow Springs, OH: fxBear, 2013.

Burkhalter, Gigi. Interview. Skype, September 30, 2015.

Clemens, Steve. Interview. Phone, October 5, 2015.

———. "Risking Arrest at the School of the Americas: November 2005." *Mennonista* (blog), November 2005. http://www.mennonista.blogspot.com/2008/10/risking-arrest-at-school-of-americas.html.

Dear, John. *Jean Donovan and the Call to Discipleship*. Erie, PA: Pax Christi USA, 1987. http://www.fatherjohndear.org/pdfs/Jean_Donovan_Call_to_Discipleship.pdf.

Fleischer, Jeff. "Too Cruel for School." *Mother Jones*, March 23, 2005. http://www.motherjones.com/politics/2005/03/too-cruel-school.

Flores-Maisonet, Anton. "Does Love Cross Borders?" *Alterna Community* (blog), February 26, 2015. http://web.archive.org/web/20160416121838/http://www.alternacommunity.com/2015/02/26/does-love-cross-borders-part-one/.

Geglia, Beth. *Not Forgotten: Street Art by the School of the Americas Watch*. Washington, DC, 2014. https://vimeo.com/95829437.

Gynther, Brigitte. "Berta Cáceres, ¡Presente!" SOA Watch: Close the School of the Americas. March 9, 2016. http://web.archive.org/web/20180718055408/http://www.soaw.org/about-us/equipo-sur/263-stories-from-honduras/4365-berta-caceres-ipresente.

Hamm, M., J. Ferrell, and C. Greer. "Provocateur for Justice: Notes on the Imprisonment of Professor Luis Barrios." *Crime, Media, Culture* 6, no. 2 (August 27, 2010): 227–38. https://doi.org/10.1177/1741659010369960.

Hanrahan, Clare Marie. *Conscience & Consequence: A Prison Memoir*. Asheville, NC: Celtic WordCraft, 2005.

Hodge, James, and Linda Cooper. *Disturbing the Peace: The Story of Roy Bourgeois and the Movement to Close the School of the Americas*. Maryknoll, NY: Orbis Books, 2004.

Inserra, Chris. Interview. Phone, October 7, 2015.

Kanner, Rebecca. Personal correspondence. May 13, 2016.

———. "Why Civil Disobedience? Prisoner of Conscience Speaks Out." *Solidarity: The Magazine for UAW Members and Their Families*, October 2010.

Knapke, Margaret, ed. *Voices for the Voiceless*. Washington, DC: School of Americas Watch, 2000.

Lamb, Betsy, ed. *Voices of Courage: From the SOA Watch Vigil and Action Prisoners and Probationers of Conscience of November 2003*. Washington, DC: School of the Americas Watch, 2004.

Leadership Conference of Women Religious. "Assembly Resolutions." https://lcwr.org/assembly/resolutions.

Lenz, OFM, Robert. *Featured Icons: Oscar Romero of El Salvador*, 2015. https://www.youtube.com/watch?v=INDYB4bX3LQ.

Loadenthal, Michael. Interview. Phone, November 11, 2015.

Magovern, Ann. Interview. Phone, September 2, 2015.

Martínez, Elizabeth "Betita." "Combating Oppression Inside and Outside." In *We Have Not Been Moved: Resisting Racism and Militarism in 21st Century America*, edited by Elizabeth "Betita" Martínez, Matt Meyer, and Mandy Carter, 74–77. Oakland, CA: PM Press, 2012.

Maxit, César. Personal correspondence. Facebook messenger, April 4, 2016.

Moakley, John Joseph. "Interim Report of the Speaker's Task Force on El Salvador." Washington, DC: US House of Representatives, April 30, 1990.

NAACP. *NAACP Policy Handbook: Resolutions Approved by the National Board of Directors, 1976–2006.* http://web.archive.org/web/20180508095050/http://action .naacp.org/page/-/Policy_Handbook_5_9_07.pdf.

Nelson-Pallmeyer, Jack. Interview. Harrisonburg, VA, October 16, 2015.

———. *School of Assassins: Guns, Greed, and Globalization.* Rev. and expanded ed. Maryknoll, NY: Orbis Books, 2001.

Parker, Darren. "A Black Man's Look at Faith Activists." In SOA Watch Anti-Oppression Working Group, *Compilation of Anti-Oppression Resources.*

Pax Christi USA. "Teachers of Peace." https://paxchristiusa.org/about/teachers-of -peace/.

Perrone, Mary Ann, and Rebecca Kanner. Interview. Ann Arbor, MI, January 15, 2016.

Puppetista.org. *Puppetista Activists @ SOAW.* Columbus, GA, 2006. https://www .youtube.com/watch?v=oHIqgqlqu_4.

Quigley, William. "Advice for Lawyers: Civil Disobedience 101." *Bill Quigley: Social Justice Advocacy* (blog), January 18, 2016. https://billquigley.wordpress.com /2016/01/18/advice-for-lawyers-civil-disobedience-101/.

———. Personal correspondence, January 26, 2016.

Richter, Robert, dir. *School of Americas, School of Assassins.* Maryknoll World Films, 1994. Documentary, 13 min.

Rubin, Zach. "The Geography of Protest at the School of the Americas." University of Missouri. http://zachrubin.com/academic-work/academic-work/the-geog raphy-of-protest.pdf.

Ruiz, Pablo. "Cry ¡Presente! Now and Forever." In *Bury the Dead: Stories of Death and Dying, Resistance and Discipleship.* Edited by Laurel Dykstra. Translated by Julia McRae. Eugene, OR: Cascade Books, 2013.

Schloss, Mike. Interview. Phone, June 5, 2015.

Shenk, Joanna. Interview. Skype, October 2, 2015.

Sisters of Mercy. "Mercy's Involvement in School of Americas." http://www.sisters ofmercy.org/resources/prayer-service-school-of-americas/.

SOA Watch. "Become a Peacemaker." *SOAW: Resist Empire & Militarization,* November 2015. https://web.archive.org/web/20151113160405/http://soaw.org /november/participate/volunteer-at-the-vigil/become-a-peacemaker/.

———. "June 15: Global Day of Action Demanding Justice for Berta." *Close the School of the Americas,* June 2016. https://web.archive.org/web/20180718053920 /http://www.soaw.org/about-us/equipo-sur/263-stories-from-honduras/44 01-june-15-global-day-of-action-demanding-justice-for-berta.

———. "Moving 2016 November Vigil to the Border?" *¡Presente!* https://web .archive.org/web/20180419175859/http://www.soaw.org/presente/content /view/418/74/lang,en/.

———. "November 16, 1997 Memorial Service Bulletin," 1997. Rebecca Kanner personal archive.

———. "Prisoners of Conscience." *Close the School of the Americas,* 2018. https://web .archive.org/web/20180115112258/http://www.soaw.org/about-us/pocs.

———. "The SOA Watch Latin America Project." *Close the School of the Americas*, 2007. https://web.archive.org/web/20070419114410/http://www.soaw.org/article.php?id=1510.

———. "SOA Watch Nonviolence Guidelines." *Close the School of the Americas*, 2016. https://web.archive.org/web/20161011192201/http://www.soaw.org/index.php?option=com_content&view=article&id=1093.

———. "SOA Watch Vigil and Witness." November 2000. Rebecca Kanner personal archive.

———. *Speaking Truth to Power*. Maryknoll, NY: Maryknoll Social Communications Department, 1998.

———. "Three Hundred Religious Leaders Hold Prayer Vigil to Close the School of the Americas." *Close the School of the Americas*, 1996. https://web.archive.org/web/20180720162257/http://www.soaw.org/take-action/action-history/166-1996/165.

SOA Watch Anti-Oppression Working Group. *Compilation of Anti-Oppression Resources: To Incorporate Anti-Oppression Perspectives into the Organizing to Close the SOA*. Washington, DC: SOA Watch, 2004.

Sullivan, Lisa. Interview. Phone, May 30, 2016.

Taylor, Gail. "Gender Equity in SOAW: Obstacles and Strategies." In SOA Watch Anti-Oppression Working Group, *Compilation of Anti-Oppression Resources*.

Tilson, Nicole. Interview. Phone, June 8, 2015.

Triggs, Bruce. "Globalizing SOA Watch." In *The Global Activist's Manual: Local Ways to Change the World*, edited by Mike Prokosch and Laura Raymond, 48–53. New York: Thunder's Mouth Press/Nation Books, 2002.

Uassouf, Gabriela, dir. *Somos Una América: Shut Down the SOA*. Documentary. SOAW, 2011. Documentary, 25:36 min.

Ubalde, Manuel. *Funeral de Pablo Neruda, 1973*. (In French.) Santiago, Chile, 1973. https://www.youtube.com/watch?v=xF7s8CM-dTY.

US Army. "WHINSEC Information Brief." Fort Benning, Georgia, November 28, 2017. http://www.benning.army.mil/tenant/whinsec/content/pdf/Information%20brief.pdf?28NOV2017.

Viscarra, Arturo. Interview. Phone, September 9, 2015.

Wright, Scott, and Jean Stokan. "Remembering Maura, Ita, Dorothy and Jean: A Scattering of Seeds and Words of Gratitude." *School of the Americas Watch* (blog), December 2, 2015. http://web.archive.org/web/20180718153423/http://www.soaw.org/news/organizing-updates/4347-scott-wright-and-jean-stokan.

Wright-Rios, John. Interview. Skype, November 10, 2015.

SECONDARY SOURCES

Ackerman, Peter, and Christopher Kruegler. *Strategic Nonviolent Conflict: The Dynamics of People Power in the Twentieth Century*. Westport, CT: Praeger, 1994.

Agamben, Giorgio. *State of Exception*. Translated by Kevin Attell. Chicago: University of Chicago Press, 2005.

————. *The Time That Remains: A Commentary on the Letter to the Romans*. Translated by Patricia Dailey. Stanford, CA: Stanford University Press, 2005.

Almond, Gabriel A., R. Scott Appleby, and Emmanuel Sivan. *Strong Religion: The Rise of Fundamentalisms around the World*. Chicago: University of Chicago Press, 2003.

Appleby, R. Scott. "Rethinking Fundamentalism in a Secular Age." In *Rethinking Secularism*. Edited by Craig J. Calhoun, Mark Juergensmeyer, and Jonathan VanAntwerpen. Oxford: Oxford University Press, 2011.

Arendt, Hannah. *On Violence*. New York: Harcourt, Brace & World, 1970.

Aristotle. *The Nicomachean Ethics*. Edited by Leslie Brown. Translated by David Ross. Oxford: Oxford University Press, 2009.

Asad, Talal. *Formations of the Secular: Christianity, Islam, Modernity*. Stanford, CA: Stanford University Press, 2003.

————. *Genealogies of Religion: Discipline and Reasons of Power in Christianity and Islam*. Baltimore: Johns Hopkins University Press, 1993.

Audi, Robert, and Nicholas Wolterstorff. *Religion in the Public Square: The Place of Religious Convictions in Political Debate*. Lanham, MD: Rowman & Littlefield, 1997.

Augustine. "Against Faustus." In *From Irenaeus to Grotius: A Sourcebook in Christian Political Thought, 100–1625*. Edited by Oliver O'Donovan and Joan Lockwood O'Donovan. Grand Rapids, MI: Eerdmans, 1999.

————. *The City of God against the Pagans*. Translated by R. W. Dyson. Cambridge: Cambridge University Press, 1998.

Aulén, Gustaf. *Christus Victor: An Historical Study of the Three Main Types of the Idea of Atonement*. Translated by A. G. Herbert. 1931. Reprint, Eugene, OR: Wipf and Stock, 2003.

Badiou, Alain. *Saint Paul: The Foundation of Universalism*. Stanford, CA: Stanford University Press, 2003.

Bakunin, Mikhail Aleksandrovich. *Bakunin on Anarchy: Selected Works by the Activist-Founder of World Anarchism*. Translated by Sam Dolgoff. New York: Vintage Books, 1972.

Bandy, Joe, and Jackie Smith, eds. *Coalitions across Borders: Transnational Protest and the Neoliberal Order*. Lanham, MD: Rowman & Littlefield, 2005.

Bass, S. Jonathan. *Blessed Are the Peacemakers: Martin Luther King, Jr., Eight White Religious Leaders, and the "Letter from Birmingham Jail."* Baton Rouge: Louisiana State University Press, 2001.

Bell, John. "The End of *Our Domestic Resurrection Circus*: Bread and Puppet Theater and Counterculture Performance in the 1990s." *The Drama Review* 43, no. 3 (September 1999): 62–80.

Benhabib, Seyla. "Models of Public Space: Hannah Arendt, the Liberal Tradition, and Jürgen Habermas." In *Habermas and the Public Sphere*, edited by Craig J. Calhoun, 73–98. Cambridge, MA: MIT Press, 1992.

Benjamin, Walter. "Critique of Violence." In *Selected Writings*, edited by Marcus Paul Bullock and Michael William Jennings, 1:236–52. Cambridge, MA: Belknap Press of Harvard University Press, 1996.

———. "On the Concept of History." In *Selected Writings*, edited by Michael William Jennings and Howard Eiland, translated by Harry Zohn, 4:389–400. Cambridge, MA: Belknap Press of Harvard University Press, 2003.

Bernstein, Eduard. *The Preconditions of Socialism*. Translated by H. Tudor. 1899. Reprint, Cambridge: Cambridge University Press, 1993.

Bilgrami, Akeel. *Secularism, Identity, and Enchantment*. Cambridge, MA: Harvard University Press, 2014.

Bivins, Jason. *The Fracture of Good Order: Christian Antiliberalism and the Challenge to American Politics*. Chapel Hill: University of North Carolina Press, 2003.

Blakeley, Ruth. "Still Training to Torture? US Training of Military Forces from Latin America." *Third World Quarterly* 27, no. 8 (November 2006): 1439–61. https://doi.org/10.1080/01436590601027289.

Boccaccini, Gabriele. "Inner-Jewish Debate on the Tension between Divine and Human Agency in Second Temple Judaism." In *Divine and Human Agency in Paul and His Cultural Environment*, edited by John M. G. Barclay and Simon J. Gathercole, 9–26. London: T&T Clark, 2006.

Boccaccini, Gabriele, and Carlos A. Segovia, eds. *Paul the Jew: Rereading the Apostle as a Figure of Second Temple Judaism*. Minneapolis: Fortress Press, 2016.

Boff, Leonardo, and Clodovis Boff. *Salvation and Liberation*. Maryknoll, NY: Orbis Books, 1984.

Bossy, John. *Christianity in the West, 1400–1700*. Oxford: Oxford University Press, 1985.

Bourdieu, Pierre. *The Logic of Practice*. Translated by Richard Nice. Stanford, CA: Stanford University Press, 1990.

———. *Practical Reason: On the Theory of Action*. Stanford, CA: Stanford University Press, 1998.

Bretherton, Luke. "Coming to Judgment: Methodological Reflections on the Relationship between Ecclesiology, Ethnography and Political Theory." *Modern Theology* 28, no. 2 (April 2012): 167–96.

———. *Resurrecting Democracy: Faith, Citizenship, and the Politics of a Common Life*. New York: Cambridge University Press, 2015.

Brown, Alexandra R. "Paul's Apocalyptic Cross and Philosophy: Reading 1 Corinthians with Giorgio Agamben and Alain Badiou." In *Apocalyptic and the Future of Theology: With and beyond J. Louis Martyn*, edited by Joshua B. Davis and Douglas Harink, 96–117. Eugene, OR: Cascade Books, 2012.

Brown, Peter. *The Cult of the Saints: Its Rise and Function in Latin Christianity*. Chicago: University of Chicago Press, 1981.

———. "Saints as Exemplars in Late Antiquity." *Representations*, no. 2 (1983): 1–25.

Burawoy, Michael, ed. *Ethnography Unbound: Power and Resistance in the Modern Metropolis*. Berkeley: University of California Press, 1991.

———. *The Extended Case Method: Four Countries, Four Decades, Four Great Transformations, and One Theoretical Tradition*. Berkeley: University of California Press, 2009.

Butler, Judith. "The Ethics and Politics of Nonviolence." 2015 Yusko Ward-Phillips Lecture. Notre Dame, IN: University of Notre Dame, 2015.

———. *Frames of War: When Is Life Grievable?* New York: Verso, 2009.

———. *Notes toward a Performative Theory of Assembly*. Cambridge, MA: Harvard University Press, 2015.

Cajka, Peter. "The Rights of Conscience: The Rise of Tradition in America's Age of Fracture, 1940–1990." PhD diss., Boston College, 2016.

Carlyle, Thomas. *The Works of Thomas Carlyle*. Edited by Henry Duff Traill. Vol. 5. Cambridge: Cambridge University Press, 2010.

Casanova, José. "Rethinking Public Religions." In *Rethinking Religion and World Affairs*. Edited by Timothy Samuel Shah, Alfred C. Stepan, and Monica Duffy Toft. New York: Oxford University Press, 2012.

Catholic Church. *Catechism of the Catholic Church*. New York: Doubleday, 1997.

Cavanaugh, William T. "The Church in the Streets: Eucharist and Politics." *Modern Theology* 30, no. 2 (April 2014): 384–402.

———. "Discerning: Politics and Reconciliation." In *The Blackwell Companion to Christian Ethics*, 2nd ed., edited by Stanley Hauerwas and Samuel Wells, 211–23. Oxford: Blackwell Publishing, 2004.

———. "From One City to Two: Christian Reimagining of Political Space." *Political Theology* 7, no. 3 (2006): 299–321.

———. *Migrations of the Holy: God, State, and the Political Meaning of the Church*. Grand Rapids, MI: Eerdmans, 2011.

———. *The Myth of Religious Violence: Secular Ideology and the Roots of Modern Conflict*. Oxford: Oxford University Press, 2009.

———. *Theopolitical Imagination*. London: T&T Clark, 2002.

———. *Torture and Eucharist: Theology, Politics, and the Body of Christ*. Oxford: Blackwell Publishers, 1998.

Certeau, Michel de. "Walking in the City." In *The Practice of Everyday Life*, 91–110. Berkeley: University of California Press, 1984.

Cerulo, Karen A. "Mining the Intersections of Cognitive Sociology and Neuroscience." *Poetics* 38, no. 2 (2010): 115–32.

Chabot, Sean. "Making Sense of Civil Resistance: From Theories and Techniques to Social Movement Phronesis." In *Civil Resistance: Comparative Perspectives on Nonviolent Struggle*, edited by Kurt Schock, 227–57. Minneapolis: University of Minnesota Press, 2015.

Chenoweth, Erica, and Kathleen Gallagher Cunningham. "Understanding Nonviolent Resistance: An Introduction." *Journal of Peace Research* 50, no. 3 (May 1, 2013): 271–76. https://doi.org/10.1177/0022343313480381.

Chenoweth, Erica, and Maria J. Stephan. *Why Civil Resistance Works: The Strategic Logic of Nonviolent Conflict*. New York: Columbia University Press, 2011.

Cicero, Marcus Tullius. *On the Commonwealth*. Translated by James E. G. Zetzel. Cambridge: Cambridge University Press, 1999.

Cohan, John Alan. "Civil Disobedience and the Necessity Defense." *Pierce Law Review* 6 (2007): 111.

Collins, Randall. "Social Movements and the Focus of Emotional Attention." In *Passionate Politics: Emotions and Social Movements*, edited by Jeff Goodwin, James M. Jasper, and Francesca Polletta, 27–44. Chicago: University of Chicago Press, 2001.

Commission on the Truth for El Salvador. "From Madness to Hope: The 12-Year War in El Salvador." *Report of the Commission on the Truth for El Salvador*. New York: United Nations Security Council, 1993.

Cone, James H. *The Cross and the Lynching Tree*. Maryknoll, NY: Orbis Books, 2011.

———. *God of the Oppressed*. New York: Seabury Press, 1975.

Connolly, William E. *Pluralism*. Durham, NC: Duke University Press, 2005.

———. *Why I Am Not a Secularist*. Minneapolis: University of Minnesota Press, 1999.

Copeland, M. Shawn. *Enfleshing Freedom: Body, Race, and Being*. Minneapolis: Fortress Press, 2010.

———. "Wading through Many Sorrows." In *A Troubling in My Soul: Womanist Perspectives on Evil and Suffering*, edited by Emilie M. Townes, 109–24. Maryknoll, NY: Orbis Books, 1993.

Cortright, David. *Peace: A History of Movements and Ideas*. Cambridge: Cambridge University Press, 2008.

Crenshaw, Kimberle. "Demarginalizing the Intersection of Race and Sex: A Black Feminist Critique of Antidiscrimination Doctrine, Feminist Theory and Antiracist Politics." *University of Chicago Legal Forum* 1989, no. 1 (1989).

———. "Mapping the Margins: Intersectionality, Identity Politics, and Violence against Women of Color." *Stanford Law Review* 43, no. 6 (July 1991): 1241–99.

Crichton, J. D. "A Theology of Worship." In *The Study of Liturgy*, edited by Cheslyn Jones, Geoffrey Wainwright, and Edward Yarnold. New York: Oxford University Press, 1978.

Davaney, Sheila Greeve. "Theology and the Turn to Cultural Analysis." In *Converging on Culture: Theologians in Dialogue with Cultural Analysis and Criticism*, edited by Delwin Brown, Sheila Greeve Davaney, and Kathryn Tanner, 3–16. Oxford: Oxford University Press, 2001.

Davies, John, and Edy Kaufman. *Second Track/Citizens' Diplomacy Concepts and Techniques for Conflict Transformation*. Lanham, MD: Rowman & Littlefield, 2002.

de Cleyre, Voltairine. "Direct Action." In *The Selected Works of Voltairine de Cleyre: Poems, Essays, Sketches and Stories, 1885–1911*. Edited by Alexander Berkman. Chico, CA: AK Press, 2016.

Deming, Barbara. *Revolution & Equilibrium*. New York: Grossman, 1971.

Dewey, John. *The Essential Dewey*. Edited by Larry A. Hickman and Thomas M. Alexander. Bloomington: Indiana University Press, 1998.

Dixon, Chris. *Another Politics: Talking across Today's Transformative Movements*. Berkeley: University of California Press, 2014.

Doggett, Martha. *Death Foretold: The Jesuit Murders in El Salvador*. Washington, DC: Georgetown University Press, 1993.

Douglas, Kelly Brown. *Stand Your Ground: Black Bodies and the Justice of God*. Maryknoll, NY: Orbis Books, 2015.

Dunn, James D. G. *The New Perspective on Paul*. Rev. ed. Grand Rapids, MI: Eerdmans, 2008.

Durkheim, Emile. *The Elementary Forms of the Religious Life*. Translated by Karen Fields. 1912. Reprint, New York: Free Press, 1995.

Dworkin, Ronald. *Law's Empire*. Cambridge, MA: Belknap Press of Harvard University Press, 1986.

Ellacuría, Ignacio. "The Christian Challenge of Liberation Theology." In *Ignacio Ellacuría: Essays on History, Liberation, and Salvation*. Edited by Michael Edward Lee, 123–35. Maryknoll, NY: Orbis Books, 2013.

———. "The Crucified People: An Essay in Historical Soteriology." In *Ignacio Ellacuría*, 195–226.

———. *Freedom Made Flesh: The Mission of Christ and His Church*. Translated by John Drury. Maryknoll, NY: Orbis Books, 1976.

———. "Latin American Quincentenary: Discovery or Cover-Up?" In Lee, *Ignacio Ellacuría*, 27–38.

———. "On Liberation." In Lee, *Ignacio Ellacuría*, 39–62.

Elshtain, Jean Bethke. *Augustine and the Limits of Politics*. Frank M. Covey Jr. Loyola Lectures in Political Analysis. Notre Dame, IN: University of Notre Dame Press, 1995.

Emerson, Ralph Waldo. *Representative Men*. Philadelphia: Henry Altemus, 1892.

Engler, Mark. "The Machiavelli of Nonviolence: Gene Sharp and the Battle against Corporate Rule." *Dissent* 60, no. 4 (Fall 2013): 59–65.

Epstein, Barbara. *Political Protest and Cultural Revolution Nonviolent Direct Action in the 1970s and 1980s*. Berkeley: University of California Press, 1991.

Esquivel, Julia. *Threatened with Resurrection: Prayers and Poems from an Exiled Guatemalan (Amenazado de Resurrección)*. Elgin, IL: Brethren Press, 1982.

Falk, Richard A. "The Nuremberg Defense in the Pentagon Papers Case." *Columbia Journal of Transnational Law* 13 (1974): 208.

———. "Son My: War Crimes and Individual Responsibility International Law." *University of Toledo Law Review* 3 (1971): 21–42.

Farmer, Paul. *Pathologies of Power: Health, Human Rights, and the New War on the Poor*. Berkeley: University of California Press, 2005.

Feuerbach, Ludwig. *The Essence of Christianity*. Mineola, NY: Dover, 2008.

Finnis, John. *Natural Law and Natural Rights*. Oxford: Clarendon Press, 1980.

Francis, Mark R. *Local Worship, Global Church: Popular Religion and the Liturgy*. Collegeville, MN: Liturgical Press, 2014.

Freeman, Jo. *The Politics of Women's Liberation: A Case Study of an Emerging Social Movement and Its Relation to the Policy Process*. New York: McKay, 1975.

———. "The Tyranny of Structurelessness." *Berkeley Journal of Sociology* 17 (March 1972): 151–64.

Gallo-Cruz, Selina. "Negotiating the Lines of Contention: Counterframing and Boundary Work in the School of the Americas Debate." *Sociological Forum* 27, no. 1 (March 2012): 21–45.

———. "Protest and Public Relations: The Reinvention of the US Army School of the Americas." *Interface: A Journal for and about Social Movements* 7, no. 1 (May 2015): 322–50.

Galtung, Johan. "Cultural Violence." *Journal of Peace Research* 27, no. 3 (August 1, 1990): 291–305.

———. "Violence, Peace, and Peace Research." *Journal of Peace Research* 6, no. 3 (January 1, 1969): 167–91. https://doi.org/10.2307/422690.

Gandhi, Mohandas K. *All Men Are Brothers: Autobiographical Reflections*. Edited by Krishna Kripalani. 1958. Reprint, New York: Contiuum, 2004.

Ganz, Marshall. "Resources and Resourcefulness: Strategic Capacity in the Unioniza-
    tion of California Agriculture, 1959–1966." *American Journal of Sociology*,
    2000, 1003–62.
George, Robert P. *In Defense of Natural Law*. Oxford: Clarendon Press, 1999.
Gill, Lesley. *The School of the Americas: Military Training and Political Violence in the
    Americas*. Durham, NC: Duke University Press, 2004.
Girard, René. *Violence and the Sacred*. Baltimore: Johns Hopkins University Press,
    1977.
Goodman, Lenn Evan. *Religious Pluralism and Values in the Public Sphere*. New York:
    Cambridge University Press, 2014.
Goossen, Rachel Waltner. "'Defanging the Beast': Mennonite Responses to John
    Howard Yoder's Sexual Abuse." *Mennonite Quarterly Review* 89, no. 1 (2015):
    52–81.
Graeber, David. *Direct Action: An Ethnography*. Oakland, CA: AK Press, 2009.
Grandin, Greg. *Empire's Workshop: Latin America, the United States, and the Rise of the
    New Imperialism*. New York: Metropolitan Books, 2006.
Grant, Jacquelyn. *White Women's Christ and Black Women's Jesus: Feminist Christol-
    ogy and Womanist Response*. Atlanta: Scholars Press, 1989.
Grimes, Katie M. "Breaking the Body of Christ: The Sacraments of Initiation in a
    Habitat of White Supremacy." *Political Theology* 18, no. 1 (2017): 22–43.
Grimes, Ronald L. *Beginnings in Ritual Studies*. Washington, DC: University Press of
    America, 1982.
———. "Emerging Ritual." Proceedings of the North American Academy of Liturgy,
    1990.
Gustafson, James M. *Ethics from a Theocentric Perspective*. Chicago: University of
    Chicago Press, 1981.
Guth, Karen V. "Doing Justice to the Complex Legacy of John Howard Yoder: Restor-
    ative Justice Resources in Witness and Feminist Ethics." *Journal of the Society
    of Christian Ethics* 35, no. 2 (2015): 119–39.
Gutiérrez, Gustavo. *On Job: God-Talk and the Suffering of the Innocent*. Maryknoll,
    NY: Orbis Books, 1987.
———. *A Theology of Liberation: History, Politics, and Salvation*. Maryknoll, NY: Orbis
    Books, 1988.
———. *We Drink from Our Own Wells: The Spiritual Journey of a People*. Maryknoll,
    NY: Orbis Books, 1987.
Habermas, Jurgen. "Religion in the Public Sphere." *European Journal of Philosophy*
    14, no. 1 (April 2006): 1–25.
Haley, Peter. "Rudolph Sohm on Charisma." *Journal of Religion* 60, no. 2 (April
    1980): 185–97.
Hauerwas, Stanley. *After Christendom? How the Church Is to Behave if Freedom, Justice,
    and a Christian Nation Are Bad Ideas*. Nashville: Abingdon Press, 1991.
Hauerwas, Stanley, and William Willimon. *Resident Aliens: Life in the Christian Col-
    ony*. Nashville: Abingdon Press, 1989.
Held, Shai. *Abraham Joshua Heschel: The Call of Transcendence*. Bloomington: Indi-
    ana University Press, 2013.

Herdt, Jennifer A. "The Virtue of the Liturgy." In *The Blackwell Companion to Christian Ethics*, 2nd ed., edited by Stanley Hauerwas and Samuel Wells, 533–46. Malden, MA: Wiley-Blackwell, 2011.

Huggins, Martha Knisely. *Political Policing: The United States and Latin America*. Durham, NC: Duke University Press, 1998.

Huggins, Martha Knisely, Mika Haritos-Fatouros, and Philip G. Zimbardo. *Violence Workers: Police Torturers and Murderers Reconstruct Brazilian Atrocities*. Berkeley: University of California Press, 2002.

Hurd, Elizabeth Shakman. *The Politics of Secularism in International Relations*. Princeton, NJ: Princeton University Press, 2008.

International Commission on English in the Liturgy, trans. *The Rites of the Catholic Church*. Study Edition. Vol. 1. Collegeville, MN: Liturgical Press, 1990.

International Committee of the Red Cross. "Principles of International Law Recognized in the Charter of the Nüremberg Tribunal and in the Judgment of the Tribunal, 1950." In *Report of the International Law Commission Covering Its Second Session, 5 June–29 July, 1950*. New York: International Law Commission, July 29, 1950. https://www.icrc.org/applic/ihl/ihl.nsf/Treaty.xsp?action =openDocument&documentId=854DDAACFDE285E4C12563CD002D6B95.

James, William. *Pragmatism*. Cambridge, MA: Harvard University Press, 1975.

Jasper, James, and Jane Poulsen. "Recruiting Strangers and Friends: Moral Shocks and Social Networks in Animal Rights and Anti-Nuclear Protests." *Social Problems* 42, no. 4 (1995): 492–512.

Jennings, Theodore W. *Transforming Atonement: A Political Theology of the Cross*. Minneapolis: Fortress Press, 2009.

Jerolmack, Colin, and Shamus Khan. "Talk Is Cheap: Ethnography and the Attitudinal Fallacy." *Sociological Methods & Research* 43, no. 2 (May 1, 2014): 178–209. https://doi.org/10.1177/0049124114523396.

Johnson, Elizabeth A. *Friends of God and Prophets: A Feminist Theological Reading of the Communion of Saints*. New York: Continuum, 1998.

Joosse, Paul. "Becoming a God: Max Weber and the Social Construction of Charisma." *Journal of Classical Sociology*, June 10, 2014. https://doi.org/10.1177 /1468795X14536652.

Katongole, Emmanuel. *Born from Lament: The Theology and Politics of Hope in Africa*. Grand Rapids, MI: Eerdmans, 2017.

Kaveny, Cathleen. *Prophecy without Contempt: Religious Discourse in the Public Square*. Cambridge, MA: Harvard University Press, 2016.

Keller, Catherine. *God and Power: Counter-Apocalyptic Journeys*. Minneapolis: Fortress Press, 2005.

Keogh, Stacy. "The Survival of Religious Peace Movements: When Mobilization Increases as Political Opportunity Decreases." *Social Compass* 60, no. 4 (December 3, 2013): 561–78.

Kertzer, David I. *Ritual, Politics, and Power*. New Haven, CT: Yale University Press, 1988.

King, Martin Luther. "The Negro Is Your Brother, or Letter from a Birmingham Jail." *Atlantic Monthly* 212, no. 2 (August 1963): 78–88.

———. "A Time to Break Silence." In *A Testament of Hope: The Essential Writings and Speeches of Martin Luther King, Jr*, edited by James Melvin Washington, 231–44. San Francisco: HarperSanFrancisco, 1991.

K'Meyer, Tracy Elaine. *Interracialism and Christian Community in the Postwar South: The Story of Koinonia Farm*. Charlottesville: University Press of Virginia, 1997.

Koopman, Sara. "Cutting through Topologies: Crossing Lines at the School of the Americas." *Antipode* 40, no. 5 (November 2008): 825–47. https://doi.org/10.1111/j.1467-8330.2008.00639.x.

Kraft, Herman Joseph S. "Track Three Diplomacy and Human Rights in Southeast Asia: The Asia Pacific Coalition for East Timor." *Global Networks* 2, no. 1 (January 2002): 49–64. https://doi.org/10.1111/1471-0374.00026.

Kroeker, P. Travis. *Messianic Political Theology and Diaspora Ethics: Essays in Exile*. Eugene, OR: Cascade Books, 2017.

Kurlansky, Mark. *Nonviolence: The History of a Dangerous Idea*. New York: Modern Library Chronicles, 2008.

Lambek, Bernard D. "Necessity and International Law: Arguments for the Legality of Civil Disobedience." *Yale Law & Policy Review* 5, no. 2 (1987): 472–92.

Lambelet, Kyle B. T. "'How Long O Lord': Practices of Lamentation and the Restoration of Political Agency." In *Bridging Scripture and Moral Theology: Essays in Dialogue with Yiu Sing Lúcás Chan, S.J.* Edited by Michael Cover, John Thiede, and Joshua Ezra Burns. Lanham, MD: Lexington Books, 2019.

———. "Lovers of God's Law: The Politics of Higher Law and the Ethics of Civil Disobedience." *Political Theology* 18, no. 7 (2018): 593–610.

———. "Mourning the Dead, Following the Living: Exemplary Dead and Charismatic Leadership." *Journal of Religious Ethics*, 47, no. 3 (2019).

———. "Nonviolence as a Tradition of Moral Praxis." Expositions, forthcoming.

———. "Nonviolent Struggle between Norm and Technique." Candler School of Theology, Emory University, Atlanta, forthcoming.

———. "Sanctuary in a Small Southern City: An Interview with Anton Flores-Maisonet." *Radical History Review*, no. 135 (2019).

Lambelet, Kyle B. T., and Brian Hamilton. "Engage Survivors More, and Yoder Less." *National Catholic Reporter*, February 26, 2016. https://www.ncronline.org/news/accountability/engage-survivors-more-and-yoder-less.

Land, Clare. *Decolonizing Solidarity: Dilemmas and Directions for Supporters of Indigenous Struggles*. London: Zed Books, 2015.

Lassalle-Klein, Robert. *Blood and Ink: Ignacio Ellacuría, Jon Sobrino, and the Jesuit Martyrs of the University of Central America*. Maryknoll, NY: Orbis Books, 2014.

Lederach, John Paul. "Justpeace: The Challenge of the 21st Century." In *People Building Peace: 35 Inspiring Stories from around the World*, edited by European Centre for Conflict Prevention, 27–36. Utrecht: European Centre for Conflict Prevention, 1999.

Lederach, John Paul, and R. Scott Appleby. "Strategic Peacebuilding: An Overview." In *Strategies of Peace: Transforming Conflict in a Violent World*, edited by Daniel Philpott and Gerard F. Powers, 19–44. New York: Oxford University Press, 2010.

Lee, Michael Edward. "Ignacio Ellacuría: A View from the North." In *Ignacio Ella-curía: Essays on History, Liberation, and Salvation*. Edited by Michael Edward Lee, 1–23. Maryknoll, NY: Orbis Books, 2013.

Lilla, Mark. *The Stillborn God: Religion, Politics, and the Modern West*. New York: Vintage Books, 2008.

Lloyd, Vincent. *In Defense of Charisma*. New York: Columbia University Press, 2018.

———. "Liturgy in the Broadest Sense." *New Blackfriars* 92, no. 1037 (January 2011): 71–89. https://doi.org/10.1111/j.1741-2005.2009.01319.x.

———. *The Problem with Grace: Reconfiguring Political Theology*. Stanford, CA: Stanford University Press, 2011.

Lloyd, Vincent, and David True. "What Political Theology Could Be." *Political Theology* 17, no. 6 (November 2016): 505–6. https://doi.org/10.1080/1462317X.2016.1241062.

Long, Thomas G. *Accompany Them with Singing: The Christian Funeral*. Louisville, KY: Westminster John Knox Press, 2009.

Lorde, Audre. "The Master's Tools Will Never Dismantle the Master's House." In *Sister Outsider: Essays and Speeches*, 110–13. Trumansburg, NY: Crossing Press, 1984.

Lovin, Robin W. "The Limits of Freedom and the Possibilities of Politics: A Christian Realist Account of Political Responsibility." *The Journal of Religion* 73, no. 4 (1993): 559–72.

Luxemburg, Rosa. *Reform or Revolution*. 2nd ed. 1908. Reprint, New York: Pathfinder Press, 1973.

MacIntyre, Alasdair. *Whose Justice? Which Rationality?* Notre Dame, IN: University of Notre Dame Press, 1988.

Macklin, June. "Saints and Near-Saints in Transition: The Sacred, the Secular, and the Popular." In *The Making of Saints: Contesting Sacred Ground*, edited by James F. Hopgood, 1–22. Tuscaloosa: University of Alabama Press, 2005.

Mahmood, Saba. *Politics of Piety: The Islamic Revival and the Feminist Subject*. Princeton, NJ: Princeton University Press, 2012.

Marion, Jean-Luc. *Prolegomena to Charity*. New York: Fordham University Press, 2002.

Markus, R. A. *Saeculum: History and Society in the Theology of St. Augustine*. Rev. ed. New York: Cambridge University Press, 1988.

Marsh, Charles. *The Beloved Community: How Faith Shapes Social Justice, from the Civil Rights Movement to Today*. New York: Basic Books, 2005.

Martyn, J. Louis. "Apocalyptic Antinomies." In *Theological Issues in the Letters of Paul*, 111–24. Nashville, TN: Abingdon Press, 1997.

Marx, Karl. "The Eighteenth Brumaire of Louis Bonaparte." In *The Marx-Engels Reader*, 2nd ed., edited by Robert C. Tucker, 594–617. New York: Norton, 1978.

Mathewes, Charles T. *A Theology of Public Life*. Cambridge: Cambridge University Press, 2007.

McAdam, Doug. *Political Process and the Development of Black Insurgency, 1930–1970*. Chicago: University of Chicago Press, 1982.

McAnany, Patricia Ann. *Living with the Ancestors: Kinship and Kingship in Ancient Maya Society*. 2nd ed. Cambridge: Cambridge University Press, 2014.

McCammon, Holly J. *The U.S. Women's Jury Movements and Strategic Adaptation: A More Just Verdict*. Cambridge: Cambridge University Press, 2012.

McCormick, David H. "From Peacekeeping to Peacebuilding: Restructuring Military and Police Institutions in El Salvador." In *Keeping the Peace: Multidimensional UN Operations in Cambodia and El Salvador*, edited by Michael W. Doyle, Ian Johnstone, and Robert C. Orr, 282–311. New York: Cambridge University Press, 1997.

McGrane, Bernard. *Beyond Anthropology: Society and the Other*. New York: Columbia University Press, 1989.

McKenny, Gerald P. "Responsibility." In *The Oxford Handbook of Theological Ethics*. Edited by Gilbert Meilaender and William Werpehowski. Oxford: Oxford University Press, 2007.

Menjívar, Cecilia, and Néstor Rodríguez, eds. *When States Kill: Latin America, the U.S., and Technologies of Terror*. Austin: University of Texas Press, 2005.

Metz, Johann Baptist. *Faith in History and Society: Toward a Practical Fundamental Theology*. Translated by J. Matthew Ashley. New York: Crossroad, 2007.

Milbank, John. *Theology and Social Theory: Beyond Secular Reason*. 2nd ed. Oxford: Blackwell, 2006.

Mische, Ann. "Finding the Future in Deliberative Process: A Pragmatist Reappraisal of the Dual-Process Model." Presented at the Annual Meeting of the American Sociological Association, Denver, CO, August 2012.

Mitchell, Nathan. *Liturgy and the Social Sciences*. Collegeville, MN: Liturgical Press, 1999.

Moe-Lobeda, Cynthia D. "Structural Violence as Structural Evil." In *Resisting Structural Evil: Love as Ecological and Economic Vocation*, 49–82. Minneapolis: Fortress Press, 2013.

Moran, Dominic. *Pablo Neruda*. London: Reaktion Books, 2009.

Morrill, Bruce T. *Anamnesis as Dangerous Memory: Political and Liturgical Theology in Dialogue*. Collegeville, MN: Liturgical Press, 2000.

Morris, Aldon D. *The Origins of the Civil Rights Movement: Black Communities Organizing for Change*. New York: Free Press, 1984.

Nepstad, Sharon Erickson. *Convictions of the Soul: Religion, Culture, and Agency in the Central America Solidarity Movement*. Oxford: Oxford University Press, 2004.

———. *Nonviolent Revolutions: Civil Resistance in the Late 20th Century*. Oxford: Oxford University Press, 2011.

———. *Nonviolent Struggle: Theories, Strategies, and Dynamics*. New York: Oxford University Press, 2015.

———. *Religion and War Resistance in the Plowshares Movement*. New York: Cambridge University Press, 2008.

Niebuhr, H. Richard. *The Responsible Self: An Essay in Christian Moral Philosophy*. 1963. Reprint, Louisville, KY: Westminster John Knox, 1999.

Niebuhr, Reinhold. "Augustine's Political Realism." In *An Eerdmans Reader in Contemporary Political Theology*, edited by William T. Cavanaugh, Jeffrey W. Bailey, and Craig Hovey, 223–39. 1953. Reprint, Grand Rapids, MI: Eerdmans, 2012.

———. *Beyond Tragedy: Essays on the Christian Interpretation of History*. New York: C. Scribner's Sons, 1937.

———. *The Nature and Destiny of Man: A Christian Interpretation*. 1st ed. Library of Theological Ethics, 1941. Reprint, Louisville, KY: Westminster John Knox Press, 1996.

Nietzsche, Friedrich Wilhelm. *The Genealogy of Morals*. Edited by Horace Barnett Samuel. Mineola, NY: Dover Publications, 2003.

O'Connor, Kathleen M. *Lamentations and the Tears of the World*. Maryknoll, NY: Orbis Books, 2002.

O'Donovan, Oliver. *The Desire of the Nations: Rediscovering the Roots of Political Theology*. New York: Cambridge University Press, 1996.

———. *The Ways of Judgment*. Cambridge: Eerdmans, 2005.

Omer, Atalia. "Modernists despite Themselves: The Phenomenology of the Secular and the Limits of Critique as an Instrument of Change." *Journal of the American Academy of Religion* 83, no. 1 (March 1, 2015): 27–71.

Pemberton, Glenn. *Hurting with God: Learning to Lament with the Psalms*. Abilene, TX: Abilene Christian University Press, 2012.

Perkinson, James W. *Messianism against Christology: Resistance Movements, Folk Arts, and Empire*. New York: Palgrave Macmillan, 2013.

Pickstock, Catherine. "Liturgy, Art and Politics." *Modern Theology* 16, no. 2 (April 2000): 159–80.

Polletta, Francesca. *Freedom Is an Endless Meeting: Democracy in American Social Movements*. Chicago: University of Chicago Press, 2002.

Porter, Jean. *Nature as Reason: A Thomistic Theory of the Natural Law*. Grand Rapids, MI: Eerdmans, 2005.

Ransby, Barbara. *Ella Baker and the Black Freedom Movement: A Radical Democratic Vision*. Chapel Hill: University of North Carolina Press, 2003.

Ratzinger, Joseph. "Instruction on Certain Aspects of the 'Theology of Liberation.'" Congregation for the Doctrine of the Faith, August 6, 1984. http://www.vati can.va/roman_curia/congregations/cfaith/documents/rc_con_cfaith_doc _19840806_theology-liberation_en.html.

Rawls, John. *Political Liberalism*. New York: Columbia University Press, 1993.

———. *A Theory of Justice*. Cambridge, MA: Belknap Press of Harvard University Press, 1971.

Riesebrodt, Martin. "Charisma in Max Weber's Sociology of Religion." *Religion* 29, no. 1 (January 1999): 1–14.

Romero, Óscar. "La iglesia, un servicio de liberación personal, comunitaria, trascendente." San Salvador, El Salvador, March 23, 1980. http://www.sicsal.net /romero/homilias/C/800323.htm.

———. "Misión de la iglesia en medio de la crisis del país." San Salvador, El Salvador, August 6, 1979. http://www.romerotrust.org.uk/sites/default/files/homilies /1979%2008%2006%20Mision%20de%20la%20Iglesia%20en%20medio%20 de%20la%20crisis%20del%20pais.pdf.

———. "La última homilía de Monseñor." San Salvador, El Salvador, March 24, 1980. http://www.romerotrust.org.uk/sites/default/files/homilies/1980%2003 %2024%20La%20ultima%20homilia%20de%20Monsenor.pdf.

———. *Voice of the Voiceless: The Four Pastoral Letters and Other Statements*. Mary-knoll, NY: Orbis Books, 1985.

Rosen, Fred, ed. *Empire and Dissent: The United States and Latin America*. American Encounters/Global Interactions. Durham, NC: Duke University Press, 2008.

Sanders, E. P. *Paul and Palestinian Judaism: A Comparison of Patterns of Religion*. Philadelphia: Fortress Press, 1977.

Satha-Anand, Chaiwat. "Overcoming Illusory Division: Between Nonviolence as a Pragmatic Strategy and a Principled Way of Life." In *Civil Resistance: Comparative Perspectives on Nonviolent Struggle*, edited by Kurt Schock, 289–301. Minneapolis: University of Minnesota Press, 2015.

Scarsella, Hilary. "Not Making Sense: Why Stanley Hauerwas's Response to Yoder's Sexual Abuse Misses the Mark." *ABC Religion & Ethics*, November 30, 2017. https://www.abc.net.au/religion/not-making-sense-why-stanley-hauerwass-response-to-yoders-sexual/10095168.

Scharen, Christian. *Public Worship and Public Work: Character and Commitment in Local Congregational Life*. Virgil Michel Series. Collegeville, MN: Liturgical Press, 2004.

Scharen, Christian, and Aana Marie Vigen, eds. *Ethnography as Christian Theology and Ethics*. New York: Continuum, 2011.

Schillebeeckx, Edward. *Christ, the Sacrament of the Encounter with God*. New York: Sheed and Ward, 1963.

Schirch, Lisa. "Ritual, Religion, and Peacebuilding." In *The Oxford Handbook of Religion, Conflict, and Peacebuilding*, edited by R. Scott Appleby, Atalia Omer, and David Little. Oxford: Oxford University Press, 2015.

Schlesinger, Stephen C., and Stephen Kinzer. *Bitter Fruit: The Story of the American Coup in Guatemala*. Rev. and expanded ed. Cambridge, MA: Harvard University, 2005.

Schmitt, Carl. *The Concept of the Political*. Expanded ed. Chicago: University of Chicago Press, 2007.

———. *Political Theology: Four Chapters on the Concept of Sovereignty*. Chicago: University of Chicago Press, 2005.

Schock, Kurt. *Civil Resistance Today*. Cambridge: Polity, 2015.

———. *Unarmed Insurrections: People Power Movements in Nondemocracies*. Minneapolis: University of Minnesota Press, 2005.

Schüssler Fiorenza, Elisabeth. *In Memory of Her: A Feminist Theological Reconstruction of Christian Origins*. New York: Crossroad, 1983.

Schweitzer, Albert. *The Mysticism of Paul the Apostle*. 1931. Reprint, Baltimore: Johns Hopkins University Press, 1998.

———. *Out of My Life and Thought: An Autobiography*. New York: Holt, 1959.

Sharp, Gene. "Ethics and Responsibility in Politics: A Critique of the Present Adequacy of Max Weber's Classification of Ethical Systems." *Inquiry* 7, no. 1–4 (January 1964): 304–17.

———. *The Politics of Nonviolent Action*. Boston: P. Sargent, 1973.

Shaw, Randy. *Beyond the Fields: Cesar Chavez, the UFW, and the Struggle for Justice in the 21st Century*. Berkeley: University of California Press, 2011.

Smith, Christian, ed. *Disruptive Religion: The Force of Faith in Social-Movement Activism*. New York: Routledge, 1996.

———. *Resisting Reagan: The U.S. Central America Peace Movement*. Chicago: University of Chicago Press, 1996.

Smith, David Norman. "Faith, Reason, and Charisma: Rudolf Sohm, Max Weber, and the Theology of Grace." *Sociological Inquiry* 68, no. 1 (February 1998): 32–60.

Smith, James K. A. *Desiring the Kingdom: Worship, Worldview, and Cultural Formation*. Vol. 1 of Cultural Liturgies. Grand Rapids, MI: Baker Academic, 2009.

———. *Imagining the Kingdom: How Worship Works*. Vol. 2 of Cultural Liturgies. Grand Rapids, MI: Baker Academic, 2013.

Smith, Ted A. "Politics in the Wake of Divine Violence." *Studies in Christian Ethics* 25, no. 4 (2012): 454–72.

———. "Redeeming Critique: Resignations to the Cultural Turn in Christian Theology and Ethics." *Journal of the Society of Christian Ethics* 24, no. 2 (2004): 89–113.

———. "Troeltschian Questions for 'Ethnography as Christian Theology and Ethics.'" *Practical Matters* 6 (2013). http://practicalmattersjournal.org/issue/6/center pieces/troeltschian-questions-for-ethnography-as-christian-theology-and -ethics.

———. *Weird John Brown: Divine Violence and the Limits of Ethics*. Stanford, CA: Stanford University Press, 2014.

Snarr, C. Melissa. *All You That Labor: Religion and Ethics in the Living Wage Movement*. New York: New York University Press, 2011.

———. "Waging Religious Ethics: Living Wages and Framing Public Religious Ethics." *Journal of the Society of Christian Ethics* 29, no. 1 (2009): 69–86.

Sobrino, Jon. *Christ the Liberator: A View from the Victims*. Translated by Paul Burns. Maryknoll, NY: Orbis Books, 2001.

———. "The Crucified Peoples: Yahweh's Suffering Servant Today." In *The Principle of Mercy: Taking the Crucified People from the Cross*, 49–57. Maryknoll, NY: Orbis Books, 1994.

———. *Jesus the Liberator: A Historical-Theological Reading of Jesus of Nazareth*. Maryknoll, NY: Orbis Books, 1993.

———. *No Salvation outside the Poor: Prophetic-Utopian Essays*. Maryknoll, NY: Orbis Books, 2008.

———. *The Principle of Mercy: Taking the Crucified People from the Cross*. Maryknoll, NY: Orbis Books, 1994.

Sohm, Rudolph. *Kirchenrecht*. Edited by Erwin Jacobi and Otto Mayer. 1892. Reprint, Berlin: Verlag von Duncker & Humblot, 1970.

Springs, Jason A. *Healthy Conflict in Contemporary American Society: From Enemy to Adversary*. New York: Cambridge University Press, 2018.

Starr, Bradley E. "The Structure of Max Weber's Ethic of Responsibility." *The Journal of Religious Ethics* 27, no. 3 (1999): 407–34.

Stassen, Glen Harold, ed. *Just Peacemaking: The New Paradigm for the Ethics of Peace and War*. Cleveland: Pilgrim Press, 2008.

Stern, Steve J. *Reckoning with Pinochet: The Memory Question in Democratic Chile, 1989–2006*. Durham, NC: Duke University Press, 2010.

Stout, Jeffrey. *Blessed Are the Organized: Grassroots Democracy in America*. Princeton, NJ: Princeton University Press, 2010.

———. *Democracy and Tradition*. Princeton, NJ: Princeton University Press, 2004.

Swidler, Ann. "Culture in Action: Symbols and Strategies." *American Sociological Review*, 1986, 273–86.

Tanner, Kathryn. "Eschatology and Ethics." In *The Oxford Handbook of Theological Ethics*. Edited by Gilbert Meilaender and William Werpehowski. Oxford: Oxford University Press, 2007.

———. *God and Creation in Christian Theology: Tyranny or Empowerment?* Oxford: Basil Blackwell, 1988.

Taylor, Charles. *A Secular Age*. Cambridge, MA: Belknap Press of Harvard University Press, 2007.

Terrell, JoAnne Marie. "Our Mothers' Gardens: Rethinking Sacrifice." In *Cross Examinations: Readings on the Meaning of the Cross*, edited by Marit Trelstad, 33–49. Minneapolis: Fortress Press, 2006.

Tertullian. "Apology." In *Caesar and the Lamb: Early Christian Attitudes on War and Military Service*. Edited by George Kalantzis. Eugene, OR: Cascade Books, 2012.

Tilly, Charles. *The Contentious French*. Cambridge, MA: Belknap Press, 1986.

———. *Regimes and Repertoires*. Chicago: University of Chicago Press, 2006.

Uvin, Peter. "Global Dreams and Local Anger: From Structural to Acute Violence in a Globalizing World." In *Rethinking Global Political Economy: Emerging Issues, Unfolding Odysseys*, edited by Mary Ann Tétreault, Robert A. Denemark, Kenneth P. Thomas, and Kurt Burch, 147–62. London: Routledge, 2003.

Vaisey, Stephen. "Motivation and Justification: A Dual-Process Model of Culture in Action." *American Journal of Sociology* 114, no. 6 (2009): 1675–1715.

Van Dyke, Nella, and Holly J. McCammon, eds. *Strategic Alliances: Coalition Building and Social Movements*. Social Movements, Protest, and Contention. Minneapolis: University of Minnesota Press, 2010.

Vásquez, Manuel A. "Grappling with the Legacy of Modernity: Implications for the Sociology of Religion." In *Religion on the Edge: De-centering and Re-centering the Sociology of Religion*. Edited by Courtney Bender, Wendy Cadge, Peggy Levitt, and David Smilde. Oxford: Oxford University Press, 2013.

Velleman, J. David. "Motivation by Ideal." In *Philosophy of Education: An Anthology*, edited by Randall Curren, 517–26. Oxford: Blackwell, 2007.

Weaver, Alain Epp. *Mapping Exile and Return: Palestinian Dispossession and a Political Theology for a Shared Future*. Minneapolis: Fortress Press, 2014.

Weber, Max. *Economy and Society: An Outline of Interpretive Sociology*. Edited by Guenther Roth and Claus Wittich. 1922. Reprint, Berkeley: University of California Press, 2013.

———. "Politics as a Vocation." In *From Max Weber: Essays in Sociology*, edited by Hans Gerth and C. Wright Mills. 1919. Reprint, New York: Oxford University Press, 1958.

Weber, Samuel. "Taking Exception to Decision: Walter Benjamin and Carl Schmitt." *Diacritics* 22, no. 3/4 (October 1, 1992): 5–18.

Weber, Thomas. "Nonviolence Is Who? Gene Sharp and Gandhi." *Peace and Change* 28, no. 2 (2003): 250–70.

West, Cornel. *The American Evasion of Philosophy: A Genealogy of Pragmatism*. Madison: University of Wisconsin Press, 1989.

West, Traci C. *Disruptive Christian Ethics: When Racism and Women's Lives Matter*. Louisville, KY: Westminster John Knox Press, 2006.

Westerholm, Stephen. *Perspectives Old and New on Paul: The "Lutheran" Paul and His Critics*. Grand Rapids, MI: Eerdmans, 2004.

Whelan, Michael. "The Litany of Saints." *Worship* 65, no. 3 (May 1991): 216–23.

Whitmore, Todd David. "Crossing the Road: The Case for Ethnographic Fieldwork in Christian Ethics." *Journal of the Society of Christian Ethics* 27, no. 2 (2007): 273–94.

———. *Imitating Christ in Magwi: An Anthropological Theology*. London: T&T Clark, 2019.

Williams, Delores S. "Black Women's Surrogacy Experience and the Christian Notion of Redemption." In *After Patriarchy: Feminist Transformations of the World Religions*, edited by Paula M. Cooey, William R. Eakin, and Jay B. McDaniel, 1–14. Maryknoll, NY: Orbis Books, 1991.

Williams, Rowan. "The Politics of the Soul: A Reading of the City of God." *Milltown Studies* 19/20 (1987): 55–72.

Wright, N. T. *Paul: In Fresh Perspective*. Minneapolis: Fortress Press, 2005.

Wybrew, Hugh. "Ceremonial." In *The Study of Liturgy*. Edited by Cheslyn Jones, Geoffrey Wainwright, and Edward Yarnold. New York: Oxford University Press, 1978.

Wyschogrod, Edith. *Saints and Postmodernism: Revisioning Moral Philosophy*. Religion and Postmodernism. Chicago: University of Chicago Press, 1990.

Yoder, John Howard. *Body Politics: Five Practices of the Christian Community before the Watching World*. Nashville: Discipleship Resources, 1992.

———. *The Politics of Jesus: Vicit Agnus Noster.* 1972. Reprint, Grand Rapids, MI: Eerdmans, 1994.

Zagzebski, Linda. *Divine Motivation Theory*. Cambridge: Cambridge University Press, 2004.

———. "Moral Exemplars in Theory and Practice." *Theory and Research in Education* 11, no. 2 (July 1, 2013): 193–206. https://doi.org/10.1177/1477878513485177.

Zotti, Mary Irene. "The Young Christian Workers." *U.S. Catholic Historian* 9, no. 4 (1990): 387–400.

Zunes, Stephen. "Unarmed Insurrections against Authoritarian Governments in the Third World: A New Kind of Revolution." *Third World Quarterly* 15, no. 3 (September 1994): 403–26. https://doi.org/10.1080/01436599408420388.

INDEX

ABOUT THE AUTHOR

Kyle B. T. Lambelet is a Louisville Postdoctoral Fellow at the Candler School of Theology at Emory University where he teaches at the intersection of political theology, theological ethics, and social change. He has a PhD in theology and peace studies from the University of Notre Dame. His work has been published in *Political Theology*, the *Journal of Religious Ethics*, *Peace Review*, and the *Journal of Anglican Studies*. This is his first book.